# Just Five Minutes

## Nine Years in the Prisons of Syria

By Heba Dabbagh

Translated by Bayan Khatib

**Published February 2007**
**Printed in Toronto, Canada**


Library and Archives Canada Cataloguing in Publication

Dabbagh, Heba, 1959-
Just five minutes : nine years in the prisons of Syria / Heba
Dabbagh; translated by Bayan Khatib.

ISBN 0-9781726-0-4

1. Dabbagh, Heba, 1959-. 2. Women political prisoners--Syria--
Biography. 3. Political prisoners--Syria--Biography. 4. Syria--Politics
and government--1971-2000. I. Khatib, Bayan, 1979- II. Title.

DS98.5.D32A3 2007 365'.45092
C2007-900507-1

# Contents

**Forward**

**A Historical Introduction**

**Part One:  December 1980**

The Arrest:  Just Five Minutes

**Part Two:  January 1981 - October 1982**

Kafar Suseh Prison:  A Journey beyond Time

**Part Three:  October 1982 - November 1985**

Katana Prison:  A Slow Death

**Part Four:  August 1985 - October 1985**

Military Interrogation Prison:  In the Depth of the Unknown

**Part Five:  November 1985 - October 1989**

Dooma Prison:  The Battle against Time

**Part Six:  December 1989**

Release

**Translator's Note**

**Glossary of Arabic Terms**

# Forward

Like the color wheel, the days of our lives feature different colors. Some days bring splashes of glorious white. Other days are stained with the darkest of hues.

My life began as bright and lively as a budding flower and the days of my childhood were filled with love from my beloved parents and feelings of belonging and warmth from my family. I flourished lifted by this love and goodness and grew to become my father's favorite, my mother's confidant and a princess among my seven brothers and four sisters, the one they went to for help. Most nights I went to bed thinking about my dreams, fell asleep trusting that my dreams would come true and awoke feeling safe and serene.

I took no part in any political activities. Although I loved my faith and spent much of my time studying it, that did not make me a political activist. My lack of affiliation with political organizations did not mean that I was blind to the injustice and cruelty of the government and its oppression of all factions of the Syrian population. When I became a hostage in the hands of the government, I saw first hand the evil that ruled my country. I shared cells and stories with people like me and others who came from a variety of different backgrounds and faiths, some from the sect of the ruling party itself.

I lived a happy, carefree life until I went to university and faced the difficulty of parting with my family. It pained us to part, but it was a parting of our choosing, a decision we arrived at together, unlike the forced parting that came later. That parting separated me from my family and landed me in the prisons of oppressors and in the depth of darkness. Then came a final parting, a permanent one. The oppressors killed my parents and eight of my brothers and sisters and forced my remaining three brothers to flee the country and live far away from home.

The picture I had created of my life blurred and darkened. The buds of all my hopes and dreams never bloomed. I sat in the depth of prisons, a hostage for my "politically active" brother, the years of my life slipping away, my heart breaking and my soul withering.

Everything that happened to me was based on informant lies. The government knew well that the allegations against me were baseless. They chose to ignore the truth. They did not want to waste the efforts of their paid informants and their mob of agents who screeched onto my street, ripping through the silence of the night to capture me. They did capture me and they dragged me from one prison to another for nine fruitless years, slamming every door of mercy and humanity shut in my face.

Nine years were long enough to kill every last one of my dreams and any hope I had in any human being. During those nine years, I had but one ray of light in my heart, my hope in God. No matter how much that hope dimmed, it never died. My hope in God knew no limits, although pains did obscure it for short periods of time. My pleas to God were my only comfort. They saved me.

When people slept and the whips retired, I prayed to God. Oh God, the only one who can, when nightly despair overcomes us, shine upon us from His light and ease our sorrows; God, who when tragedy befalls us, can bring relief; God, who when all roads for help are blocked, can send ships of rescue through means unbeknown to the oppressors; God, who in Him is safety and comfort and stability and under his protection we find peace. I prayed to God to grant me the patience to bear any test that he gives me. I prayed to Him, to conform my will to His and to fill my heart with acceptance for the path He chooses for me. I prayed to God to assist me in His praise during times of ease and strain. Oh God, in patience we grow and in your praise and acknowledgement of your blessings we rid ourselves of selfishness and pride. In hardship we find virtue. Grant us good character and peaceful hearts. Your power encompasses everything.

The Kind and the Almighty bestowed upon me invaluable blessings. He grounded me, protected me and sent to me from amidst the blur of sticks and whips that which eased my pains and sorrows. He gifted me with my cellmate and soul mate, Majida. Majida always found more patience and peace than I could muster and was always more ready to give and sacrifice.

God showered his mercy upon us both in the form of our other cellmates, a group of women with many virtues. We will never forget their goodness, their love and their open arms. We were partners in our imprisonment, our worries and our suffering. I would like to thank them here and ask God to grant all of us his forgiveness and his blessings. I would also like to ask for their forgiveness and pardon if I mentioned anything in this book that may hurt them in any way. But the duty I feel to speak out against the oppression of the Syrian regime overpowers my worries of the consequences of doing so. I feel entrusted with the task of documenting these events. As painful as it is to bring the past to light, it seems easy in comparison to keeping the secrets of the oppressors and allowing all of our suffering to be in vain.

I lived in the hell of Syrian prisons for nine years, a hostage. The pen would tire before I could describe every detail of what took place and every pain I felt while I was imprisoned by this evil regime. But I lived through it all and in the end I can say that the days of our lives come in black and white and every shade in between. Some days are easy; others are hard. Some days pass with ease; others with friction. But all of our days are products of a predetermined destiny.

While the ruling dictators thought that they held the reins over the land and people, it was, and still is, God's will that holds ultimate power and final say. Today the rulers of our lands use their power to oppress. Tomorrow they will stand with the rest of us in the hands of the Ultimate and Just Ruler.

Although my unjust imprisonment and the loss of nine years of my life pain me, today I live in the midst of God's bounties. God's kindness has healed my wounds and replaced anxiety with peace and deprivation with blessings. I feel these blessings in my beloved husband who planted hope in the hearts of the deprived and kept his promises. My husband is a light and hope that shines in my soul and makes up for all I lost. I also feel these blessings in our lovely daughter Wafa, who introduced new happiness to our lives, and in our other two children Jabir and Sarah. Jabir and Sarah's mother, Hanan, left her children in our care for she had taken under her care the fight for justice and honor. Although she is gone, her life remains a shining example for the rest of us.

I feel now, as I felt before, that th e end of my story has not come. The chapter of accountability is yet to come. The oppressors who rule the land today will stand in the hands of God in this final chapter. I put my trust in God and there I find comfort.

Heba Dabbagh

# A Historical Introduction

Syria, an ancient nation rich in culture and history, has been home to many civilizations. Until today, Syria remains the homeland of people from many different backgrounds, religions and sects including: Sunnis, Shias, Druze, Alawis, Ismailis, Christians and Jews. In the beginning of the last century, Syria's division left it vulnerable to French occupation. Syria struggled to regain its independence from France and did so in 1945 with an army that reflected Syria's diversity.

In 1963, the Baath party took power in Syria. They ignited trouble by slowly weeding out non-Baath factions of the army, including Sunnis, who made up the majority of the Syrian population. Hafiz Al-Assad of the Baath party gained the presidency in 1970. President Al-Assad further alienated the multitude of sects by putting together a government of Alawis, the religious sect he belonged to, and personal friends. This pushing aside of the Sunni majority and other factions who desired to have a voice in the governing of their country aroused feelings of anger and resentment that soon led to the desire to overthrow the government.

Certain groups from within the myriad of oppositionists considered revolution and armed resistance as the best means to end Hafiz Al-Assad's dictatorship and exclusive government. As those opposition groups watched their government destroy the democratic process, forbid the forming of political parties and terrorize its own people through martial law, military court and cold blooded murder, they grew certain that an armed resistance was the only way to make their voices heard; so they began to take action.

The government reacted to the threat of opposition by instituting the complete eradication of the armed faction of the resistance movement. This cleansing began with the persecution and execution of the armed resistance, but quickly expanded to include non-militant factions, until identities blurred and no family felt safe from government persecution, imprisonment and murder. The government's wrath, executed largely by the Mukhabarat, the notorious secret service agents, spread terror throughout the country. Often, a friendly conversation or a mere cup of tea with an oppositionist landed people in jail. In addition, the

Mukhabarat commonly took hostages in place of "wanted criminals". Soon, the prisons of Syria filled with members of the resistance movement, as well as innocent men, women and children whose only crime was being related to or casually associating with someone from the resistance movement.

The Syrian government acted under a veil of darkness, with the international community turning a blind eye to the atrocities and human rights violations. Fueled by a systematically ingrained fear, the Syrian people learned to never speak of their government's crimes. As a result, the shocking stories of mass imprisonments and slaughter, including the 1980 Hama massacre, which according to some reports took the lives of 25,000 people, remained a muffled cry. Human rights organizations estimated that during this period of turmoil, the Syrian government killed tens of thousands of men and women and imprisoned tens of thousands more.

Although many political prisoners have been released over the years, Mukhabarat agents continue to show up at people's door steps and take them away, with no regard for due process or basic human rights. Until today, few Syrians dare to speak out against the crimes of their government, for they have learned well the consequences of such boldness.

Bayan Khatib

## Part One: December 1980

The Arrest: Just Five Minutes

On one of the coldest nights in Damascus, Wednesday, December 31, 1980, I kept awake while my roommates drifted to sleep. I spent half the night struggling to stay awake, struggling to understand the sentences in my *Sharia* textbook, and struggling to absorb information for my final exam in the morning. The winter chill, my sleepy eyes, and my cozy mattress fought against my will to stay awake, against my ability to concentrate and comprehend the words I read. My mattress called me to its comfort and warmth. Somehow, I resisted.

I stared at the words in my book. Scenes from the past swirled in my mind. My stomach cramped. The memories came back blurry and elusive, but still I could no longer study, still I could no longer sleep.

I spent the entire first semester at the University of Sharia living in this anxiety. When the semester ended, I went back to Hama, my city, to spend my break between semesters with my family and loved ones. During the visit, my mother surprised me with a request.

"Heba, your brother wants me to talk to you. He wants me to convince you to drop your courses and leave the country right away. He wants you to go to Amman as soon as possible."

Safwan, my brother, fled to Amman, Jordan, several months ago, seeking refuge from the Syrian government who accused him of being a member of the Ikhwan, an outlawed opposition group.

"I'm afraid the Mukhabarat will arrest my sister instead of me. I'm afraid they'll take her as a hostage," Safwan told my mother when she visited him in Amman.

I knew that Syria's secret service police, the Mukhabarat, commonly held hostages in place of wanted members of the political

11

resistance, but still Safwan's worries sounded unreasonable to me. I never in my life imagined that his fears might be justified.

"Sorry mama. I just don't see why I need to go."

My break ended and I returned to Damascus to begin the second semester at university. My roommates and I renewed the lease on our apartment in Al-Baramka. I immersed myself in my second semester courses and began to forget my brother's warnings. But I couldn't completely forget, for the atmosphere around me began to change. I began to feel unsafe. Armed men and search blockades, like I had seen in Hama, appeared throughout Damascus and quickly spread to our campus. Security officers appeared at the doors of our university and demanded to see identifications. Whispered rumours spread throughout the campus about the arrest, imprisonment and even murder of many members of the resistance movement.

Day by day, the situation deteriorated. Soon the sounds of gunfire and explosions became an everyday occurrence in Damascus. Newscasts and newspapers could no longer keep up with their reports of every "criminal" hideout the police raided, of every "criminal" the police arrested, and of every "criminal" the police shot dead. In the midst of all the chaos, and as every heart in Damascus filled with fear, I felt the danger inch closer and closer toward me.


## God Will Help

Two days ago Majida, my close friend from university, and I shopped for a get-well gift for my aunt in Al-Hameediya, an area of town lined with tiny shops. As we walked from one shop to the next and from one street to the other, I felt more and more anxious. *Someone was following us.*

Majida and I got onto a bus to Al-Makhim, where my aunt lived. The man I suspected of following us got onto the same bus. Fear filled my body. I wanted to tell Majida, but my lips froze. Somehow, I managed to whisper my worries into her ear. Majida smiled.

"You're just imagining things."

That morning when I arrived at the university, security guards had stopped me as usual. They had taken my identification card, examined it carefully, and returned it to me. After my classes, I had walked back to our apartment with Majida. Even then, I had felt someone following us. Even then, Majida had chastised me for my silly imagination.

"Everything seems normal. Don't worry so much."

I couldn't not worry. Worries spun in my mind, until they overtook all of my thoughts, like a hurricane sweeping up everything in its path.

That December 31$^{st}$, the silence of the cold night seemed deafeningly loud and I could not read another word. The chilling silence soon turned my worries into pure fear. Slamming car doors in the streets broke the silence and startled me out of my thoughts. The distinct sirens of the Mukhabarat vehicles blared from below.

Something was wrong and this time I was sure it was not just my imagination. *Maybe the police are going to raid a hideout nearby. Maybe they are here to arrest another wanted "criminal".* I ran to the window to watch. Before I could sweep the curtain away, I heard violent knocking at the front door. I looked out the window. Mukhabarat vehicles occupied the entire street.

"Open the door now or we'll break the lock with gunfire," a man shouted from behind our apartment door.

Quickly and almost automatically, I slipped my scarf on and ran for the door. I gripped the doorknob and froze. *Should I open the door even though the girls are all asleep or should I warn them first?* Without thinking, I found myself running to Fatima, a teacher and the eldest of my roommates.

"Wake up. Come on. I think the Mukhabarat are here for you," I shouted and shook her, unaware of how careless my words sounded.

13

I remembered Sausan, another one of my roommates, who was a dentistry graduate doing her internship in Damascus. I remembered that her brother had been executed that morning in Tadmur Prison. *Maybe they came for her*.

Mukhabarat officers banged on our door with fists and rifles. Fatima ran for her scarf and wrapped it around her head. She pulled the door open. Officers charged into our apartment. They moved with unbelievable violence. One of them jumped up onto the roof of the building to search it. Another ran to the window. A third one to the kitchen. And a fourth and a fifth… and a tenth... spread throughout our apartment.

One of the officers forced his way into our bedroom. He saw a copy of the Quran on a shelf, grabbed it, threw it onto the ground, and stomped on it with both feet like an enraged maniac. The other officers smashed and damaged many of our belongings. They searched every corner of every dresser and every closet. *Why are they searching our apartment? What are they searching for?*

I heard a deep monstrous voice from the living room call out, "Waheeba Dabbagh".

My body froze. *They're here for me.* I stepped forward.

"No one here by that name," I quivered and shook my head.

"Take every girl back to her room and check their identifications," the leader of the group instructed.

We followed his orders immediately. We walked into our rooms, trembling with every step. One of the officers, a young man, who I think was performing his mandatory military service as an officer for the Mukhabarat, took my identification. He looked at it, looked up at my face, and then back at my identification as if to make certain it was really me in the picture. His gaze went back and forth between the picture and me. His eyes swelled with tears.

"You're from my home town," he said and blinked back tears.

"God help you."

"Why? What's going on?"

"God will give you patience. What can you do? God will help."

"Why do I need help? Have they come for me?"

I felt as if I was sinking into a deep dark well.

He looked down at the ground and whispered, "Yes."

The young man slowly shuffled back into the living room and handed my identification to the leader of the group who continued to shout, "Waheeba Dabbagh". The leader looked at me, his eyes filled with fury.

"You told me with such nerve and shamelessness that there's no one here by that name". He turned to one of the officers and said, "Take her to her room and search her well."

## Coffee or Tea?

The officer took me and one of my roommates to a different room.

"Search her," he ordered my friend.

"What do you think you are going to find? They already searched us and the whole apartment when they first came."

The voice of the leader masked my own trembling voice as he spoke to another man on the walkie-talkie.

"We found her," he said.

"Come on, get dressed. You're coming with us - just five minutes."

I wrapped my long coat around me and tucked my scarf into it. I remembered that I had some money in my drawer. I took it out and started to give it to my friends, but the officer said, "No, leave it with you. You might need it."

"I won't need it. You said just five minutes, so why would I need it?"

He assured me that I would need it, but I gave the money to my

15

friends anyway. An officer shoved me out the door.

"Hold her hand," the leader said.

The staircase that led down the building was dark. The electricity was out, as it often was. I resisted the officer as he struggled to grab my hand.

"That was an order!"

"Hand cuff me, but don't hold my hand."

The officer let me walk down the stairs by myself. When we got to the entrance of the building, he pushed me towards a car that was waiting for us. The car's open door felt like a monster's open jaws, waiting for me to walk in, waiting to capture me.

"Who does she share her room with?" I heard a man's voice through the walkie-talkie.

The leader recited the names of my roommates.

"Bring them with her," the man ordered.

The leader climbed back up the stairs and brought down Majida and Malak. We got into the car. Mukhabarat vehicles from all over the street surrounded us.

Within seconds, we found ourselves near Tashreen Stadium, in the part of town called Abbassiya. We stopped in front of the Assadat building, a Mukhabarat branch. The officers led us into the building and into a room stacked with electronic devices that flashed red and green lights. *Maybe they're communication devices.*

"What would you like to drink, coffee or tea?" one of the officers asked.

None of us could answer.

"I will bring you some strong coffee so you can clear your heads." The officer walked out.

# The Interrogation

After a few minutes in the room with the electronic devices, someone called my name. An officer led me to the office of the leader of the division, whom I later discovered was the nephew of President Hafiz Al-Asad. His name was Maeen Naseef. I stepped into Naseef's office. A man with bloodshot eyes sat behind an elegant desk. He wore a traditional Arab man's dress. The dress was white, thin and transparent. Naseef crossed his legs, revealing his hairy calves.

"Sit here," he ordered with a rough voice.

Before I could sit, he began to toss accusations.

"You're from the Ikhwan. Isn't that right?"

"No."

"Then what is your connection to the Ikhwan?"

"I have no connection to them."

"Then how come you distribute the *Natheer* magazine and where did this letter come from?" He swayed his upper body from side to side.

I had heard of the *Natheer*, the banned Ikhwan publication. I noticed a small paper in Naseef's hand. I recognized the paper. It was the letter my brother Safwan had written to our family, entrusting us to care for our father. My father had attempted to visit Amman with one of my other brothers to get treatment for a blood disease he developed after spending months in fear and sadness over the Mukhabarat's pursuit of Safwan, but he never made it to Amman. The border guards refused my father and brother entry. They said my brother was not allowed to leave the country until he completed his two and a half years of obligatory military service.

My father never found treatment for his disease in Syria. That day, Safwan met my father and brother at the border and gave them a letter to take home to the family. I wanted to keep that letter in memory of Safwan. The officers found it when they searched my room.

In the letter, Safwan wrote: "The carrier of this letter is the father of a *mujahid*."

Naseef began to read out parts of Safwan's letter, his voice saturated with sarcasm.

"The father of a *mujahid* ha?" he said. "Your father acts like a socialist, but he's in the high ranks of the Ikhwan. I'll show him. I swear to you I will fill his body with bullet holes."

Naseef's words remained engraved in my mind until I heard about the Hama massacre years later. The Mukhabarat kept their promise. They tortured my father and then filled his body with bullet holes.

## The Evidence is Lost

"I am not a member of the Ikhwan," I insisted.

I trembled with terror for myself and for my father.

"What about the letter?"

"I don't know. Maybe somebody forgot it at my apartment or left it there on purpose."

Naseef turned the letter in his hand. It seemed like he was thinking of a different approach.

"Who do you know from your brother's friends?"

"No one. I haven't seen my brother for a long time and I have nothing to do with his friends."

"What about Abdul-Kareem Rajab?" Naseef's eyes glimmered.

"Who is he? I don't know him."

My reply sent Naseef into a rampage.

"So you will not admit that you are a member of the Ikhwan?"

"How can I admit to being a member of the Ikhwan when I am not?"

He slid one of his slippers off his feet and flung it at me. I jerked

18

my head to the side. The slipper smacked the transcriber who sat behind me. Naseef went bezerk.

"You say that you are not a member of the Ikhwan, but your behaviour is the behaviour of the Ikhwan!"

Naseef went back to talking about the letter and swinging it back and forth in front of my face. He got nowhere. Frustrated, Naseef left the room. *He must have gone to fetch someone to torture me.* When he returned, I thought he wanted to talk about the letter again, to swing it in front of my face, but instead he fumbled through a pile of papers the officers had picked out of my garbage can. They had tried to put the pieces of papers back together, hoping to find incriminating evidence. Naseef frantically ruffled through papers as if looking for something in particular.

"Did anyone enter this room while I was gone?" Naseef snapped at the transcriber.

"No sir."

"Did this bitch move from her spot?"

"No."

"Did you leave the room?"

"No."

Naseef lost the letter from Safwan. I have no idea how. He searched and searched, but found nothing. Naseef grew angrier and angrier and yelled louder and louder, threatening me with dirty and disgusting language.

"Your friend in the room next door admitted that you are a member of the Ikhwan. If you do not voluntarily confess, we have ways to make you confess."

"No matter what your ways are, they cannot make me a member of the Ikhwan. I will continue to state that I am not a part of the Ikhwan, no matter what."

# A Long List of Accusations

When Naseef finished with me, officers took me to another room similar to the room with the electronic devices that continuously flashed colourful lights. It was Majida's turn to face Naseef. Before I could calm myself, the officers called my name again and led me back to Naseef's office. A long list of accusations awaited me - a list long enough to convict three men.

"You are charged with being a member of the Ikhwan, with distributing the *Natheer* magazine, with giving lectures about Sayid Qutb in the mosques of Damascus, with helping to purchase a house where the Ikhwan met and conspired against the government, and with transporting an ammunitions vehicle containing a broadcast device through Al-Muhajireen."

Naseef assured me that they have a definite confession from one of my friends confirming all of the charges.

"Your friend is certain of all of her information. She knows you and she has studied with you and lived with you and she does not lie."

"She is lying. I have nothing to do with anything she said. I haven't done any of those things. I was never a part of such acts."

As I spoke, things began to clarify in my mind. I realized from Naseef's words that someone had helped him craft these accusations and fill my file with lies. I knew who it was. It was a person I had never actually seen with my own eyes, but a person who my friends at university constantly warned me about. It was Abdul-Kareem Rajab, a spy for the Mukhabarat, planted in the high ranks of the Ikhwan. My realization encouraged me to stick to my responses and assured me that Naseef's accusations had little to stand on. Although the situation seemed grim, I felt confident.

Naseef's questions and threats continued.

"If you do not confess voluntarily, we have ways to make you confess," he threatened again.

# Waiting for Execution

The interrogator ordered one of the Mukhabarat officers to take me to a hidden room. A short while later, they brought Malak to join me. Malak had arrived in Damascus less than a month ago. She was in her first year of university. She hadn't even gotten to know the city yet, nor anyone in it; but she knew me and that was enough to drag her down. They left us in the room with a guard and took Majida for more interrogation. When they finished with Majida, it was my turn for another round. For the rest of the night I listened to the same ridiculous questions and accusations over and over again.

"Your first friend gave us a definitive confession about your activities and your other friend Majida has just admitted to the same accusations against you. They both said that you are a member of the Ikhwan, that you are armed, that you have helped the Ikhwan with many of their activities and that you distribute the *Natheer* magazine."

When he said "your first friend," I knew he meant the informer Abdul-Kareem Rajab. Before I could answer him, the interrogator ordered an officer to take me away. The officer led me out of the room, down a hall and asked me to face the wall, raise my arms and bend one of my legs back. *It's over. They're convinced that I'm guilty and they're probably going to execute me. Or maybe they want to shoot me right here, right now.*

An officer brought Malak out and ordered her to stand beside me in the same position, with two arms up and one leg bent back. *They're going to shoot both of us right now.* My body numbed. I contemplated my death. *How will I die? Will they shoot me from the back? Will they hang me? What will they do to me?* I needed to know. I gathered what little courage and will power I had left and turned my head to the guard.

"Why are you making us stand like this? What did we do wrong?"

"You know exactly what you did."

"Will they kill us?"

"No," he smirked. "You think execution comes that easy?"

## To the Beatings

We stood in that hallway for another half hour, maybe more. Time lost its value. Later, an officer took me back to the room with the electronic equipment.

"Sit," he ordered.

I sat. Soon they brought Malak to the room and sat her in a couch in front me, a couch that faced the slightly ajar door. Malak leaned her head onto the arm of the couch and fell asleep instantly. *Sleep will shelter her. It will protect her from this nightmare, at least for a little while.* I wished I could sleep, but fear kept me awake. The sounds coming from Majida in the interrogation room down the hall kept me awake. They clawed at my heart. I heard her cries, but I could not hear her words. I wondered how they were torturing her.

"Malak. Malak," I whispered. I longed to scream, to wake her up, to make her hear me. I wanted her to peek out of the door. Maybe she could find out what was happening, but Malak would not wake up. Morning light began to seep in, but still I could not sleep, still I could not wake Malak.

During this time, officers came in and out of the room. Some asked meaningless questions, others sufficed with just a look to make sure we hadn't moved. One officer smiled at me. At sunrise, an officer asked us if we'd like breakfast.

"No," I answered.

"Do you want a drink?"

"I don't want anything. Thank you."

"I will bring you a cup of tea to clear your head."

A moment later, he placed a cup of tea in front of me. I couldn't drink. I wasn't sure whether it was fear or exhaustion that prevented me from holding the cup up to my lips. At eight o'clock, officers awoke Malak. It was time for another interrogation session, this time in the basement.

"They're going to torture us now. I know it," I whispered to Malak as we walked down the stairs to the basement.

"Don't say that. Please, don't say that," she quivered.

"Why did you sleep the whole night? Why didn't you stay up so you could hear what they were saying to Majida? We could have benefited from knowing what they said to her and what she said to them. Maybe we could have found out what's going to happen now."

## Against My Country

In the basement, we walked down a long dim hallway that led to an interrogation room. I saw a new face sitting in the middle of the room, waiting for us. I sat on the edge of a small army cot in the corner of the room. For the next half hour, a new interrogator recited the same accusations, asked the same questions and I responded with the same answers. He recorded everything in a file.

I couldn't follow his words anymore. Fatigue and sleep deprivation finally conquered my fears and I felt my eyes close. I would almost fall asleep, but then the interrogator's rough voice and his thick language would shake me back to wakefulness and I would lift my eyelids for a while. I felt like my insides were about to come hurling out.

When the officer finished interrogating me, my only desire in the world was to find anything, a tile, a slab of concrete, anything I could collapse upon and sleep. But before I drifted off again, an officer forced me up and led me down that same dreadful hallway to another room in the basement where yet another man awaited me. The man greeted me with dirty language drenched in the accent of the ruling Alawi party. For the next hour, he repeated the same old accusations.

"You are a member of the Ikhwan. Everybody has confessed to it. You have committed many crimes against your country. You deserve no less than execution."

He spoke on and on, his words like a tape recording, like a machine, a robot, anything but human. I could not tell where his sentences began or where they ended. He made sarcastic remarks, taunted me, swore at me. Every disgusting word that came out of his mouth felt like a rock crashing against my head. My head throbbed all over. I could no longer focus on his words. I heard only fragments.

"Confessions against you…you're a criminal…against your country... execution! execution! execution!"

I lost awareness for the next while. Then, an officer walked into the room with Majida and Malak.

"Aren't you girls hungry?"

"No. We are not hungry," I answered.

"Well, we are going to feed you some barbequed chicken anyways."

*He means torture. I know it.*

"We don't need your food."

He grabbed all three of us and led us back down the hall and all the way to the entrance of the building.

"Where are we going?" I asked.

"You'll see."

Malak, Majida and I stepped into an army vehicle and huddled. Two armed men climbed in behind us. The second they slammed the door shut, the car took off and accelerated at an unbelievable rate as if it wanted to fly over all of the cars on the road, as if it wanted to fly over the road itself. A police car drove in front of us with wailing sirens and flashing lights. Traffic, near and far, swerved out of our way.

Another police car drove behind us for security. The car jerked at sharp angles, bumped up and down and sped wildly through the streets of Damascus.

Malak became nauseous. She vomited all over the place. The putrid smell suffocated us. Majida and I turned Malak's head to the back. Malak vomited some more. Her vomit made a puddle between the two guards who sat in the back. She vomited over and over again, all the way from the Mukhabarat branch in Abbassiya to the prison in Kafar Suseh.

## Part Two: January 1981 - October 1982
Kafar Suseh Prison: A Journey beyond Time

The three cars transporting us from the Mukhabarat branch to Kafar Suseh Prison passed through the entrance gates and sped to the main building. The building had three floors. The driver went around the building through a maze of alleyways and stopped in front of one entrance. He gripped our hands, led us through an automatic door, through the main lobby, through another door, down five steps and into a dark basement - a different realm. The officer's rough hands squeezed my own and pulled me through the hallways.

In the dim light, we could barely see the metal bars of the cells. Our gasps of exhaustion seemed to echo in the silence of the prison.

"Moneera!" a harsh voice hollered.

Before we had a chance to catch a glimpse of the man calling out, a girl appeared at the end of the hallway. She wore a traditional Syrian dress and her long hair was pulled back in a braid. She swayed towards us.

"Search them one by one," Abu Adil, the head guard, said. He kept his gaze firmly on Moneera.

Abu Adil pushed me into the room first, the room we later learned was the interrogation and torture chamber. Moneera walked in behind me.

"So, what's your name?" she asked casually.

I wanted to reach out and strangle her with my bare hands.

"Why do you want to know my name?"

"Why so angry?"

"Hmmm… I don't know. How do you expect me to feel? Is it possible for a human being to feel happy in such a place?"

"Okay. Okay. Don't get all upset. I'm a prisoner just like you."

"Why are you lying to me? You don't look like a prisoner."

"I swear to God I am a prisoner. I'm in a cell filled with women

26

from the Ikhwan."

I didn't want to say another word to her. She spoke with the Alawi accent, like all the guards. *I'm sure she works here. She just wants to squeeze information out of me.*

"You don't believe me? Tomorrow we'll meet in the cell and I'll remind you that you didn't believe me."

*Could she possibly be telling the truth?* I let my guard down for a moment and asked her a question.

"Who from the Ikhwan is in your cell?"

"There is an old woman from Aleppo and another woman called Um Shaima and…"

She listed many names. I didn't recognize any.

"I am the only communist in the cell. The rest are all Ikhwan," she said.

Moneera searched me and then she searched Majida and Malak. An officer took us back up the stairs. He led us through many hallways and doors until we reached the south building of the prison where our interrogation at Kafar Suseh Prison would begin.


## In the Hands of the Torturer

I heard doors open, doors close, and locks turn. Some of the sounds seemed close, others sounded like echoes from a distant part of the prison. Every sound made me tremble. Every prison employee who walked by carried something in his hands: a walkie-talkie, a chain, a whip, a cable… I felt the world I know fade away. I felt myself enter a new world, one that gave life to all my nightmares.

They took me to Naseef Khairbek's office, the leader of the Kafar Suseh division. Khairbek's office looked spacious and warm with fashionable furnishings, complete with a desk, a bookshelf, a sofa and a luxurious rug. A bust of President Hafiz Al-Asad sat on the desk. In the corner of the room was another bust of the president, a bronze life size one.

Khairbek was busy conversing with another man on the walkie-talkie. He glanced at me from the corner of his eyes and motioned to the officer to take me away. The officer led me to a room across from Khairbek's office. A young man tied with rope lay on the floor. A group of officers shouted questions at him and beat him. Khairbek strolled in. He spoke into his walkie-talkie, talked to the officers in the room and shouted at the young prisoner all at the same time. Khairbek motioned with his hand, and the officer who had brought me into the room grabbed me and ordered me to wait outside.

I hadn't slept for days. I could no longer focus on the faces around me, on the sounds of the officers swearing, name calling and cursing, or on the sounds of pain that echoed throughout the prison. Sounds spun together in my head. Everything blurred.

A couple of minutes later, they brought me back into the room. They wanted me to watch. *They want to terrify me into confession.* Khairbek and about four other men tortured the young prisoner with whips, sticks, cables, and electrocution devices. One of the men was called Abdul Aziz Thalja. Thalja was huge, monstrously huge. A young man probably still in his teens also participated in the torture. I later came to know that young man well. His name was Hussain. He was a soldier from the town of Daraa.

I never found out the name of the young prisoner they tortured that day or why they tortured him. I only remember that throughout his torture session he continued yelling the same thing over and over again: "I swear to God it wasn't me. It wasn't me." But in the end, he gave in. He confessed to the murder of an officer, probably thinking his confession would end the torture. But the torture did not end. The torture not only continued, but became even more brutal. I could not stand to see or hear anymore.

"Why am I here?" I cried out to the guard beside me.

28

"I don't know. Why are you here? Why don't you ask them?" He smiled.

"I don't want to ask them. I have nothing to confess. Why are they making me watch this man's torture?"

"I don't know. I have nothing to do with any of this," he shrugged casually.

The torture went on for another half hour. When they finished with the prisoner, they chained his wrists and ankles, picked up his bruised and bloody body and carried him out of the room. They made me follow to watch the grand finale. Officer Thalja dragged the man to the top of the stairs and with one powerful kick sent the young man tumbling down. The prisoner groaned as he bumped and banged against each step.

"Put him in solitary confinement," Thalja hollered down the staircase.

Thalja ordered an officer to take me back to the room where they had tortured the young man. The officer ordered me to stand in the corner of the room. Khairbek and Thalja spoke into their walkie-talkies. They all left the room. Thalja came back in. Thalja pressed a button. The door closed. The door fit into the wall like pieces of a puzzle. The door disappeared. My hopes of ever getting out of this room unharmed disappeared.

Thalja didn't ask me any questions. He didn't say a word. He marched up to me and smacked my head. My head crashed into the wall. My head bounced back. The world spun. I saw four of everything. I saw four Thaljas. I felt like I was hanging upside down.

"Listen up. If you don't talk, if you don't confess, you have no idea what's coming to you."

# The Magic Carpet

Thalja left for a little while, only to return with Khairbek, the officer who led the raid in my apartment and a fourth man I did not know.

"You! You don't want to talk?" You don't want to confess? You don't want to tell us where your brother is?"

"My brother is not here."

"So, where is he?"

"I don't know. I think he went to continue his studies somewhere."

I remembered that when my mother had visited my brother in Jordan, he had told her that if our father asks about his whereabouts, she should tell him that he had gone to Pakistan to continue his education. I had no idea that just minutes ago Thalja and the other men had interrogated my mother and asked her the same questions about my brother's whereabouts. I had no idea that my mother had responded with the exact same answer.

"We both know that your brother is here and you are going to lead us to him and his friends. You are going to take us to the house where they hide out."

"I have no idea what you are talking about."

Khairbek called an officer.

"Go bring her a pair of pants. Let her cover up and then put her on The Magic Carpet."

The officer grabbed me, forced me down onto a wooden board, and strapped my neck, wrists, stomach, legs, knees and ankles onto the board. He checked the straps to make sure they were secure. He lifted the bottom of the board up into the air. The board created a right angle with the floor. He strapped me so tight that I couldn't move a single joint. My legs hung in the air. My coat fell to my waist revealing the long underwear that I always wore in winter and tucked into my thick knee highs.

30

"Look sir," the officer smirked, "she says she isn't from the Ikhwan, but look, she's fully prepared for a beating. She doesn't even need the pants."

I tried to wiggle out of the straps. The officers sneered. I was about to ask them to put the board right side up just so my legs wouldn't show, but before I could, they attached the board onto a chain that hung from the ceiling. The officer who had taken me from my apartment walked toward me, gripping a long thin whip.

"You don't want to talk, ha?"

"I have nothing to say."

Thalja hovered over my head. He held a square shaped box, an electric generator. He plugged it into the wall. Two clamps hung from the box. Thalja grabbed the clamps. He clipped them onto my fingers. Another officer began to whip my feet. Thalja did not wait for the whipping to stop. Thalja flicked the switch. Electricity travelled through my body. I screamed. None of the men even flinched.

"So, you still don't want to talk?"

"I told you I have nothing to say. Nothing!"

"Did you feel how powerful that electric shock was? Well let me tell you, that was just the lowest setting."

"It doesn't matter. I can't confess to something I didn't do."

"No. No," he shook his head, "You're lying. You're hiding things from us. Would you like to get up right now and take us to the house where your brother and his friends live? Otherwise, you're going to Tadmur Prison."

The words "Tadmur Prison" send shivers down every Syrian's back. Tadmur Prison was notorious for severe torture and large scale massacres.

Thalja shoved a picture in front of my face.

"Do you know this man?"

"No."

"But he is your brother's close friend. His name is Abdul-

Kareem Rajab. Don't you know him?"

*The rumours about Rajab must be true. I'm sure of it now.*

"No. I don't know him."

Thalja smiled, a cold twisted smile. He began to read from a bunch of papers in his hand, while keeping an eye on me, watching for my facial expressions.

"Heba Dabbagh is an active member of the Ikhwan. She purchased a house for the Ikhwan. She gives lectures about Sayid Qutb in the mosques of Damascus. She…"

"Ahhhhh……" I screamed. "Lies! Lies! Those are all lies. I have nothing to do with any of those things."

Thalja tossed the papers at my face.

"Don't you see? It's all documented. It's all from the confessions of Rajab. He ratted you out. And I'm a hundred percent sure that he is a member of the Ikhwan and that he knows everything about you and I am sure that you know him too.

"No! No!"

The torture continued. One of the officers returned to whipping my feet. He seemed to put every ounce of strength in him into each fling. The whip whistled as it travelled through the air. Another officer with a whip joined in. Thalja put the clamps back onto my fingers. Electricity flooded my body. I screamed and called out to God, but after a while my voice faded, then vanished. My head wobbled in the air. I lost all feeling. About ten minutes later, they stopped. I heard their voices in the background. I heard cursing and swearing, but I could not focus on the words.

"…to Tadmur," I heard.

They unclipped the straps and pulled me off The Magic Carpet. Officers dragged me out of the torture chamber, down many hallways and out of the building. A car awaited me. I saw Majida already in the car with an officer guarding her. I didn't dare say a word to her. The car took off at an insane speed. The driver slammed the breaks at the exit gates.

"You still don't want to talk?"

I felt every part of me scream, "I have nothing to say! I have nothing to do with the Ikhwan. Do you want me to lie to you? Do you?"

The driver turned the car around back to Kafar Suseh Prison, back to the torture room and back to the beatings. They repeated the same questions. They recited the same list of accusations. But the torture wasn't the same this time. This time, many more officers were present, so many more that I could no longer keep count of how many men surrounded me, how many sticks beat me, or how many whips flogged my feet. It looked like the whole room was filled with sticks, whips and clamps. It sounded like the whole room was filled with men questioning and accusing me. I lost the will to respond.

"You are armed. Look at her. She claims that she is innocent, that she is not from the Ikhwan, that she is not an active member, but she is and she is an armed member too," I heard Thalja shout.

I could not bear to hear those accusations anymore.

"I have nothing to do with any of this and I am not armed!"

"But your friend Majida told us you were."

"Don't believe her. Bring her here. Let's see if she can say that to my face. She probably said that to avoid your torture."

"No. Your friend doesn't lie. She's honest, not like you. She confessed everything. We didn't torture her, but we are going to continue beating you until you talk."

Thalja stomped up to me. He placed the clamp on my lip.

"Are you going to talk?"

"I have nothing to say. No matter how much you beat me, no matter how much you electrocute me, I will not lie against myself."

Khairbek shouted, "Pick her up, give her a paper and let her write down all the information she is hiding. Then we'll see."

Khairbek turned to me.

"In case you decide not to talk, I just want you to know that we

33

have men here so huge and monstrous that one of them could block that whole door. Have you ever seen a man from the village of Al-Deer? If you haven't, I will bring one here just for you. Then we'll see."

## Death is a Believer's Comfort

They removed me from The Magic Carpet once again. I felt wet. They had dumped water on me to awaken me when I fainted during the torture. I looked around the room. Most of the officers had left. I looked out the window. It was night. The torture must have lasted for about two or three hours. Before I could regain my balance, an officer brought me a pen and paper and sat in front of me.

"Listen," he said, "If you talk, you can help yourself get out of this mess. If you stay silent, you will sink deeper and deeper."

"I have nothing to say."

"They don't bring anyone here who has nothing to say. Nobody ends up here unless they have sinned."

"But, I didn't do anything."

"You're free to write whatever you want."

He instructed me to write about myself in general, about my schooling, my studies and about my relationship with the Ikhwan. I wrote what I knew. I wrote the truth. I gave the paper to the officer. He left the room. Minutes later, Thalja came into the room ready to explode. He waived the paper in my face.

"These are your answers? You sister of a fag. You… " Thalja spewed out a long stream of curses.

"I know that you know where that house is, the one where your brother and his friends are hiding and you are going to take us to it now. I know what you're trying to do. You're stalling. You're trying to buy them time to escape."

I did not say a word, yet he still scribbled more things into my

34

file. He left the room, but returned minutes later.

"If you don't talk now, we are going to take you down into the basement and if you go down into that basement you will never leave it until you…"

"Good. Death is a believer's comfort."

"How dare you talk back? How dare you be so smug? Don't you realize what you are doing to yourself? Did you not feel the beatings you just got? Have you no mercy on your own body? Why don't you just confess and spare yourself more torture?"

"Because I have nothing to confess. I told you I have nothing… nothing!"

Khairbek walked into the room just in time to hear my outburst. The look on his face sent shivers of fear through my body. He swore at me and called me words I had never been called in my life.

"If you don't confess everything right this minute, I will strip you naked."

A new terror gripped me.

"But I have nothing to confess," I whimpered. I knew my pleas were useless.

"Take your coat off," he ordered.

I stood there staring at him, feeling fear like never before.

"If you don't want to take it off yourself, I'll take it off for you."

Khairbek reached for the buttons on my coat. He found nothing. My coat was designed with hidden buttons. He slid his hands down my body, searching for the buttons. I swiped his hands away. He grabbed my long ponytail from beneath my scarf and pulled it towards him. My head bumped against his chest. He tugged my hair the other way and my head crashed against the wall. He banged my head against the wall over and over again and shouted more foul words.

Khairbek clutched my scarf and yanked hard. I had tucked my scarf into my coat and the bottom of it had slipped into my sleeves.

Khairbek pulled and tugged, but the scarf would not come off.

"You claim that you're not from the Ikhwan! Look at you. Your clothes are stuck to your body like glue and you have secret, hidden buttons on your coat. You came perfectly prepared for this, didn't you?"

I kept silent. I couldn't fit in a word even if I wanted to.

"Bring me the whip," he hollered.

My feet were so bruised and swollen from the previous beatings that I couldn't wear my shoes.

"You don't want to talk? You'll see."

An officer handed Khairbek the whip. He walked toward me. I ran away from him and stood behind the table. He came after me. I ran around the table. He chased me.

"Damn you! After all those beatings you still have the energy to run around. Catch her," Khairbek yelled out to the guard at the door.

The guard caught me from the other side of the table.

"Get her out of my face. Take her to solitary confinement. I don't want to see her anymore."

I couldn't believe that he let me go. The guard threw my shoes at me and pushed me out of the room, through hallways and down several staircases. I wondered what solitary confinement would be like.

"Why didn't you talk? Wouldn't that have been better for you? You could have saved yourself from all this. Look at how swollen your face is. Your hands are blue, your feet are bruised and you can't even wear your shoes anymore," the guard said.

"I have nothing to say."

I was so tired of repeating those words over and over again. Every time they forced me to repeat them, I felt as if they lost more meaning. *God punish you all!*

"You could have lied and told them what they wanted to hear to save yourself."

It sounded like he was reciting lines from an act he had

memorized.

"I don't lie. Anyways, I know that in this place the result will always be the same, whether I lie or tell the truth."

"How do you know that?"

"Because they didn't believe me. I told them the truth, but they didn't believe me and you know what they did to me. So I wonder what they would have done if I had lied."

In the basement, I saw Hussain with a silly smile on his dim face. He was missing a tooth and the gap in his mouth looked like a window in a broken down house.

"Welcome. Welcome," he said as he twisted a whip in his hands. "You lighten up this place."

## A Chicken's Coop

Hussain gripped my shoulders and pushed me down five stairs. He led me through a hallway so dark I could not see its end. He pointed to the second cell in the hallway and said, "Here's your lovely new room. Good night and sweet dreams."

I looked into the tiny cell, my new room. I saw darkness and nothing else.

"No way! I won't go in there," I said, unaware of how pathetic I sounded.

"Are you going to go in or do I have to shove you in myself and break your head?" Hussain pushed me into the darkness.

I looked around at the other cells. I glimpsed the faces of my roommates peeking out of the peepholes. Without thinking, I ran towards them, calling out their names. Hussain caught me and hauled me back to the cell.

"Get back here. You think you're in some kind of hotel or something? You think you can just go around and make visits?"

I heard a voice calling out from the end of the hallway, from cell number 24. I recognized the voice. It was my mother.

"These are women you tyrant. You're flexing your muscles on them? Have you no mercy? My whole life I've been hearing about your merciless hearts and now I see your evil with my own eyes."

My heart jumped at the sound of her voice. I ran towards it.

"My mother is here? God damn you. What are you doing with her? My brothers and sisters are all young and my father is sick and they're all helpless without her," I yelled and ran.

"What do we care about your brothers and sisters and your father? We just want your mother." Hussain laughed hysterically.

Hussain slammed the tiny doors shut on all the peepholes and then caught up with me and dragged me back to the cell. I reached out for the walls, the doors, anything I could cling to, anything to keep me out of that cell.

"If you don't get in there right now, I'm going to call officers to force you in."

"But it's so dark in there."

"And now *you* will light it up. Now get in there."

I peeked into the tiny cell. It looked barely over one metre square. In the corner, I saw two metal cans, one with a mush of watery rice and the other with water.

"This cell is like a chicken's coop. You're treating me like an animal."

"That's dinner for tonight. You can go ahead and eat it, if you have the appetite."

"You know very well that anyone who sets foot in this place will never have an appetite again."

One of the other prison workers, an old man, shuffled down the hall. He stepped close to me and whispered, "Just go in there my sister, and trust in God. Don't give him more opportunity to hurt you."

That old prison worker was the only prison employee at Kafar

Suseh Prison to ever treat me well. I took a deep breath and stepped into the tiny solitary confinement cell. I could still hear my mother's voice yelling, but soon the sound of the guards' hollering and laughing overshadowed her calls. The guards were celebrating the New Year. The smell of alcohol and the sounds of drunken men filled the prison.

I couldn't move. I was sitting in an uncomfortable position, but still I couldn't move a single muscle. I knew they had taken Majida for interrogation after me. I knew that now she was going through what I went through. I knew that going through such things could make her say things they wanted to hear, things about me.

In the middle of the night, before I was able to get any sleep, an officer came to my cell, yanked me up, and dragged me back through the hallways, back up the stairs and back into the interrogation room.


## Lemon Yellow


Thalja awaited me in the interrogation room.

"You are not a member of the Ikhwan, right? You did not do any work for them, right? And you do not want to confess, right? That's okay, because tonight God sent someone to confess on your behalf. Your own friend told us that you are armed and she saw your weapons with her own eyes."

"Bring her here so I can gouge her eyes out! Come on. Bring her to me. I want to hear her say that in front of me."

"She does not lie. I told you. She does not lie. She is honest, not like you. And I know you're lying because you've just turned lemon yellow right in front of me."

My eyes widened in disbelief.

"I have spent two entire days without food, without sleep, and without going to the washroom. I have spent two entire days being beaten and tortured and feeling scared to death, so how on earth could I

39

look anything but lemon yellow?"

Thalja shook his head.

"Take her back to solitary confinement," he called out to an officer.

The officer led me back to the cell, back to the anxiety and fear. I looked at the blanket they had tossed into my cell, but left it crumpled on the floor. I didn't want to be warm. I didn't want to fall asleep. I didn't want anyone to open my cell and find me vulnerable.

I sat in the middle of the cell. I watched cockroaches climb the walls around me. *They're staring at me. They're checking me out. I'm their new guest.* The sound of a latch opening broke the short stretch of silence. It was the latch of the door that led to the solitary confinement block. I heard the guards shove a new batch of prisoners down the hallway. I looked out the peephole and saw six or seven boys between the ages of twelve and fifteen. Later, I found out that they had rounded the boys up at a mosque. The guards tossed them into a solitary confinement cell near mine, all of them together in a one-meter square cell.

One of the boys was sick, probably because of what they had just finished doing to him. He told the guards that he needed to go to the washroom. The guards ignored him. He begged. They ignored. He begged harder.

"Please. My stomach hurts. I need to go to the bathroom. Anybody? Please. I can't hold it anymore."

The guards were too drunk to care.

"Shut Up! Shut your damn mouth up!" they shouted.

"Please. Please," he continued to plead and plead.

An officer came up to their cell, opened the peephole, stuck his arm in and whipped the boy with a cable.

"I told you to shut up, you animal."

Then there was silence. Soon, a suffocating smell wafted through the prison. The officer marched back to the boys' cell swearing and cursing.

"You did it in the cell you son of a bitch?"

The officer dragged the boy out into the hallway. From the way he beat him, I could tell that the officer had lost every last bit of sobriety, sanity and compassion he ever may have had.

My mother's shouting started up again.

"May God destroy you, you heartless monsters. He begged you to take him to the washroom. He begged you, but you didn't listen to him. What was he supposed to do? You gave the poor boy no choice but to do it in his pants."

After this episode the prison fell silent again, a restless silence. The hours of the night dragged by as if chained to a mountain. I didn't dare close my eyes or fall asleep, but slowly I began to lose sense of my surroundings. I felt cold. I felt as if the entire prison was covered with snow. I felt as if the officers were going to come to my cell any minute now and they were going to take me outside and drag me through the snow and strip me of my clothes and torture me one final time before they would shoot me and I would die and leave this world.

At dawn, I heard a soft knocking. It came from the cell next to mine, where they held Majida. I realized she was trying to wake me up for *fajr* prayer. I hadn't performed any of the five daily prayers since I arrived at Kafar Suseh Prison. I was anxious to start praying again, but I had no water to wash with for *wudu* and I didn't even know which way to face for the *qibla*. I knocked on the door. Hussain turned up.

"Can you tell me which way the *qibla* is?"

"Sure," he smiled. "Remember when we were beating you and you were hanging upside down? Well the way you were facing then, that was the *qibla*."

"Please! Please tell me which way it is."

Hussain's smile faded.

"I don't pray, so how would I know? But I saw the men in the other solitary confinement cells pray this way," he said and pointed to

41

the back of my cell.

I prayed in the direction he told me, with my back facing the door of my cell. My heart pounded against my chest as I prayed. I worried that a guard would open the door and find me in prayer. Who knows what the consequences of that might be? My fears came true. In the middle of my prayer, a guard named Ibraheem opened the door to my cell to give me my breakfast.

"What are you doing? Are you praying?"

I didn't answer. I continued to pray, but I felt as if my heart was going to drop into my hands. Thank God, Ibraheem left me alone and continued to distribute breakfast to the other prisoners. Later, he returned.

"You're finished? Well, may God accept your prayers," Ibraheem snickered.

I nodded and said nothing. He pushed a plate of food at me and left. Before my heart could slow down, the door opened again. It was Abu Ahmad, the old, kind guard.

"Don't you need to go to the washroom?"

I nodded. I got up and stepped out of my cell. The hall was empty.

"How come I never hear anyone around here anymore? And where is my friend Malak? Isn't her interrogation over yet?"

"They're out. They're all out. No one's here anymore but you, you and your friend Majida."

"What about my mother?"

"You, your friend and your mother only. You're the chosen ones."

*That's it. This must be the end. It's over. Everybody's out, but us.* I burst into tears.

"Why did they let everyone out but us? They haven't proven anything against me. I'm innocent," I sobbed.

"I swear to God, I don't know anything. Ask them. I just work here."

"Aren't you going to eat? Aren't you hungry? I bring my own lunch here. I have bread with jam and butter and other things too. I have some left if you want."

I realized that I had not eaten since I got to this place, but I didn't want to eat someone else's food. I thanked him, but didn't take his food.

The next day, I couldn't handle the hunger anymore. I picked away at the crust of the bun they brought me for breakfast. The inside of the bun was soft and gooey. I also ate the tiny piece of cheese that came with my breakfast. Cheese was a rare commodity in Kafar Suseh Prison. I spent the rest of my eight days in solitary confinement sitting in the middle of my chicken's coop, scared and waiting.

## The *Khat* and the Cow Herdsman

Several days passed. I still felt terrified. I still sat and waited in my solitary confinement cell. I felt severed from the world, from life, from my life. I replayed the arrest and interrogation over and over again in my mind, forcing myself to face the fact that this was not the kind of nightmare that I would eventually wake up from. I looked around my new home. The cell looked more like a grave than anything else. The only signs of life were the spiders and cockroaches that crept along the walls searching for moisture with their creepy antennas.

At first, I saw nothing in the darkness except for the spiders and cockroaches, but after a while, the dim lights of the hallway filtered through and my eyes began to adjust to the darkness. I noticed lines carved into the wall. I squinted and tilted my head closer. Lines formed letters. Letters formed words: *"Allahu akbar wa lillahi alhamd."* God is great. Praise be to God. Engraved around those words were the names of many people who had inhabited this cell before me.

On the adjacent wall, someone had engraved a mosque. Around the mosque it said: *"La ilaha illa Allah, Muhammad rasool Allah."* There is no God but Allah and Mohammad is his messenger. Below it was a signature. I also noticed an engraving of the map of Palestine with *"Allahu akbar wa lillahi alhamd,"* God is great and praise be to God, inscribed below it.

Less than two hours after sunrise, the daily routines of prison life commenced. The interrogators, guards, and whip-bearers didn't sleep until dawn and awoke in mid-morning. The cursing, swearing and blasphemy began the minute they awoke, mixed in with the sounds of whips against flesh as the guards led the prisoners to the *"khat"*. The *khat*, literally means the line, but in prison language it signified the morning line-up for the washrooms.

Yaseen, an Alawi soldier, and one of the most ignorant and dim-witted creatures of God, was always the first to volunteer for the job of taking the prisoners to the *khat*. He gripped his whip, strolled along the line-up of prisoners like a lion tamer and lashed out at the prisoners, whipping them and scarring their legs, backs and arms. No one dared to whimper, let alone scream. Noise brought worse pain. Yaseen trained the men well.

"My son, do you think that you are still living in that little village you came from and that these people are the flock of cows you used to herd?"

It was my mother's voice.

Yaseen let nothing get in the way of his enjoyment of the morning ritual. He ignored my mother and continued to whip the young men. He gloated at the horrifying scenes he orchestrated. My mother pounded and kicked the door of her cell. She cried out and begged Yaseen to stop. She did all she could, but there was nothing she could really do.

Soon after the morning ritual ended, but before we could enjoy much of the calm that followed, interrogation time began and the yelling, cursing and swearing of the guards, the officers and the

44

interrogators started up again. Torture in prison never ends. When they stop torturing your body, they begin to torture your heart. Every day, my heart ached as I listened to the sounds from the torture chamber. After the interrogation sessions ended, the prison fell silent again.

A guard opened my door and asked if I needed to go to the washroom. I said yes and followed him out. I shut the washroom door firmly behind me and listened. *There's nobody here.* I splashed water on my face. I felt a presence behind me. Slowly, I turned around and stood face to face with my mother. We froze in shock for a long time before my mother threw her arms around me and held me tight.

"Did they hit you? Did they torture you?" Mama asked quickly.

I looked up and saw rage and terror in her eyes.

"No. I'm fine." I couldn't add to her pain.

I continued to wash my face, my arms and my feet. I lifted my foot into the sink.

"What's this? Your foot is blue. Your fingers are blue too and so swollen. Did anybody touch you? Did anybody hurt you?"

"No. Thank God. Nobody touched me."

"Why did they arrest you?"

"I swear I have no idea. I know they want Safwan. They wanted me to tell them where he is."

My mother then told me that she had told the Mukhabarat that Safwan was in Pakistan studying and we realized, with relief, that we had both given the same answers. Mama examined my bruised and swollen body parts with her eyes. She pushed the washroom door open and ran out into the hallway screaming with all her might. She called out to God. She begged him to avenge our pain. Hussain came running.

"How could you let her in when the other one was already in there? Don't you know that only one person at a time is allowed in the washroom?" he yelled at the other guard.

"I didn't know anyone else was in there. Why did you close the door of her cell if she was still in the washroom?"

The two guards grabbed my mother, each from one side, and forced her back into her cell. Mama continued to shout prayers to God to punish them.

For the next few days, I didn't see my mother. I never found out why they had arrested her until after the interrogation process was over and they put us all in a joint cell with a big group of women. That's when Mama told me the whole story.


## The Ambush


My mother wanted to visit my brother in Jordan. On her way, she thought she would stop by Hama and drop off some things I had forgotten at my parents' house during the break. My brother decided to settle down in Jordan with a group of young men who were all wanted by the Syrian government for being members of the Ikhwan. The Marka family, who were friends of ours and who also had an outlawed son in Jordan, tagged along with my mother on her trip.

"On the day you were arrested, your father woke up from a bad dream about your brother," Mama told me. "He dreamt that something bad happened to Safwan. He asked me to visit your brother, to make sure he was all right. I spoke to the Marka family and they agreed to go with me to Jordan. We decided to stay at your place for one night and leave for Jordan in the morning. When I was a few steps away from the entrance of your building, I heard a soft voice warning me not to go into your building, pleading with me to stay away. It was one of your neighbours. I couldn't see him, but he begged and begged for me not to go into your building. He'd watched your arrest the night before. I figured he couldn't possibly be talking to me. I didn't listen to him. I went into your building, walked up to your apartment and knocked on your door. The door flew open and a cluster of guns pointed at me. A man grabbed me, pulled me into your apartment and slammed the door shut. One hour later, I found myself in Kafar Suseh Prison."

## The Most Just of Judges

As I listened to my mother's story, sadness clenched my heart and the sadness only grew as my mother relayed to me what happened to the Marka family. The police arrested them along with my mother at my building. When Mrs. Marka found out that the police had shot her 18 year old son, Ayman, and her 14 year old daughter, Majd, in the middle of the street, she went into shock. She never recovered from that shock. The Mukhabarat shot her children in revenge for the many wanted men who had escaped from them.

Mrs. Marka could not bear it. She lost her mind. She took off her *hijab* and tied a band around her head so tight, as if to block out all pain. Her mental condition did not stop the Mukhabarat from arresting her. The arrest set off her first nervous breakdown.

"During my first day in solitary confinement, I heard the interrogator shout at Mrs. Marka at the top of his lungs, but she never answered him. She didn't have the mental capacity," Mama told me.

Mr. Marka was over seventy years old. His wife and two daughters had dragged him along when the police arrested them. During the arrest, the two daughters lost consciousness. My mother, in her desperation to wake them up, slapped their faces over and over again.

"The Mukhabarat realized that the two girls and their father were of no use to their investigation, so they sent them straight down to the overflowing basement cells to spend the night. The police found no space in any cell for Mr. Marka. They left the seventy-year-old man on the floor in the hallway at the door of my solitary confinement cell. I remember praying to God to help the poor old man whose family had been inflicted with one tragedy after the other," Mama said.

My mother also told me about her interrogation, and like I knew she would, she had answered all of the officers' questions with stubborn courage.

"Tell us about your criminal son. Where is he?" the interrogator asked her.

"I do not have a criminal son. Watch what you say."

"That's right. You don't just have a criminal son, but a criminal son who lured the rest of his siblings along into a life of crime."

"All I know is that I raised my son to go from our home to the mosque from the mosque to university and that's all."

"May God give you strength. May you live and raise more children," they sneered. "So you don't want to talk?"

He turned to another officer and said, "Prepare her for some beatings."

"God help you. I am your mother's age and you want to beat me?"

"Well, you refuse to talk."

"What do you want me to say? Nothing pleases you, not the truth and not lies."

They did not beat my mother that time. Thank God, something made them leave her alone. During the entire length of her imprisonment, she argued with them, confronted them, and prayed to God to punish them. Yet, they treated her better than all of the other prisoners.

Mama almost never slept. She stayed awake as much as she possibly could. She kept an eye and an ear on everything that happened in the prison. Nothing got past Mama.

When they first put her in solitary confinement, she would call out for Abu Isam, the warden from the town of Daraa.

"What did I do? Why am I in prison?"

"I have nothing to do with this," he answered.

"You have everything to do with this. It's all in your hands. I want to write a letter of complaint to the leader of this whole division. Give me a pen and paper."

"That is not allowed. It would never reach him. That is against the rules."

"Then I will complain to God, the one and only, the most just of judges and God willing one day you will sit in my place, but you will not have the patience to bear it as I do."

After a month or two, we heard about Abu Isam's death. He died in a car crash. The steering wheel tore into his stomach.

## More Hostages

Even after arresting my mother and her friends, the Mukhabarat continued their ambushes in my building. They arrested and imprisoned ten other people, including the rest of my roommates and other visitors who came to our apartment. Some of those arrested were: Fatima, a student from Kara who lived with us, Susan, a dentistry graduate from Aleppo who was in the middle of her residency, two sisters from the Jamoos family who studied science at the university and who were from Al-Till, Yusra, a medical student from Jordan and her father who was visiting her in our apartment at the time, Maha, another medical student who was half Palestinian and half Lebanese, a girl from the Darweesh family who was from Latakiya, and Ghada, a student who lived with us and her brother and his friend who were visiting her at the time.

They interrogated all of these people after they finished with Majida and me. Eventually, they realized that none of them were of any use. Although I did not sleep a single second of that night, I had no idea that all of this was happening around me.

## My Mother and the Strike

Before two days without interrogation could pass, an officer came to my

49

cell to take me for another round. I had spent the last few hours, alone in my cell, thinking and trying to piece things together. At this point, I had already tasted the severest of torture and the harshest of threats. This new round of interrogation would bring nothing new. They recited the same questions. They hollered the same threats. They used the same intimidation techniques. Nothing changed. For a whole week, they repeated the same routine over and over again every single day.

The only thing that changed slightly from day to day was the way they chose to beat me. Sometimes, they used sticks. Sometimes, they used whips. One time, they tried to squeeze me into a wheel, another one of their torture methods, but the wheel did not fit me. That frustrated them and they took out their frustrations by whipping me. Everyday I grew new bruises and new scars. Everyday I felt new pain. But their questions never changed, nor did my answers.

From the tiny window in my solitary confinement cell, I watched new scenes of horror everyday. I listened to the desperate pleas of prisoners that went on and on, day and night. The greatest horrors arose when a guard would catch one of the male prisoners in prayer. The guards patrolled the hallways constantly on the look out for those men who dared to pray. If they caught one, they would drag him out of his cell and beat him in the hallway without a shred of mercy, all the while hollering blasphemous phrases and sickening curses. Such language was a part of the guards' everyday speech, even when they spoke to one another. Thank God, they never beat the women prisoners for praying. They caught us praying many times, but never said a word about it.

Majida and I often communicated by knocking on the walls of our cells. Sometimes when we felt sure that none of the guards was there, we spoke through the walls. One time at night, a guard heard us. He jumped up from his post and dashed to our cells.

"I heard voices. Who was talking?"

"Me," Majida said.

She didn't want to be the cause of torture for any of the young men.

"With who?"

"With my friend. Is it illegal to talk?"

The guard said nothing and walked away.

My mother had more courage. She never let a chance to talk to me go by without taking full advantage of it. She didn't care about consequences. Sometimes she would ask to go to the *khat* and the guards would take her out of her cell and walk her down the hallway and when she passed my cell, she would grab onto the bars and insist that they let her see me and talk to me, even if it's just for a second. The guards would try to pull her away, but her grip would be so tight that two men couldn't pull her away. Sometimes they would give in and they would open the peephole and let her see me.

"But no talking," they'd warn, "not even for a second."

"No, I want you to open the door and let me in. I want to talk to my daughter."

"No, that is not allowed."

My mother pushed the limits as far as any prisoner possibly could. On the second day of her imprisonment, after they released the rest of the girls and left only us, my mother decided to go on strike. She refused to eat, use the bathroom, or even sleep until they allowed her to see me. I didn't know about my mother's strike until Abu Adil came to me and said, "Next time you see your mother, give her a couple of lessons on religion. Tell her that her body has a right over her. Did you not study that in your *Sharia* classes at university? Tell her to start eating."

"She is a mother and you know a mother's heart. She has the right to do this."

During the second day of her strike, an order came allowing us to meet. Abu Adil came to my cell to take me to my mother.

"Remember what we talked about yesterday? Tell her to start eating."

"It doesn't matter what I say. I can't force her to do anything."

"Don't you want to help us end her strike?"

"What can I do? Can't you see the state she is in? God help her."

When we got to her cell, he turned to my mother and said, "Here, do you see your daughter now?"

"No." Mama did not look up.

"Then what do you want? We don't know what to do with you anymore."

"You know what I want and God willing, I will get it. God is greater than all of you. He is the most just of judges and if he wanted to, he could break all your necks and end your miserable lives, all of you."

Abu Adil laughed like a wild animal and shoved me back to my cell. God only knows for sure, but I felt that because of my mother's strike, they ended our interrogation period earlier than planned and after eight days in solitary confinement, they transferred us to the joint cell.

## The Joint Cell

During the eight days my mother and I spent in solitary confinement, we had no contact with any of the other prisoners. We never even saw Moneera, the woman who searched us when we first arrived. But the other women in the prison had seen us through a small crack in the wall. One time, on my way to the washroom, Hajja Madeeha, one of the prisoner's in the women's joint cell, caught a glimpse of me passing by. She knocked on her door and called out to one of the guards to open up so she could air out her blanket. Hussain pushed me into the washroom quickly and went to open her door. She called  to the other women to come  and air out their blankets too. She spoke loudly so that I could hear her and know that there were other women here.

"Is someone in the washroom? I thought I heard a woman's voice," she asked Hussain.

"No. There's nobody there. If there were more women, we would have put them with you in your cell."

Hajja Madeeha continued to question Hussain with her unbending stubbornness that I would soon grow to know and love.

"Tell me, what is wrong with your blanket? You've been airing it out for an hour," Hussain said.

"I saw a cockroach on it and I swear I have no idea where it went now."

"Sure. Whatever. Get back into your cell and let's get this over with."

"There are more women here aren't there?" she whispered to Hussain as she folded her blanket.

"Yes, there are. Don't worry. They're going to join you tomorrow."

He thought she would leave him alone now, but her questions persisted.

"Do you know where they're from?"

"You'll find out tomorrow when they join you. Tomorrow you can sit together and talk your hearts out."

Hajja Madeeha went back to her cell. I went back to mine. I overheard the entire conversation and even got to see Hajja Madeeha through a crack in the bathroom door. The sight of another woman consoled me.

The next day, the warden came to my cell. He handed me a piece of paper. On it was my name, the date, the time of arrest and imprisonment, the duration spent in solitary confinement and the list of accusations against me, accusations that had now turned into convictions.

I wrote back to them on the same paper that I had been wrongfully accused of everything:  wrongfully accused of being a member of the

Ikhwan, wrongfully accused of being armed, wrongfully accused of actively circulating anti-government literature...

Half an hour later, Hussain came to my cell and asked me to stand. I thought he was going to take me for another round of threats and torture.

"Where are we going? To interrogation?"

"No."

"To execution?"

"You'll see."

"I'd rather execution."

"No. We're not going to execute yet."

"Then when?"

"When you finally admit that you are from the Ikhwan."

"Fine. Will you really execute me if I confess?"

"First confess. Then it's up to the head of interrogations."

He led me down the hall and through a big black door. I felt sure that another torture session awaited me. I didn't want to step past that big black door. Hussain pushed me through the door and down the hall to a cell. I looked up and saw a room filled with women in *hijab*. I sighed, stepped into the room and greeted the women. I felt relieved to see other female prisoners, but I still couldn't let go of the fear. Hussain closed the door behind me. A minute later, he returned with Majida and my mother.

At first my mother, Majida and I felt uncomfortable. We didn't know what to do, what to say to each other. We worried that the Mukhabarat had planted a spy among the women, but it didn't take long for my mother to break down into thundering sobs. I held her tight. It felt as if they had put us into this room with no intention of ever letting us out. My mother sobbed harder and louder and called out for justice. She prayed as loud as she could so that the guards would hear her. One of the women approached my mother and put an arm around her shoulder.

"Hey, don't cry. Don't worry. Don't let them get to you. There is no peace for a believer until she meets her Lord."

That was Hajja Madeeha, one of the female prisoners from the resistance movement. We spent many days together in that cell, enough days for each of us to tell her story, to relay every detail of injustice, frustration and pain.


## Hajja Madeeha's Story

Hajja Madeeha was a well-known lady from Aleppo and in her forties. She led many religion classes for women, although she herself couldn't read or write. She harboured members of the Ikhwan on the government's list of "wanted criminals". One day, she stepped out of her house to deliver a letter. The Mukhabarat caught and arrested her. They had discovered her ties to the Ikhwan through a government informant who had infiltrated the Ikhwan. His name was Samih Kiyalee.

The officers took her to the Mukhabarat's security division. Hajja Madeeha infuriated the head of the division, Omar Hameeda. She withstood severe and continuous torture to give the men time to escape from the hideout. She made a pact with the men that if she was ever arrested, she would hold off from confession for a certain period of time, long enough for them to escape.

Hameeda was on to her game. He decided to make her pay dearly for such criminal courage. Hameeda grabbed a pair of scissors and snipped off the tip of Hajja Madeeha's tongue. But the tongue snipping was not the worst of Hameeda's plans for Hajja Madeeha.

During her interrogation, Hameeda stripped Hajja Madeeha naked, tied her arms behind her back and hung her upside down from the ceiling. He hollered and cursed and beat her. When Hajja Madeeha thought that the Mukhabarat could do no more, Hameeda ordered an officer to bring in Hajja Madeeha's younger brother. They shoved him

55

into the room where his sister hung naked and bloody.

"Do you know who this is?" Hameeda asked the young man.

"No. I can't tell. Who is it?"

"It's your sister, Madeeha."

Hajja Madeeha's brother blacked out and dropped to the ground. Officers dragged him back to his cell and left him unconscious. Hajja Madeeha's torture continued for hours until she decided that she had given the men enough time to escape. She confessed and led the Mukhabarat to her house. The officers found remnants of the men's belongings in the hideout.

Hameeda dragged Hajja Madeeha back to the division in a fit of fury. He swore to cut off the tongue that deceived him. He did. Hajja Madeeha recovered quickly; her tongue grew back. Years later, Hajja Madeeha met the manager of civil prisons. He said to her, "We cut off your tongue so that you'd stop talking so much, but from what I see, you grew it back longer than ever."

After one month at the security division, the Mukhabarat transferred Hajja Madeeha to Kafar Suseh Prison, along with several other women. She wasn't lucky enough to be from the group they decided to release, the group they felt they no longer had use to detain. Among the lucky ones was Sana, a young girl who was like a daughter to Hajja Madeeha and who had lived with her in an apartment with several other students.

The police also released a woman, whom we knew as Abd-Alqadir's wife, and her mother. Abd-Alqadir's wife was sixteen and a newly wed. The Mukhabarat arrested Abd-Alqadir after retrieving information against him from Samih Kiyalee, the informant. The interrogators tortured Abd-Alqadir for information on the location of the Ikhwan base he managed. Hameeda ordered for Abd-Alqadir's wife to be brought to the police division. Hameeda allowed officers to rape Abd-Alqadir's wife and forced Abd-Alqadir to watch. Hameeda ordered Abd-Alqadir's transfer to Tadmur Prison, where he was later murdered in a massacre. After his death, they released his wife. She was no longer of any use.

## Aysha's Story

While Hajja Madeeha comforted my mother and me, Aysha, Um Shaima and the others gathered around us and extended warm hugs and embraces. Moneera, the young woman who searched us when we first arrived at Kafar Suseh Prison, sat against a wall, watched and smiled.

Aysha was a doctor from Aleppo. The Mukhabarat arrested her for treating a man from the Ikhwan.

"I'm a doctor. I'm just doing my job. When patients come to me, I treat them. I don't know who they are and I don't care. I'm just a doctor," she told the Mukhabarat.

Her reasoning meant nothing to them. The Mukhabarat preferred to assume that Aysha worked for the Ikhwan, treating their wounded. They arrested her. Their assumptions quickly turned to convictions. Mustafa Al-Tajir led Aysha's interrogation.

"Are you willing to go out without your *hijab*?"

"Of course not."

"What about your overcoat? Will you take that off?"

She knew he wasn't going to like her answer, so she looked around, searching for somewhere to run, somewhere to hide. Al-Tajir slapped her. He picked up a whip and beat her. He tore off her clothes piece by piece. Aysha tried to wiggle and squirm out of his grip, but could do little with her arms cuffed behind her back. Aysha stood naked except for the socks on her feet.

"I'll leave your socks on for you, so you don't get cold."

Al-Tajir ordered officers to strap Aysha onto The Magic Carpet. They strapped her in tight and tortured her using every tool they had: whips, sticks, cables, electricity... They even took her glasses away and

57

Aysha couldn't see a thing without her glasses.

When Al-Tajir and his crew finished with her, Omar Hameeda wanted a turn. Hameeda stepped into the room, tied Aysha onto a chair, stood in front of her, lit a cigarette, sucked in several puffs of smoke, and twisted the cigarette into her chest. The rage in his eyes cooled as her skin sizzled. Officers threw Aysha into a cell at the security branch for a few days before transferring her to Kafar Suseh Prison.

## Um Shaima's Story

As Um Shaima walked back home with her husband, who carried their seven month old baby, she felt something strange, something not right. As she neared her apartment, Um Shaima grew certain that something was wrong. She stood in front of her apartment door, pulled out her keys and pushed them into the lock. Before she could turn the key and push the door open, she heard the click of metal. With her hand still on the key, she turned her head to her husband, who was still making his way up from the bottom of the stairwell, and motioned with her other hand for him to run away.

Um Shaima wondered if she would ever see her husband and her baby again, her baby who still nursed from her. Officers swung the door open, grabbed Um Shaima and pulled her in. They threw her into the bedroom. The officer in charge marched in.

"Where's your husband and the other men who were staying here? How come we didn't find anybody?"

We later found out that this too was the work of the informant Samih Kiyalee.

"I don't know anything. I don't know where my husband went

and I don't know who was with him."

The officer in charge threatened Um Shaima with rape if she didn't talk. Um Shaima said nothing. The officer pressed his body against hers. Um Shaima kicked and wrestled with him with a sudden surge of strength that scared the officer off. The Mukhabarat took Um Shaima to Omar Hameeda's division.

Hameeda was well known for his wild creativity when it came to torture. Hameeda tied Um Shaima's hands behind her back and hung her upside down from the ceiling, like a lamb awaiting slaughter. Slaughter would have been a mercy. Instead, Hameeda and several other men beat and flogged her. Hameeda brought in the electrocution device. He placed the clamps on Um Shaima's breasts. Her breasts dripped with milk. When the interrogation ended, the Mukhabarat knew that they had no evidence for a conviction, but that did not stop them from sending Um Shaima to Kafar Suseh Prison.

## Dragging the Dead

The fourth inmate, Fawziya, was a mother of five children, five children now living without parents in Idlib. Mukhabarat officers killed Fawziya's husband during a raid of the Ikhwan base in Aleppo. Just another martyr for the cause, people thought, but for Fawziya, his martyrdom was like the fall of the first domino. Soon nothing in her life remained standing.

The Mukhabarat made Fawziya watch as they shot her husband dead. They made her watch as they dragged his corpse around town behind an army tank. After the show, they threw her into prison and scheduled her for regular sessions of severe torture.

Fawziya didn't like to talk about it. She didn't talk much about anything. She didn't have to. Her scarred and swollen feet and her blue fingertips, which had still not grown nails back, told us all we needed to know. Fawziya spent the first few months of her imprisonment in a sombre silence, mourning her husband's death. When a guard opened our door, she covered her head quickly with a blanket and turned to the wall.


## Moneera

Those four women, Hajja Madeeha, Aysha, Um Shaima and Fawziya were accused of being members of, or aiding the Ikhwan. The fifth woman in our cell, Moneera Kamil Mustafa, came from a different cause. Moneera was from an Alawi town along the coast and barely eighteen. Her father, her brothers and some of their friends had formed a communist group and published anti-government leaflets.

The Mukhabarat arrested her and her brother, who was sixteen. The government considered them adolescents who didn't really understand what they were doing and their prison stay was supposed to be a short-term arrangement just until they matured and began to think more clearly.

Moneera had it easy at Kafar Suseh Prison, with guards bending all sorts of rules for her. They allowed her visitors and a radio and they even let her visit her brother in the south section of the prison. When the men in her brother's cell found out about the visits, they began to send us stuff, stuff that their families sent to them. At first, we all had our suspicions about Moneera; she could have been an informant, but after spending many months together, we grew to trust her as she consistently treated us with gentleness and kindness.

"You know, we don't talk about things in front of you. We're afraid you'll rat us out to the warden," Hajja Madeeha once said to Moneera, half joking, half serious.

"I assure you I am not that type of a person. If I was an informant I wouldn't be here with you," Moneera said.

We spent a lot of time arguing with Moneera about communism, but our conversations proved useless. She held on to her beliefs tightly, although at the same time, she remained respectful of our faith. When we prayed or recited Quran, Moneera lowered the volume on her radio. When we went on hunger strikes, Moneera joined us and stuck by us to the end.

## Suffocation

I lived with those five inmates for many months before others joined us. We lived in cell number two, a medium sized cell in the north section of the prison. Our washroom was to the right of the cell. It had a shower, but no door or shower curtain. The women and I pulled the elastics out of our skirts, tied them together, hung them up like a rod in front of the shower and threw a blanket over them. We also had an electric heater in the washroom, a privilege the men did not enjoy. The men lived without heat. They lived without washrooms or even a single pipe of water in their cells. The men could only use the washroom two or three times a day after meals when the guards took them out to the *khat*.

Our cell door rarely opened and we had no windows, except for a so-called window so high up, it was close to the ceiling. It opened up to the main prison gate. Metal bars and screens layered the window so that barely any air or light came through. Even in the middle of winter, we would sit in our cell, sweat and suffocate.

We begged the guards to at least open the peephole or to bring us a fan or anything to circulate the air. One of the guards, Yaseen, consistently refused to bring us any relief, even if it just meant cracking the peephole open. Sometimes, out of desperation, we would beg him repeatedly and he would respond like a robot programmed to repeat the same phrase over and over again.

"There is no peephole. There is no peephole."

"Okay. There is no peephole, so bring us a fan or something to

61

move the air in here so we don't suffocate to death," Hajja Madeeha would say.

"There is no peephole. There is no fan. There is no door."

It was a day of grand celebration, the day they decided to let us out for a breath of fresh air – after eight months of living in an underground cell. Eventually, they began to take us out for fresh air once or twice a week. Two years later, they decided to accept our requests for a fan. By then, new prisoners had filled our cell to the rims. The overcrowding caused such suffering and suffocation that some of the women nearly died.

## Whispers are Forbidden, Time is Meaningless and to Complain is to be Humiliated

Our days in prison passed slowly and tediously, so slowly that we soon forgot about time and its passage. We no longer differentiated between night and day. We guessed at the time in order to perform our five daily prayers by keeping track of the guards' changing shifts and by trying to keep count of how long each of us had been in prison.

The light in the hallway outside our cell did not turn on and off with the rising and setting of the sun, adding to our blurred sense of night and day. Somehow, winter time seemed to bring even more darkness to our already dark existence, and it felt as if we were drowning in all this darkness, slowly suffocating, slowly dying, along with our dreams of freedom.

We were only allowed to whisper. If a guard heard us speak, he would slam his stick against the door and startle us back into silence.

"Shut up!" he would yell, and we would shut up.

When one of the guards wanted to call on any of us, they would call us by a man's name. The guards called me Mohammad.

After two weeks of living in this state of terror and tension, my mother decided she had had enough. She wanted to lighten things up, to soothe the tension. She knocked on the door and called out to Hussain, the guard, and asked him to please bring us a copy of the Quran. Hussain's eyes widened. He looked at my mother as if she had completely lost her sanity.

"Do you happen to think that you are at home or in a palace where you can demand what you please? Do you not know that the Quran is forbidden in this place?"

"Why?" She tried to stay calm and polite.

"Because we don't keep copies of the Quran here."

"I saw some with my own eyes. They were stacked in the interrogation room. They belonged to those young men in the solitary confinement cells."

She was talking about the group of boys they had rounded up at the mosque and dumped into one solitary confinement cell.

"Those Qurans are for burning, not for reading," Hussain answered with a look of disgust on his face. "Forbidden!" he yelled and slammed the peephole shut.

My mother gently knocked on the door again and pleaded with Hussain. He opened the peephole, shouted that it was forbidden and slammed the peephole shut in my mother's face. At that point, my mother lost her poise. She banged and kicked the door. This time, Ibraheem showed up. Mama asked for a copy of the Quran.

"The Quran is forbidden here. Forbidden."

"Fine, give me a paper then. I want to write to the warden."

"I don't have any paper."

My mother insisted that she get a piece of paper right away and went on and on with her arguments, until Ibraheem couldn't take it anymore. The warden received my mother's letter and sent for her to come to his office. We had no idea that he had sent for her not to discuss her request, but to humiliate her. He yelled and screamed at her and told her that they didn't keep any Qurans in prison.

63

"Why do you want one anyway? So you can read it and pray to God to send us to hell?"

When Mama returned, she told us about her meeting and we all decided to go on a hunger strike. That day we refused breakfast and lunch. A guard came to warn us that if we didn't end the strike, they'd put all of us back in solitary confinement. To show us they were serious, they cut off our water supply.

This was our first attempt at a strike and we hadn't yet built up the courage to persist, so we ended the hunger strike. The next day, my mother asked for another paper. She wanted to write to the head of the division again. Abu Asim, the warden, personally came to our cell this time.

"What do you want?" he asked.

"We're so bored in here and we just want a copy of the Quran so we could have something to do."

"Why don't you occupy yourselves with something else?"

"Like what?'

"Like making things with dough, like the men."

"Fine, teach us how."

"Okay, I will go find out how the men work the dough and I'll come back and tell you."

One hour later, Abu Isam, came back with a copy of the Quran so old and worn, I wondered where he got it from. The truth was, we didn't care how old or worn it was; we felt thrilled to have it. We immediately divided the large copy of the Quran into different chapters and used a piece of cardboard - I don't know where that cardboard came from - to cover each chapter. We numbered the chapters and started reading and memorizing and we felt overjoyed. Some time later, an officer came from Abu Isam's office and taught us how to make things with dough, like the men did.

# Prayers, Supplications and Games

The young men in the prison used to save the soft insides of their bread. They would save and save bits of bread, until they collected a large enough chunk of gooey dough for their art. The men substituted saliva for water to help knead the dough. After kneading, they left the dough to rise. After the dough rose, the men kneaded it again, until it became malleable enough to shape into small sculptures or beautiful rosary beads.

The warden kept one of the men's airplane sculptures in his office. When I had first seen that airplane on Abu Isam's desk, I thought it was made of silver. Some of the guards brought in dyes for the men, to add colour to their amazing creations, but their seeming acts of kindness turned out to be purely selfish. The guards always came back for the final products.

We embraced this new activity with great enthusiasm, grateful to have something to break the monotonous routine of prison life. We started out making rosary beads and spent hours and hours kneading, moulding and shaping the dough until we got it just right. Eventually, we progressed to making necklaces, key chains and other simple objects.

Later, we began to use colours. We invented our own ways of dyeing. The guards agreed to give us their coffee grinds and we used them to dye our beads and key chains. Towards the last few years of my imprisonment, the guards even brought us medicinal pills they didn't need so that we could melt or grind them and use them to colour our art.

One day, Hajja Madeeha magically pulled out knitting needles from God knows where and held them up for us to see. We stared in utter shock. We couldn't believe that she had snuck knitting needles into prison during her transfer from Al-Muslamiyah Prison to Kafar Suseh. We got even more excited when one of the other women found an old woollen sweater among her things. We undid the wool and knitted a brand new sweater. Knitting became our new favourite pastime. We knitted, undid and re-knitted that old sweater more times than I can count.

As time went by, we invented more and more ways to amuse ourselves. We collected olive pits, sanded them against the coarse walls of our cell and turned them into rosary beads. One time a guard caught us sanding the pits against the wall and forbade us from doing it again. He was afraid that we were trying to inscribe a message on the wall or create some sort of signal. We started to sneak our olive pits out during outdoor breaks so we could sand them against the walls of the field.

My mother was a well of creativity when it came to keeping us occupied. She invented games and taught them to us. We played spin the cup, where we would sit around in a circle, place our one and only plastic cup in the middle, spin the cup and wait for its mouth to stop at someone. That person would have to answer any question we wanted to ask them, quickly and honestly. We all loved this game, except for Hajja Madeeha. She was older and constantly frowned upon our immaturity. Our recreational activities clashed with her serious nature.

We tried to organize our time, to schedule time for reading and memorizing the Quran, time for reciting and memorizing special supplications, and time for night prayers. The women held competitions to see who could recite the largest amounts of Quran during the night prayers. At dawn we prayed *fajr* and then sat down to recite supplications. Everything we did was in the dark. We stuck to this routine every single day hoping and praying for God to help us. In the evening, we would repeat the entire routine of praying, reciting and supplicating all over again.

After our morning routine, Majida and I sat together and reviewed what we had memorized of the Quran. We reviewed and reviewed until our eyes watered and drooped. Some days, sleep would overcome us. Other days, we stayed awake the entire day. My mother always stayed up after dawn, until it was time for her to perform her mid-morning, *duha*, prayers. Only then would she lie down for a short while.

## Conversations Through a Wall

Sometimes we found amusement outside of our cell walls. After breakfast, when the men went to the *khat*, we stood against the crack in our door and tried to steal glances at the men that passed by, wondering if we would find our brothers, our uncles or our fathers among the prisoners. Some of the women in our cell also discovered a crack in the wall where our heating pipe poked out, a pipe that connected to the men's cell. The women requested a hose from the guard and told him they needed it for the washroom. The request was granted.

My cellmates pushed the hose through the opening in the wall, all the way to the men's cell. They whispered messages through the hose and sometimes even passed the men some water. The men had no water source in their cells and the guards forbade them from requesting water or using the washroom except during appointed times in the day.

We enjoyed our new invention until, Um Kamal, a new cellmate, accused of conspiring with the Iraqi government against Syria, ratted us out to the guards. The guards immediately covered the crack with cement. We went back to talking through the metal pipe. We waited for the guards to fall asleep and then we knocked on the pipe. Hajja Madeeha always spoke first. Her bed was the closest to the pipe. She shouted through the pipe as quietly as she could and the rest of us stood on high alert for the guards.

During that period of our imprisonment, the guards treated the men in horrifying ways. Everyday, they shipped a new group of men to Tadmur Prison. The person responsible for assembling the shipment to Tadmur was Abu Talal. He arrived at the men's cells before dawn everyday, pounded on the cell door like a lunatic and called out twenty to thirty names. The men lined up in the dark. Abu Talal handcuffed each two together from their hands and feet.

Some of the men faced their destinies with courage, but not every man could. Some screamed and pleaded. Some vomited. Some wet their pants. Others fell unconscious. The guards dragged the men across the prison floor, all the way to the vehicles that awaited them at the gates.

We heard everything that went on in the men's cells after dawn. We listened and cried and prayed. We could do nothing but cry and pray. They replaced every group of men transferred to Tadmur Prison with three or four more groups of prisoners. During those days, the guards stuffed the cells until the cells looked ready to explode with men. They did not care about cell capacity or breathing space and when they couldn't possibly fit another man into any of the cells, they resorted to stuffing men into the washrooms.

## Fake Tears Turn Real

Here's the story of one of the most amazing events that happened during my stay in prison. The first time I met my mother in prison, she told me that Warif, my brother, planned to leave Syria for Lebanon and from there travel to some other country and never return to Syria. But Warif only told Mama this so she wouldn't worry about him. They both knew that as long as he stayed in Syria, his life was in danger. Warif never left.

One night my mother stayed up to pray *tahajjud*, as she often did. She prayed all night until it became time for *fajr* prayer. After *fajr* prayer, she managed to stay up until sunrise for *duha* prayer. Only then did she lie down, but before she could fall asleep, she heard something and jolted up from her mattress, threw her blanket off her body and sat upright with her eyes wide open and full of terror.

"I heard Warif's footsteps!"

I took a quick breath, held it in and listened. I heard nothing. I released my breath. The men had returned from the *khat* long ago and most of the guards were fast asleep.

"What are you talking about? There isn't a single sound in the prison."

I got up, walked towards the crack in the door and peeked out into the hall. My lips trembled. I blinked hard to squeeze out the tears that blurred my vision. In front of our cell door stood Warif with his hands handcuffed behind him and his eyes blindfolded with a black cloth. Hussain pulled him by his coat, that worn out brown coat that I'd know anywhere. I looked down and saw his white running shoes. I bit down on my lip to keep myself from crying out.

"Move! To solitary confinement," Hussain ordered Warif.

I felt a fire erupt in me and I felt such a need to sob aloud, to cool that fire. I was desperate to share the burning news with somebody, but my mother was sitting there behind me, wide eyed and waiting for me to turn around and assure her that there was nobody there. I cleared my throat.

"There's nobody here," I whispered. I felt as if my voice had come from another world, from somewhere not within me.

A few weeks later, my cellmates and I went on our second hunger strike. The guards threatened us with solitary confinement and when we didn't give in, they followed through on their threat. They put my mother and Um Shaima in one cell, the same cell that they had kept Warif in just a few weeks ago. My mother and Um Shaima cried all the way to solitary confinement, trying to squeeze sympathy from the guards. Later, my mother told me that her and Um Shaima had agreed to fake cry and were actually both about to erupt into giggles on their way to solitary confinement, but contained their laughter by stuffing their towels into their mouths.

It only took my mother a few seconds in the new cell to notice the engravings on the wall. Someone had engraved a mosque. Beneath it, it read "There is No God but Allah and Mohammad is His Messenger. All praise be to Allah." Below that the artist had signed: "The martyr Mahmoud Warif Dabbagh." When my mother read the name of her son engraved on the solitary confinement cell wall, she turned to the door, pounded on it and screamed out to the guards to tell her where her son was and what they had done with him and why they arrested him in the first place. The fake tears turned real. The guards never answered her calls. My mother told me that not knowing what had happened to Warif hurt her the most.

Some time later, I found out that the Mukhabarat had arrested two of my brothers, Warif and Ghassan, more than once. The first time was in Hama. They released them after a few days due to lack of evidence. The Mukhabarat arrested Warif a second time and brought him to Kafar Suseh Prison, but again released him for lack of evidence. Some time later, they killed him.

One time, an officer was chatting with Majida and told her Warif's story. "We arrested him the first time when we suspected him of being a criminal. It turned out that he was innocent, so we let him go. The second time we arrested him, we gave him the benefit of the doubt again and let him go a second time. When we found out that he really was a criminal and that his big brother had dragged him into a life of crime, we gave him what he deserved. A murderer must be murdered, sooner or later."

## Half a Tile to Sleep on

As time went by, my troubles continued to pile up. I began to feel deep pain in my back. The pain intensified day by day and just when I thought I could no longer bear it, the diarrhoea and vomiting began.

It all started one day when I felt as if I was slipping away, slowly dying. I slept next to the heating pipes, which blew in cool air. Water condensed on the pipes and added humidity to the cool air, but I had no choice in my place of sleep. By now, the cell was packed beyond any humane limits. Each woman's share consisted of half a tile. If one of us wanted to turn over, everyone had to turn over. I didn't notice the cold air that blew over my body at first, but one day I just found my back unable to budge and the diarrhoea and vomiting followed soon after.

That day, the women all banged on the cell door and begged the guards to bring a doctor for me. The guards paid no attention. Aysha, who was a doctor, pleaded with them to at least bring us a plastic bowl. She pleaded and begged until they gave in and brought her one. After two days of continuous warm water baths, my pain began to ease.

## A New Strike

Every passing day created new stories, new experiences and new lessons. My mother snatched every opportunity she could to bring us comfort and to annoy the guards, and made those two things her main objectives for the duration of her imprisonment. She bombarded the guards with complaints and requests all strategically targeted at achieving her goals.

One day, after we realized that the guards had allowed Moneera to write the high school graduation exam, it occurred to us to make the same sort of request. We wrote a letter to the warden requesting him to provide us with our university books and an environment suitable for studying. Our demands were of course met with refusal, mockery and ridicule.

Um Shaima suggested a hunger strike. My mother quickly supported the idea and the rest of my cellmates agreed. When the guards brought dinner that evening, we refused to accept it.

"What now?" Ibraheem, the guard, asked.

71

"We're on a hunger strike."

"For what?"

"We want to write our exams too."

"If you don't take your dinner, you're all going to solitary confinement."

"Good. At least we'll be able to breathe," my mother replied.

Ibraheem slammed the door and left, only to return a few minutes later, laughing hysterically.

"The boss said get ready for solitary confinement in half an hour."

In less than half an hour, Ibraheem came back and led two of us at a time into solitary confinement cells. He put my mother and Um Shaima together, Majida and Aysha together, and Fawziya and me together.

He looked at Hajja Madeeha and said, "What about you? Don't you want to write your exams too?"

Hajja Madeeha lifted her brows. "I don't even know how to read or write."

Ibraheem left Hajja Madeeha in our cell. My mother saw my brother Warif's name engraved on the wall again, and began to yell and scream and bang on the door. A couple of hours later, they walked us back to our cells. Although our requests were denied, we felt triumphant in our ability to cause a scene and raise some trouble in spite of the pressure and fear we lived in.

## Gunshots in the Middle of the Night

One night, after dinner and after most of the guards were already asleep, the sound of gunshots tore through the silent prison, so close to where we lay, we felt as if the bullets were flying over our heads. Guards rushed around closing all windows and peepholes, turning off all the lights and shouting warnings to all the prisoners not to move. We could barely hear the guards' voices above the blasting of gunshots and shuffling of weapons.

We had no idea what was happening. Could there be an exchange of fire between the guards? Or was the prison under attack? One of the walls of our cell faced the outside grounds and we heard bullets pierce into it. There were but a few yards between our cell wall and the street, with only one fence in between. My mother got up, made her *wudu* and prayed the farewell prayer of a martyr and then took cover with us behind the wall.

A loud piercing scream rose above the sounds of guns and bullets. Guards began to shout names. We figured that one of the guards had been shot. After about an hour of chaos, the prison calmed.

Hajja Madeeha tried to find out from Ibraheem, who was on guard duty during the incident, what happened, but he sternly forbade her to ask such questions and warned her of severe consequences. In a few days, everything returned to normal. We never did find out what actually happened that day.

## Release, but to Tadmur

One day, as Hajja Madeeha spoke to the male inmates in the adjacent cell through a pipe that connected our cells, a man asked her, "Is there anyone from Hama in your cell?"

"Yes," she replied.

"My dear aunt, we are from Hama too and we are being released tomorrow. If anyone from Hama would like to send a letter to their families, write it up and stick it through the crack in the peephole. We will pull it out when we go out to the *khat*. We'll make sure no on sees anything and we'll get it to your families."

The guards had actually promised the poor men their release

73

the next day, but neglected to mention that the release was to Tadmur Prison. That morning, the head of interrogations requested my mother's immediate presence with no hint as to why. After the meeting, my mother shuffled back into the cell, her eyes red and puffy. She gazed at me and burst into tears. My heart throbbed with fear. I rushed to her, held her in my arms and asked her to tell me everything.

"They told me they are going to transfer me to another division today, but I have a feeling they're lying to me. I have a feeling they're going to let me go today." Mama unbuttoned the sweater she wore over her blouse. "The first thing the interrogator said to me was to pack up my things and get myself ready quickly." She pulled off her sweater and laid it beside me. "I asked him what about you? What about my daughter?" Mama's eyes shone with tears. "He said you have to stay here as a hostage for your brother. He told me that if Safwan doesn't give himself up soon, I may as well pretend that I never gave birth to you." Mama pushed down the pants she wore under her skirt. She laid them over the sweater. "I'm leaving these for you." She pointed at the pile of clothes. Mama knew just how badly we needed clothes.

"Does anybody want to send a message or a letter?" my mother asked.

Majida jumped up, borrowed a pen from Moneera and scribbled a note to her family on a napkin. Mama folded the napkin and tucked it into her sleeve. *She's really leaving. She's really getting out.* My mother gazed at each of us, embraced us, kissed us, prayed for us and we hugged her back, kissed her and prayed for her and then she left.

Mama barely got to the door at the end of the hallway before she began to beg Hussain to tell her when we would be released. He answered her with his usual mocking humour, but she begged and begged and we listened helplessly until she pulled herself out of his grip, ran back to our cell, lifted the peephole cover and blurted out, "I forgot, those men, our neighbours, what was their family name?"

We barely had a chance to answer before Hussain caught up with

74

her, yanked her form the collar and howled at her with his dirty language. My mother was never one to take what came her way passively. She not only reciprocated his insults and accusations, but outdid them. That was the last time I saw or heard my mother. May God have mercy on her soul.

We found out some time later that my mother had stopped by our apartment in Damascus first, the apartment where my friends and I used to live, and she had met with our old roommates and told them our stories. They asked to see Majida's letter. They copied it onto paper fearing that the napkin would wear out and the writing on it fade, but when my mother brought the copied letter to Majida's family, they refused to believe that the letter came from their daughter, for they did not recognize the writing. Majida's family had lost hope of ever seeing their daughter again. They didn't even know for certain whether she was alive or dead, until years later, when we gained visitation rights in Katana Prison, and Majida's family came to see her.


## Dear and Dignified

We found out that the Mukhabarat had indeed released my mother on February 16th 1981. We knew this because one week later, the leader of the division asked to see Majida. She had requested to meet with him to discuss possible solutions to our situation.

"Look," Khairbek said, "You will never find any place better than your place here. Here, you are dear and dignified. You will never find a division like ours. Heba's mother, when we released her, sat on the steps of this place crying and not knowing what to do with herself, until I gave her some money for a cab from my own pocket."

My mother did sit on the steps. She did cry and refuse to leave. She couldn't bear to leave without knowing what lay ahead for the rest of us. She begged for just a hint of good news, anything to keep her hope alive, to tell her that we would not be in this dear and dignified place forever. After my mother left, a new group of prisoners joined us, bringing along with them new stories of pain and tragedy, and opening a new chapter for us in our book of sorrow and suffering.

## More Guests, More Suffering

Two or three days after my mother's release, Abu Adil, the head guard, came to our cell early in the morning, opened our door and shoved a woman in. She wore a black scarf that had faded into a dingy greyish-yellow. A thick black jacket hung over her shoulders and a black pouch, like that of a beggar, held her belongings. She glanced at us and quickly stepped back out of the cell before we caught a glimpse of the red scars on her face that looked like the remains of a severe chickenpox infection, and the deep wrinkles that looked like folds along her tired face. *They brought a beggar to share our cell!* But quickly, a surge of compassion subdued my revulsion, and even though I resented having them top our long list of suffering with the looks and smells of beggary, I couldn't help but feel for the old woman.

"Get up and welcome your new guests," Abu Adil hollered as he pushed the beggar back in.

The woman took tiny steps back into our cell and then several other women, who looked and smelled like her, followed her in. They looked homeless, with raggedy old coats draped over them. One of the women wore a skirt that dragged on the ground, tied her scarf tightly on top of her head and wore a sweater so tight that it clung to her body like a wetsuit. The buttons on the back of the sweater were missing and the sweater hung open, exposing her back.

My cellmates and I looked down at the ground and said nothing, until one of the women, the one who had walked in first, sprung towards Hajja Madeeha, grabbed her in a tight embrace and cried out, "My God!

You are here!"

The two of them burst into tears and clung to each other.

"Hajja Riyad! Thank God. You're okay. Finally… finally I have found a friend in this place."

Hajja Madeeha recklessly pushed over the prisoner who sat next to her and made room for her new friend. Hajja Riyad claimed her place next to Hajja Madeeha and kept that place for years. The rest of the new inmates stepped in slowly and looked around. They took but a few minutes to relax and settle into their new home and then began to tell us the tales of the journeys that brought them to our joint cell in Kafar Suseh Prison.

## The Metal Door

Five of the new inmates, Hajja Riyad, Lama, Raghda, Montaha and Eman came from Maslameya Prison in Aleppo. Mukhabarat officers had handcuffed each two women together, stuffed them into a car and told them that they were being released. Sixteen other women, whom the Mukhabarat had jailed with them, had been released just days before. As the driver headed out of the prison and got onto the road, the women noticed the large monument, a globe of the earth, that marked the end of Aleppo and the entrance onto the road that headed out of town. Even in the darkness of the night, Hajja Riyad noticed that globe.

"I'm pretty sure you already passed my house," Hajja Riyad told the driver. "My house is in the part of town called The Metal Door. Maybe you're lost."

"No. Don't worry. We haven't gotten to The Metal Door yet. I want to give you all a tour of Aleppo before I take you to The Metal Door."

Hajja Riyad realized she wasn't going home. Lama turned pale. She figured they must be taking them for execution. Hajja Riyad fainted. The driver and other officers ridiculed the women, mocking them for believing that they were actually going home. By the time the women got to Kafar Suseh Prison, they were exhausted and edgy, but it only took a few moments for them to calm down and open their hearts to us.

## Life Savings

Hajja Riyad was a kind and simple woman. She left school in grade six and never married, although she looked over forty. Like Hajja Madeeha, she came from a religious family. Her brothers ran a carpenter shop in Aleppo; they allowed the Ikhwan to use that shop as a hideout. When the government discovered the hideout, they arrested one of her brothers, but the other one got away and escaped to Amman, Jordan. One time, as Hajja Riyad prepared to visit her brother in Amman, a woman came by and gave her money for the widows of men whom the Mukhabarat had executed, widows who had escaped to Amman and had no means of supporting themselves. Hajja Riyad felt obliged to comply with the request. She felt it was her humanitarian duty. She took the money to Amman and gave it to the widows.

Shortly after, someone mentioned Hajja Riyad's name during a confession. The Mukhabarat arrested, imprisoned and tortured her severely. They searched every square inch of her house, looking for that money. They didn't believe her when she told them the money was already gone. They told her to lead them to the money or else... Hajja Riyad tolerated as much of the continuous torture as she could, but then lost the strength to bear anymore and led the officers to the box under her couch where she kept her life savings.

Every time she mentioned her lost savings, she wept and said to Hajja Madeeha, "They stole my sweat, my pain, my hard work. They stole it and called it Ikhwan money. Damn the Ikhwan. Damn them."

78

Hajja Riyad made up a song, a song that she often sang with such sorrow, but sometimes I also sensed a touch of humour in her voice.

*Dear God, I sit here a prisoner,*
*because I delivered Ikhwan money…*

Hajja Riyad told us what the Mukhabarat did to her in Aleppo. They did to her what they did to most of the women arrested in Aleppo. Officer Omar Hameeda stripped her down to her bare skin. He dragged her by her hair along the floor and banged her head on the floor and wall, breaking her nose and causing her irreparable breathing difficulties. We realized that was why she snored so loudly at night. Hajja Riyad fainted, but Hameeda was not done with her.

Hameeda brought a powerful hose and sprayed her face with cold water. The spray of the hose was so powerful that it got into her ears and burst one of her eardrums. Her burst eardrum brought a blessing. She slept on her good ear and couldn't hear her own snoring, the snoring that tormented the rest of us every night. Sometimes when we couldn't take it anymore, we woke her up and asked her to change her position so that maybe we could get an hour's worth of quiet.

Hameeda also plied out Hajja Riyad's nails. Even after her transfer to Kafar Suseh Prison, Hajja Riyad's nails hadn't grown back. For a long time, her fingertips consisted of dark, purplish-blue bruises without nails.

After plying out her nails, breaking her nose and bursting her eardrum, Hameeda positioned Hajja Riyad in the corner of a room and called to her, "Come here you cow, come here cow," and motioned to her with his hand to come. Hajja Riyad couldn't hear his words, but responded to his motioning and crawled to him. When she reached him, Hameeda along with the rest of the officers exploded into laughter. Hameeda leaned down and spoke into her good ear, "So, you know that your name is cow."

# Eight Years for 400 Liras

Montaha, who was barely sixteen years old, was the wife of one of the men who was executed in 1979 with the accusation of being a part of an armed anti-government movement. Montaha had married him without her parents' consent, so when he was executed, her parents refused to take her and her unborn baby into their home.

"I don't even want to look at her," she heard her father say. "That's what she gets for disobeying me."

Montaha spent her customary four months of mourning at her in-laws. After that, she lived off charity, charity like the kind Hajja Riyad distributed in Amman. One night, the Mukhabarat dragged Hajja Riyad out of prison and forced her to lead them to Montaha's house. She did not dare refuse their request after the torture she endured.

When the Mukhabarat raided the house where Montaha lived, Montaha tried to escape. She ran out of the house clutching to her newborn baby, but the Mukhabarat caught her, snatched her baby out of her arms, threw the baby back into the house and drove off with Montaha to the Mukhabarat headquarters.

At the worst possible timing, some other detainee mentioned Montaha's name during a confession. The Mukhabarat discovered that Montaha had recently received a marriage proposal from Mustafa Kassar, a wanted member of the Ikhwan, and for that they punished her like they punished Hajja Riyad. They stripped her, chained her to the ceiling and tortured her in all the ways they knew how. During the torture, Montaha admitted to receiving the letter with the marriage proposal. They didn't care when she told them that she had refused the proposal.

Montaha also confessed to receiving four hundred liras as a gift from the Ikhwan for her baby, to help her out after her husband's execution, but she insisted that she had nothing to do with the anti-government movement. They believed her admission, but not her plea to innocence. After more torture, the Mukhabarat imprisoned her in Al-Maslamiya Prison in Aleppo and later transferred her to Kafar Suseh Prison.

Along with Hajja Riyad and Montaha came another girl from Aleppo; her name was Eman. She was in grade nine. She was convicted with delivering the marriage proposal letter from her brother, Mustafa Kassar, to Montaha. Because that was the only accusation against her, they did not torture her in the ways they tortured Hajja Riyad and Montaha. The Mukhabarat considered her "sin" an act of juvenile delinquency. They released her in 1984, along with Um Shaima.

The Mukhabarat arrested the fourth and fifth of our new inmates, Raghda and Lama, in Beruit. Raghda and Lama had gone to Beirut to meet a man who promised to help them join the Ikhwan movement. However, the Mukhabarat found out and raced to the meeting place and arrested the women when they arrived. Their torture was not as severe either. Like Eman, they were only in grade nine.

Lama told us that during her interrogation, they brought her cousin into the room, her cousin who allegedly recruited her into the Ikhwan, so that he could testify in front of her. Her cousin walked into the room with one of his eyeballs in the palm of his hand and blood gushing out of his empty socket.

After her transfer to Kafar Suseh Prison, the Mukhabarat put Lama through another round of interrogation. They brought her back to our cell puffy eyed and sobbing uncontrollably.

"What happened?" asked Hajja Madeeha.

"He slapped me and he cursed my father." Lama's voice quivered with rage. That was the worst of what she encountered.


## The Harmooshiya Party

Torture in prison takes many different shapes and forms. A slap across the face, a beating with a stick, curses, and insults are only some of the forms. Other ways include stuffing tens of people into one cell, where they can find no air, no escape. They include forcing a large group of individuals, each of whom has her own distinct habits, opinions, and background to become intimate neighbours.

A new prisoner joined us one day, a woman from the town of Daraa who was convicted with smuggling and trading weapons. She stepped into our cell and without any introduction glared at us and said, "I don't like the way you look." I wondered what her problem was. None of us understood, until we thought to ask her about that initial comment some time later.

"From my first glance into this room, I noticed that the older women you call Hajjas were sitting on this side of the room and the rest of you were sitting by yourselves on that side. So, I thought that you guys were different from them and that each group sat with their kind," she explained.

Her name was Um Jibri. She was tall, broad and big in every way except for her brain. She was an ignorant woman, ignorant in everything, from politics to cleanliness. She left everything filthy: her body, the place she sat and the bathroom after she used it. And we were all crammed into this tiny space with her. Lice quickly spread from her head to the head of every woman in the cell. Moneera suffered the most for she slept head to head with Um Jibri. Soon, Moneera couldn't bear it anymore.

"I have just the medicine for her," said Hajja Madeeha.

She knocked on our door, called for Hussain and asked him to lend us a jug of gas. Hussain brought us a jug of gas. Hajja Madeeha took the jug in one hand and Moneera's head in the other and poured gas all over her head. Hajja Madeeha poured the entire jug of gas, but the lice on Moneera's head remained as active and alive as ever.

The lice did not leave Moneera's head until Um Jibri left. A month or two later, they released her due to some connections she had to Mahmoud Al-Zobi, a minister in the government. Um Jibri had managed to drive all of us mad during her short stay, and not only us, but the entire team of interrogators too.

"Which party do you belong to?" the interrogators asked her, thinking that there might be a whole party involved in her weapons smuggling activities.

"I'm from the Harmooshiya party," she replied over and over again. Harmooshiya was the name of her village. The interrogators tortured her more and more, thinking that she was trying to avoid the truth, but Um Jibri had no clue why her answer was making the interrogators so angry.

## Levels of Suffering

Um Jibri seemed like a blessing compared to some of the other prisoners, whose mere presence caused us severe suffering. During the end of 1981, while the Mukhabarat pursued every woman in *hijab*, they also arrested one of the female leaders of the communist organization in Syria. Her name was Fadya Lathkani. She was in medical school in the same university as my brother. The government convicted her with distributing anti-government literature produced by the Ikhwan. In prison, Fadya became an informer for the leader of the division, relaying to him every move of every woman in our cell.

Fadya loved to stand on her communist high horse and argue about our different value systems. Our arguments never went anywhere. It wasn't the arguments that prevented us from befriending her though; it was her consistent efforts to annoy and irritate us. The warden allowed her a radio, like Moneera, and several other things forbidden to us and Fadya took total advantage of her privileges. When we prayed or read Quran, she blasted the volume on her radio and the loud music broke our concentration. When we read Quran aloud, Fadya grabbed her earphones, pressed them over her ears and glared at us. Many times, we asked her to please stop treating us that way and to respect our ways, but she would huff and scowl at us.

When the Mukhabarat murdered my family during the 1982 Hama massacre, the leader of the division delivered the news to Fadya personally. That day, Fadya came back to our cell smiling and giddy. We asked her why she was so excited and she told us that the leader of the division allowed her to have a tape recorder, but that didn't convince us. She already had a radio and a tape recorder wasn't such a big step up.

Hajja Madeeha approached her by herself and asked her what had happened to make her so happy? This time she told the truth – shamelessly.

"The leader of the division told me that Heba's entire family was murdered in Hama. That's why I am so happy."

Fadya listened to the radio. She listened to the news about the events in Hama and we begged her to tell us what was happening, but she refused to share a word. She stayed up all night listening and we watched her face as she listened and wished for a way to find out what was happening out there. We remained cellmates with Fadya until the day they transferred us to Katana Prison. Soon after that, Fadya was released. One of the first things she did after her release was visit us in Katana Prison. Fadya gloated as she told us how she was going on vacation and that when she came back she was going to live in France and continue her studies there.

## The Spying Game

We heard about a new solitary confinement prisoner, who was to join our group soon, a Palestinian woman. We later discovered that the government had planted her amongst us as a spy, like Fadya. One day Fadya told us that the leader of the division, Khairbek, had asked her to befriend the new inmate. He had guards place Fadya in a solitary confinement cell with the new inmate so that Fadya could talk to her, create a bond with her and report to the leader of the division all of the new inmate's secrets. He wanted Fadya to analyze her personality and her state of mind.

For a whole week, Fadya came back to us from the solitary confinement cell and repeated to us everything she reported to the leader of the division. Fadya went on and on about the poor Palestinian woman's suffering and sorrow, until our hearts nearly melted for the woman. A few days later, the guards brought the woman to our cell. We embraced her with open arms and open hearts. The Palestinian woman made her way from one woman to the other, listening to each of our stories and subtly extracting our secrets.

Not long after, the leader of the division ordered her release. We felt thrilled for her and we bid her a warm farewell. Naturally, she offered to deliver any letters or messages we wanted to send to the outside world. She promised to take the letters to whomever we trusted on the outside. I thought about sending a letter to my family with her, but felt reluctant when she persisted in her offer. Something in my heart told me not to trust her. The opportunity to communicate with the outside world tempted me and I almost did pick up a pen and begin to write a letter, but in the end, I decided to listen to my instincts. I thanked her for her kind offer and told her I didn't want to send anything.

Most of the other women did send letters with her. Those letters fell straight into the hands of Naseef Khairbek and he used them to piece together much of what went on in our cell and in our minds, things like who was speaking out against the government or complaining about the Mukhabarat's treatment and who the prisoners trusted on the outside.

The moment we found out that the Palestinian woman was a spy, we all looked at Fadya knowing that she had deceived us as well. Fadya played innocent and pretended to be shocked at our accusations. She persisted in her claims of innocence and even took part in our next hunger strike. She not only took part, but she was actually one of the toughest ones on herself and on those who weakened and wanted to break the strike. But we saw through her entire act and knew that her participation in the strike was nothing but a last move in her spying game.

Around that same time period, another new inmate joined us, Tarfa. Like Fadya, she didn't share our values or our religion, but unlike Fadya she was quiet and kind; she didn't like to hurt anybody with words or actions. She was a twenty-five year old Christian lady from the town of Tooma in Damascus.

Tarfa told us that she had travelled with her husband to Jordan and to Iraq, hoping to seek medical help for her infertility. On their way back to Syria, the Mukhabarat arrested her husband and accused him of working for the Iraqi government. They arrested her for being his wife. She said she didn't know anything about the Iraqi government and had no idea whether her husband actually did have any involvement or not. All she knew was that she was dragged out of her home and brought to Kafar Suseh Prison where she was tortured for days and then thrown into a cell with us.

We felt as if Tarfa was one of us. When we decided to go on a hunger strike, she joined us and stuck with it to the end. When we were transferred to Katana Prison, Tarfa was transferred with us, but when we were released she stayed in Katana Prison for many more months.

## A Guest of God

Officers continued to cram our cell with new groups of prisoners, topping our suffering with more tragedies. One group of women included two sisters, Mona and Lama, from the city of Latakiya. Mona was thirty-five years old and had two daughters and one son. Lama was single and eighteen. Mona was a kind and simple girl. Her story began with a bullet that accidentally killed her husband while he passed through an exchange of fire between the Mukhabarat and the Ikhwan in Latakiya. The bullet pierced into his shoulder - the shoulder where he had perched his young daughter - and travelled through to his heart. His daughter fell to the ground and lay barely harmed next to her dead father.

A few days later, a man knocked on Mona's door claiming to be a gas salesman and Mona said she'd buy some gas from him. The man came in to fill her tank. He asked Mona if he could stay in her place, because he had nowhere else to go and she, due to her good nature and simplicity, agreed to allow the stranger in. She had no idea that the stranger was one of the most wanted men in Latakiya, known as Abu Antar or Ahmad Antar.

The secret police found her out, raided her house, found Abu Antar hiding in one of her closets, shot him dead and dragged Mona to prison. During her interrogation, when they asked her who the man in her closet was, Mona replied, "a guest".

"A guest? A guest?" they screamed at her. "That man was the biggest criminal in the city and you claim he was a guest in your house!"

"Any guest is a guest of God," she replied.

"A guest of God?" The officers shouted at her, baffled.

"Yes, I swear. The man came to me, told me he had nowhere to go and nobody to go to, and pleaded for refuge. How could I refuse him?"

Mona and Abu Antar had agreed that if anyone asked about him, she would say he was her sister's fiancé. The police found out about this agreement and arrested Mona's sister, Lama, who had no idea about anything. But the police did not stop at Mona's sister. They also arrested Mona's parents and her brother. A short while later, they released her father, but kept her brother.

We recognized Mona's innocence and simplicity from the moment she walked into our cell crying and heaving like a child. We huddled around Mona and her sister and tried to comfort them. Mona wore *hijab* like us, and the commonality quickly created feelings of comfort between us.

"What are your names? Why did they bring you here?" we asked them after they calmed down; and that's when the sisters told us their stories.

"Why are you crying so much? They didn't even torture you and you've been here for quite a while already."

"The officer told me to go into the cell and I didn't go in right away, so he cursed my father," Mona whimpered.

"So what?" Hajja Madeeha snapped.

"Nobody can curse my father!"

Mona stayed with us until 1985, when they transferred her to a prison in Latakiya. We met her again in Katana Prison, about one year later and from there they transferred us together to Dooma Prison. We shared the same cell for years, until they released us at the same time. Lama was released from Kafar Suseh Prison in 1984.

## Squeezed in Graves

Another one of our inmates was Um Yaseen Sareej, whose son was accused of being behind the 1981 *Azbakiya* incident, a suicide bombing in Damascus. They brought his picture to our cell and asked us if we knew the man in the picture, but his face had been so disfigured that we couldn't tell whether we knew him or not. We said no, we didn't know him. The guards passed his picture throughout the prison. No one admitted to knowing him.

That night, they took his mother and asked her about her son, about the government's pursuit of him. She said she knew nothing. They brought in her son's corpse and displayed it in front of her. Um Yaseen said nothing but, *"Hasbina Allah wa ni'ma alwakeel."* I seek support only from Allah and he is the best supporter.

The Mukhabarat had imprisoned Um Yaseen's husband and her other two sons along with her. Her sons were only sixteen and twelve years old. They put the father and sons together in the south section of the prison and they put Um Yaseen with us. They didn't release Um Yaseen until after our transfer to Katana Prison.

I remember once when we were on our way to one of our bogus court hearings, Officer Soliman Al-Habeeb showed us a clipping from a newspaper of the *Azbakiya* bombing and said, "We are holding this trial for the blood of those innocent people killed in that bombing. We will avenge their blood with blood from your necks."

After the ridiculous trial, on our way back to prison, Officer Soliman Al-Habeeb said to us, "The Ikhwan were behind that incident and you should know that every move your people make on the outside will be reflected on you."

His words were not idle threats, but bitter truths. Every time the Ikhwan took action on the outside, things grew worse for us. Sometimes, they closed our peephole for days and we nearly suffocated. Other times, we listened to the screams of the male prisoners. Their screams pierced the air and grew louder as the Ikhwan on the outside grew bolder.

"Damn the Ikhwan. Damn your rise to power. Why don't you come here and see what is happening to us. You're out there. You do whatever you want. But we're in here. We're the ones being squeezed in graves," Hajja Riyad would lament.

## Prison or Convent?

Life in prison exposed me to many sorrowful sights, sounds and stories, but the most sorrowful story of all was the story of Hala. One day, I pressed my body against our cell door and peeked out the peephole. I saw a new face.

"It looks like they've brought in a new girl, a foreigner, I think."

I turned to my cellmates.

"She doesn't seem to understand Arabic. Hussain is talking to her and pushing her around and she's just staring at him like she has no idea what's going on. But she must be a Muslim foreigner because she's wearing *hijab*."

Hussain's probably dragging her out to the *khat*, I thought. Moments later, I looked out the peephole again and watched Hussain shove the young woman back into a solitary confinement cell. Everyday, for about a month, I stood at the peephole and watched guards drag Hala back and forth from solitary confinement to the *khat* and back. The guards pushed and shoved Hala and she stumbled along the hallway, never taking a step on her own or speaking a word. I also watched guards drag her to interrogation and hours later, shove her back into her cell, like an animal, a stiff lifeless animal. The only thing Hala ever did was stare with a blank face.

About a month later, the officers gave up on Hala and brought her to our cell. Ibraheem opened our door, pushed Hala in and said, "Heba. Get up. Take her. She's your job now."

Ibraheem shoved her again, with both hands, toward me. Hala wore an old scarf and huge pants that spread on the floor in two circles around her feet, the same scarf and pants I had seen her in a month ago. Her clothes looked filthy. They smelled filthy. I wondered how long she had gone without a washing. I waited for Hala to come closer. I waited and waited. Hala didn't come closer. Hala didn't move at all. After a few moments, my cellmates and I inched toward her.

"What is your name?" we asked.

Hala said nothing.

"Where are you from?"

Hajja Madeeha crept closer to Hala.

"Move back girls. You're crowding her." Hajja Madeeha

90

motioned for us to move back.

"What's your name, dear?" Hajja Madeeha asked.

Hala parted her lips and a strange sound, like an echo from a deep abandoned well, screeched out. Hala stared past all of us, as if a focal point far away demanded her undivided concentration. Nothing could break her focus.

"Who are you? What's your name?" We asked and asked, but Hala never answered.

An hour later, we stopped asking. We decided she must be scared and needed time to relax.

Moneera spent a lot of time listening to her radio. Sometimes when they aired Quranic recitation on a show called, "Growing up with the Quran," Moneera turned up the volume and let us listen. The day Hala joined us, "Growing up with the Quran" was airing and Moneera let us listen to a young boy's recitation of the Quran. When Hala heard the young boy recite, she sprung up, grabbed the radio and shrieked.

"Turn it off. Turn it off. This boy is messing up the Quran. That is forbidden. It's all lies. All lies."

We looked at each other, our eyes wide.

"May God forgive him." Um Shaima turned off the radio.

"Something is wrong with her," Um Shaima whispered to us.

After her outburst, Hala stepped back to where she was standing by the cell door and reset herself into the stiff position she was in. Hala didn't move again for hours. Night fell. Hala didn't move. Daybreak neared and Hala still stood beside the door motionless. We tried to move her, but she felt like a nail hammered to the ground. Hajja Madeeha couldn't take it anymore. She banged on the cell door. Ibraheem came.

"My son, there is something wrong with this girl. Why is she stuck in the same position? We eat, drink, sit and sleep and she just stands there doing nothing."

"Don't believe her. She's acting."

"Has she been like this from the time she got here?"

"Yes, but she's just putting on a show. It's all a grand act. She just wants to squirm out of confessing to the long list of charges against her, but she's dreaming if she thinks we're going to fall for it," Ibraheem shouted at Hala.

Hajja Madeeha stood in front of Hala, took Hala's hands in her own, pulled her gently, step by step towards her mattress and pressed Hala down into a sitting position. Hala sat beside Hajja Madeeha. We asked the guards to turn off the hallway light and we lay down and tried to sleep.

Moments later, I opened my eyes. I saw Hala crouching over my legs, examining my face with wide open eyes. I bit my lips hard. I screamed.

"Hajja. Please for God's sake. Come take her off me."

My cellmates bolted from their sleep.

"What? What happened?"

They saw Hala crouched on top of me. Hala sprung up and went back to her spot on Hajja Madeeha's mattress. She sat with her arms wrapped around her knees and looked at us with terror in her eyes.

"Come here dear, my daughter." Hajja Madeeha wrapped her arms around Hala and slowly pulled her in closer and closer until they sat side by side. Hajja Madeeha squeezed Hala to her. My cellmates and I eased back into a calmness and fell asleep.

Before sunrise, we awoke for *fajr* prayer, prayed together and lay back down to sleep. I closed my eyes. I heard heavy breathing. I opened my eyes and saw Hala's face over mine, her eyes focused on mine. Hala had lifted my blanket up to stare at me. I pictured Hala with her hands around my neck, strangling me. I screamed once and froze. Hala moved back and sat against the wall. Her face looked expressionless, as if nothing had happened.

"What do you want? Do you want something?" Majida asked Hala.

"What is this place? Is this a convent?" Hala asked.

Hala spoke with a strange accent. She spoke like a machine.

"No this is not a convent," Majida said. "This is prison!"

Hala sat stiff and silent and didn't speak another word.

## The Shooting Potato

Hala's clothes and scarf had been filthy since the day she joined us, and now after several weeks in our cell, they looked and smelled disgusting. Every time one of us came close to her or tried to touch her clothing, she pulled back and wrapped her arms around herself. For eight months, Hala didn't talk, eat, drink or use the bathroom like the rest of us. My cellmates and I forced water and a few morsels of food into Hala's mouth everyday, but we couldn't force her to chew. She often kept the same morsel of food in her mouth for hours.

Sometimes, Hala went to the washroom at night, left the curtain open, sat still and watched us. All of us lay motionless, pretending to be asleep, for if she heard any of us move she'd bolt out of the washroom without lifting her pants back up.

One day, Aysha sat beside Hala with a boiled potato in her hand.

"Here, eat this," Aysha said. "This potato is nice and sweet."

Aysha peeled the potato, broke off a tiny piece and held it up to Hala's mouth. Hala grabbed the potato out of Aysha's hand, swung her arm back and lunged the potato forward with full force. I was standing in the washroom over the sink, washing my clothes, when I felt something round and hard bang against my head and fall into the toilet.

## Burns, Rape and Fabrications

One month later, we decided we must change Hala's clothes, no matter what. For one whole month, Hala's body did not touch water. She startled and withdrew every time we neared her. Hajja Madeeha and Um Shaima decided to make the attempt.

"Look, we have some nice clean clothes for you here. You're clothes are too dirty now."

Hala motioned with her hand for them to go away. Um Shaima came closer and gently lifted Hala's shirt. Hala screamed eardrum popping loud. She punched and kicked and refused to let anyone touch her clothes, but Um Shaima and Hajja Madeeha tore her pants and shirt off her body and quickly redressed her into a clean set of clothes.

Now, Hala wore clean clothes, but her body was still filthy. She dug long dirty nails through her long hair and scratched her scalp for hours. She scratched and scratched and scratched. We realized she must have lice and we came to a concensus: Hala must bathe.

Hajja Madeeha and the women gathered around Hala and coaxed her into the washroom. Hala screamed and yelled and flung her arms and legs wildly as the women tried to take her clothes off once again. Guards rushed into our cell.

"What's going on?" they asked.

"Nothing, we just want to bathe her. We're afraid she's going to rot if we leave her like this," Hajja Madeeha said.

"You should know that she's deceiving you. She's a manipulator, a liar."

Throughout our imprisonment at Kafar Suseh, the guards and officers maintained that Hala's behaviour was an act. While bathing Hala, we discovered burn marks on her feet, her thighs and all over the back of her body, marks that looked imprinted with a hot metal rod, but the burn marks revealed little. Hala's story remained buried within her, beyond our reach.

Five or six months after Hala joined us, her stomach began to swell. It grew bigger and bigger and Hala whimpered and groaned in pain. Soon the whimpers and groans turned to hollers and screams and we suspected that Hala might be pregnant. My cellmates and I took turns guessing at Hala's story.

"Maybe she was married and maybe she lived with her husband in one of the Ikhwan hideouts and the police found them out and raided the place. Maybe she watched her husband die at the hands of the Mukhabarat and maybe that sent her into a deep shock. And on top of that she was pregnant," Hajja Madeeha speculated.

The guards too noticed Hala's swelling stomach. They went to the leader of the division, Khairbek, with the news. Abu Faris, the head of interrogations, came to our cell to investigate.

"We want to examine her. She may actually be pregnant," Abu Faris said.

"Please allow me to perform the examination and I'll inform you of the results," Aysha said.

During the examination, Hala's screams echoed throughout the prison. Aysha discovered clear signs of rape, but no permanent damage and no sign of a pregnancy. Hala remained in severe pain, moaning and wailing for two days. We felt that Hala would die soon. We knocked on the door and called out to the guards.

"Get a doctor! Quick! Hala's dying."

"What's going on," one guard opened the door and asked.

"She's dying of pain."

"So what? The law says 7% of prisoners are allowed to die."

We begged and begged for a doctor, until the guards finally fetched one. They brought us the prison workers' doctor.

"There's nothing wrong with her," the doctor said after examining Hala, "It's simply a really really bad case of constipation."

The doctor gave Hala suppositories and a lubricant. I applied them for her. A short while later, Hala hurried to the washroom. The smell that seeped out nearly killed us. None of us will ever forget that day or that smell. Hajja Madeeha knocked on the door and begged the guards to come.

95

"Please open the door, before we all suffocate to death."

The guard opened the door.

"What is that smell?" the guard asked, his eyes wide. "What did you women do in there? What on Earth do you have in there?"

"The princess finally did it," Hajja Madeeha said.

## Sizzling Flesh

Because Hala persisted with her "deceitful manipulations" for so long, the leader of the division, Khairbek, decided to test her. Khairbek planned to reunite Hala with her cousin, who was also imprisoned at Kafar Suseh Prison. Hajja Madeeha requested to accompany Hala, so that Hala might feel more comfortable. Abu Faris, the head of interrogations, agreed. Hala walked out of the cell without her *hijab*. Her long hair tangled wildly over her head and her torn and faded clothing hung on her thin body. Hala stared into space, into the world she lived in, the world we couldn't see.

Hajja Madeeha told us about the reunion. Hala's cousin stepped into the room and yelled out, "Hala! Hala! Why are you doing this to yourself?"

He grabbed her shoulders, shook her and pleaded with her to respond, but Hala stood still, her face wooden.

"Oh Hala. I'm Omar. I'm your cousin."

Hala remained frozen.

Ibraheem brought Hajja Madeeha and Hala back to our cell. He opened the door and shoved Hala in. Hala didn't budge. She gripped the doorknob and froze. Ibraheem pushed and shoved. Hala didn't budge. Ibraheem called on four officers and the five of them pushed and shoved Hala together. Hala didn't move. One of the officers pulled a cigarette from his pocket, lit it and twisted the cigarette into Hala's hand. Hala kept her grip on the doorknob. The officer dug the cigarette into Hala again and again, pressing harder and harder into her skin, until the smell of sizzling flesh stung our nostrils.

"Please for God's sake, stop. This is wrong. Wrong. Wrong. Wrong," I shrieked.

The guards lifted Hala off the ground and tossed her into our cell like a slab of meat.


## Hala Speaks

Three months after Hala joined us, my cellmates and I sat in our cell with the cell door slightly cracked to allow some fresh air in. Hala sprung up, stuffed her clothes into her bag, wrapped a scarf around her head and rushed out the door. Haitham, the guard on duty, ran after Hala, but slipped and fell on his behind. Several other guards joined the chase. They caught Hala and dragged her back to our cell.

"Where were you going?" Hajja Madeeha asked Hala.

"It's my mother's birthday. I'm going to my mother's birthday party."

Ibraheem stomped into our cell, his face burning with rage. Hala sat on the ground frozen in the position she had fallen into after the guards shoved her back into the cell. Ibraheem stood in front of Hala, swung his arm back and smacked Hala's cheek. Hala's head banged the wall. Ibraheem slapped her other cheek and Hala's head pounded the wall again. Ibraheem squeezed Hala's arm, pulled her close and hollered into her ear.

"You want to fool us? You want to run away?"

Ibraheem twisted Hala's arm behind her back and slapped her. He tightened his grip and slapped her again and again and again. My cellmates and I screamed and begged Ibraheem to stop. Hala sat like a corpse, eyes unblinking, starring into space. Ibraheem slapped and hit and kicked Hala until his rage cooled. We watched and wept, but could do nothing to stop him.

A few days later, I sat by Hala and examined her as she lay down. Her nails had grown grotesquely long. I had tried to cut them for her several times, but she never let me. I wanted to try again. I leaned closer to Hala.

"Tell me, my sister, what's your name?"

"My name is Ali Kizmy. My name is buried in me."

Hala's voice sounded like a distant echo.

I jumped up and yelled, "Hajja. She spoke! She spoke!"

*Did Hala really speak or did I hallucinate?*

"What do you think if I cut your nails for you?" I asked Hala.

I reached out and tried to take Hala's hand in mine. Hala snatched her hand away as if my fingers were burning coal. I jerked back. My heart pounded. *Forget it. I'm never going to go near her again.*

Some time later, my cellmates and I resolved to bathe Hala again. We thought maybe if we took her out to the men's roomier showers, she'd feel more relaxed. The guards agreed, so we packed clean clothes for Hala and took her out to the men's showers.

"Where are you taking me?" Hala asked. "To the television?"

Hala erupted into screams and sobs. We turned back and took Hala back to our cell.

Several attempts later, Hala began to show more acceptance to the idea of a shower. One time, Hajja Madeeha sat in front of Hala and asked her, "How about a shower today?"

"No," Hala said, "Not unless she gives me her dress."

Hala poked her finger at Majida.

"But, she has nothing else to wear. I have a new dress in my bag. My family sent it to me. It's brand new and it's very very special to me."

Hajja Madeeha pulled out the new yellow and blue dress, hoping Hala would like it once she saw it. Hala shook her head.

"I want that one," she said and pointed to Majida's dress.

Majida lifted her dress, pulled it over her head and handed it to Hala. Hajja Madeeha had no choice but to give Majida the new yellow and blue dress her family sent her.

## No Red, No Water

The colour red terrified Hala. When Hala stared at the red light on the washroom furnace, her eyes widened and her face tensed. We couldn't comprehend how a tiny red light could provoke such terror. Majida wore flower shaped earrings with a red dot in the middle. That tiny red dot terrified Hala as much as the light on the furnace. My cellmates and I searched for something to cover the red furnace light with. We found a paper bag and placed it over the red light. Majida took off her earrings and stashed them out of sight.

Aysha wore prescription glasses. Hala spent hours sitting in front of Aysha and starring at those glasses, starring at the reflection of herself.

One day, Hala said, "I'm thirsty."

We filled a cup of water for her from the washroom sink, in the same cup and from the same tap we all drink from.

Hala turned her face up and frowned.

"Does one offer their own urine for others to drink?" Hala asked.

We looked at each other and lifted our brows.

"Okay. We'll bring you the best cup of water in the whole prison," Hajja Madeeha said.

Hajja Madeeha got up and knocked on the door. Abu Adil came in.

"What?"

"We would like a cup of water for Miss Hala. Miss Hala would like to drink."

Abu Adil looked confused.

"Don't you have water in there?" He pointed to our washroom.

"The water we have in here is not good enough for Hala."

Abu Adil frowned, left and returned a moment later with a cup of water. Hajja Madeeha offered the water to Hala. Hala looked into the cup, looked up at us and said, "This is dirty." She spit in the cup. Hajja Madeeha asked Abu Adil to bring another cup of water. Abu Adil, smirked, left and came back with another cup. Hajja Madeeha offered Hala the new cup of water. Hala looked at the water, scrunched her nose and spit into the cup. Hajja Madeeha asked Abu Adil to please bring one more cup of water. Abu Adil brought one more cup of water. The experiment seemed to amuse him. By the end of the experiment, seven cups of water mixed with spit lined the wall beside Hala.

During one of our entertainment sessions, we pretended to be Palestinian refugees sending messages to our families via radio. We liked this game because it gave us a chance to express all of our pent up emotions and yearnings for our families.

"I send my greeting to my mother, my beloved mother. What are you doing now my dear mother? You must be just sitting there crying and falling apart," Hajja Riyad said and burst into tears, setting off a chain reaction of crying. Crying soon turned to sobbing and we all sobbed for ourselves and for each other.

"Hala, would you like to participate in our radio broadcast?" we asked.

"Come on, Hala. Sing a song for us," Um Shaima said.

Hala sang a song called, "One God". She sang as loud as she could and didn't stop until she finished the whole song. Guards rushed into our cell.

"What's going on here? Are you guys having some kind of religious celebration or something?"

"Leave us alone," Hajja Madeeha said. "Just shut the door and go away."

We wanted to savour every second of this joyous event. Hala's song brought such pleasure to our hearts, a pleasure like the kind a new mother feels when she first holds her baby in her arms. We prayed to God together and thanked him for breaking the silent spell, for breaking the barrier that stood between Hala and us.


## Suicide Attempt

Hala's silence slowly withered and died. After eight months of suffering, Hala's awareness returned and we finally learned her story. We described to Hala how she used to behave, but she remembered nothing. Her last memory was of her trip from Latakiya to Damascus.

Hala came from a religious family in Latakiya and studied science at college. One of her cousins, Omar, came to her for help with his grade ten math homework. Omar had a connection to the resistance movement. When the government arrested one of the men from Omar's group, the man mentioned Omar's name during interrogation and the police arrested Omar shortly after.

During Omar's interrogation, the police asked him routine questions like, 'Who is your teacher?' Of course the young boy did not realize that when the police asked about his teacher, they meant his religion teacher or the head of his activist group. Omar told the Mukhabarat that Hala was his teacher. The police arrested Hala immediately after that.

During Hala's interrogation, the police handcuffed her hands and feet and stripped her. They tortured Hala for days. Two or three officers, along with the branch president, gang raped Hala. When they finished, they picked her up and dumped her bruised and bloody body into a cold room. Wind whirled and whistled in the room. Hala lay on the floor freezing and convulsing. She heard footsteps going back and forth outside her room. Cold, fear, and indignation at the loss of her honour kept Hala in shivers all night.

Officers dragged Hala back and forth from the cold room to the torture chamber. Every time they opened the door to drag her to another session of torture, Hala feared they would rape her again.

One time, after they brought her back to the cold room, Hala caught sight of a piece of glass on the floor. She lifted the glass from the floor and gripped it in her palm. To Hala, that piece of glass was a saviour. Hala held on to her sanity long enough to slit her wrists. She lay in a growing puddle of blood and waited to die.

When the officers came back to take Hala for another round of interrogation, they found her a few breaths away from death. The officers called an ambulance and transferred Hala to Damascus. On the way to Damascus, Hala regained consciousness and found herself the only female in a car full of young men, including her cousin, Omar and several of his friends, all of whom she knew. She thought they were all in this car together on their way to execution. Hala went into shock and lost her ability to speak, along with any grip on reality she had left. After one month of solitary confinement and regular sessions of interrogation and torture, the interrogators at Kafar Suseh Prison gave up on Hala and brought her to our cell.

## My Heart Burns for My Children

The guards continued to stuff our stifling cell with more and more prisoners. Um Mahmoud, a woman who joined us after Hajja Riyad's group, came from the small town of Hiryatan, near Aleppo. Her husband, a house foundation layer, came from another small town, Hayan. Um Mahmoud was an intelligent and alert farmer. You would never guess that she was uneducated. Her husband had built a hideout for wanted men in his house. The Mukhabarat found out and arrested him, but they did not know where the hideout was located.

The Mukhabarat set a trap at Um Mahmoud's house, while she and her children were home. The Mukhabarat waited for the Ikhwan men to come out from the hideout. They waited and waited and eventually the men had to come out, but unknown to the officers, they were armed. After a long exchange of fire, the men killed all of the officers and escaped unharmed.

Um Mahmoud had no choice but to flee her house. She set out in the middle of the freezing night with her five children, carrying the younger ones and dragging the older ones behind. She headed for her parent's house in a nearby town, unaware of her new status as a wanted criminal. The Mukhabarat were now on Um Mahmoud's track. They had discovered the bodies at Um Mahmoud's house, followed her to her parent's house and arrested her. They charged her with conspiring to cover up the hideout and with being an accessory to the murders of the officers.

The Mukhabarat transported Um Mahmoud to the Central Security Branch in Aleppo, where they tortured her, breaking her nose and smashing her hand so badly that even years later, she couldn't move her hand normally. After three months at the Central Security Branch in Aleppo, the Mukhabarat transferred Um Mahmoud to Kafar Suseh Prison, where they forced her through another round of interrogation. Um Mahmoud denied everything. She told the Mukhabarat that her husband had built the house while she was away and she had no knowledge of a secret hideout. Um Mahmoud never found out what happened to her husband, but most likely, he was executed at Tadmur Prison. Her five children, who were between four and nine years old, stayed with her elderly parents. The greatest source of pain for Um Mahmoud was being torn from her children.

"My heart is burning for my children. My heart is burning…" she would repeat again and again.

Her eyes would swell with tears, but she never broke down. In 1984, they released Um Mahmoud from Katana Prison.

# Spies, Agents and Hostages

After Um Mahmoud's arrival, the guards crammed two more women into our cell. Georgette, the younger one, was 35 years old. Her husband, Zohair, led a small Alawi unit in Kirdaha. Um George, Georgette's sister, was in her sixties. Um George's husband served in the Alawi police force. The government accused the sisters of spying for the Israeli government. Although we shared the same cell for years, the sisters never opened up to us and we never put together their whole story. They spoke cautiously and clung to their secrets. I figured out enough to know that their stories were very complicated. First, the secret police arrested the two sisters and Georgette's husband. Their arrests led to the arrest of most of the other people in their unit.

The interrogators tortured Georgette every single day. Her screams echoed throughout the prison. They always brought her back one breath from death. Aysha nursed her after the torture sessions. She sat beside her and massaged her blue and green legs with a cloth that Aysha dipped in a bowl of water to keep warm and damp. Aysha gathered whatever pieces of cloths we could muster and used them to wrap Georgette's wounds. When Georgette's pain calmed, she would leap up, as if nothing had happened and play cards with the communist women. She got so wrapped up in these games that we couldn't believe that it was her screams that just hours ago filled the prison.

"How could you cheerfully celebrate your victory in a card game when just a few hours ago you were screaming in pain?" Hajja Madeeha asked.

"I'm always a winner," she grinned.

After our transfer to Katana Prison, we were reunited with Um George. Only then did she begin to tell us more of her tale. She told us about her sister, Georgette. Um George blamed Georgette for their arrests, their demise, for everything. She burned with hate for her sister and prayed to God to burn Georgette in her grave. Before Um George's transfer to Katana Prison, Georgette and her sister were transferred to Miza Prison. Georgette was executed. Um George was transferred to Katana Prison. One day, as we listened to the Lebanese broadcast on the radio, we heard about Um George's husband's execution.

The cramming of our cell didn't stop with Georgette and Um George. Guards continued to pack more women into our cell. Some of them were in different categories from the rest of us, like these two sisters, who joined us in 1982, from Arman Aleppo, Camilla and Jameela. They came from a political opposition group that supported Iraq. The younger sister, Jameela, was pregnant when the Mukhabarat arrested her on her way back from Iraq. These two sisters clung to their stories even more tightly than Georgette and Um George. Although we stayed together in the same cell until our transfer to Katana Prison and their release, they never shared their stories and secrets.

Another woman who joined us in Kafar Suseh Prison, stayed for only a short time. The Mukhabarat held her as a hostage for her husband, who had escaped from them. They only held her for a short time though, thanks to a cousin of hers with valuable connections, who led an intelligence division in Latakiya.

## Treatment by Insults

The barely existent health care and nutrition at Kafar Suseh sparked all sorts of sicknesses. Worse than the illnesses themselves was the way the prison workers treated us. During the beginning of my imprisonment, I fell ill with dysentery. I felt severe pains in my stomach, pains that intensified steadily until I began to vomit repeatedly. I couldn't keep a morsel of food down. Aysha diagnosed me with an ulcer. When the guards brought our meals to our cell, the women picked out the most nutritious portions of the food for me, but their efforts were useless. Everything served at Kafar Suseh Prison was empty of nourishment.

My stomach pains became unbearable. My cellmates decided to write a letter to the leader of the division, Khairbek, requesting an appropriate and nutritious diet for me. Khairbek generously offered me a few moments of his precious time. An officer escorted me to Khairbek's office. It didn't take long for me to realize that the purpose of the invitation was not to listen to my complaints, but to insult me and curse my "criminal" brother.

Anaemia and rotting teeth spread like a plague amongst us. Um Shaima's cavities caused her severe pain; she begged for pain relief, but the guards ignored her pleas. We felt she was going to die from this pain and so we all participated in pleading for a doctor. After days of begging, the guards came into our cell, handcuffed and blindfolded Um Shaima, led her to a special car reserved for prisoner transportation and drove her to a dentist. The dentist yanked Um Shaima's rotten tooth out – without anaesthetic.

The infection in Um Shaima's tooth had spread to the bones in her jaw. After pulling out her tooth, the dentist performed dental surgery to remove the infection, again without anaesthetic. Um Shaima staggered back into our cell in more pain than when she had left. Her jaw ached for a long long time.

Calcium deficiency afflicted many of the prisoners, but Raghda suffered the worst of its symptoms. Raghda constantly felt dizzy. One time, she went to the washroom and after she finished using it and wanted to get up, she couldn't. She fell to the ground and banged her head against the wall. We heard the thud. We ran to the bathroom and carried her back to her spot. From then on, we took up eating eggshells and potato peels. We'd grind the eggshells into a fine powder, sprinkle the grind into our mouths and quickly swallow.

Some time later, the guards allowed us to use a water heater. They offered us their leftover tea. We accepted it gladly and heated it back up with our water heater and savoured every drop. The guards let us borrow a gas burner to cook our own food or reheat the meals they served us. Once a week, the guards brought us one chicken to share between the fourteen of us, but only after cutting off the best pieces of the chicken for themselves.

We yanked out whatever was left of the chicken, cooked it on the gas burner without seasonings, tore up the cooked chicken pieces into slim strings and divided them among ourselves. Our shares consisted of a half a spoon of chicken each. We seized that half a spoon of chicken, like it was gold, added whatever spices we could find to it, spread it between two slices of bread, chewed each bite slowly and pretended we were eating real chicken sandwiches.

## Punishment According to Mood

Although the guards made our lives in prison a living hell, the male prisoners lived an even uglier hell. We complained of overcrowding and suffocation after the number of women in our cell exceeded ten, while the guards used to pack over fifty men into one cell. The men's suffering soared beyond suffocation. They couldn't rest, move or breathe - day or night. They took turns sleeping. To sleep, the men had to lay down with their legs up against the wall.

Guards constantly walked back and forth in front of the men's cells and if they heard the slightest sound, they would bang the cell door with their sticks and shout at the men to shut up. Even at night, guards constantly patrolled the men's cells, leaving the peepholes open so that they could keep an eye on every move the men made. If an officer saw any movement or heard even a whisper, he would punish the men according to his mood that night. Sometimes, the men got away with insults and curses, but most of the time the guards beat the men ferociously and their screams kept us up night after night.

The men had to act according to the guards' temperaments. The guards gave orders according to their whims and the men instantly obeyed.

"Sleep."

"Wake up."

"Eat."

"Time for the *khat*."

The men slept, awoke, ate and used the bathroom according to the will of the guards. The men tired of playing puppets and one day decided to start performing their prayers in congregation. They recited from the Quran loudly, so loudly that Hajja Madeeha often prayed along with them. Sometimes, the guards pretended not to hear. Other times, the guards punished the men, but the men took the beatings and persisted in their congregational prayers.

One time, one of the men asked to go to the washroom after they had already come back from the *khat*. The guards shouted and cursed at him. The man quieted down for a while, but then pleaded with the guards again, until one of them pulled him out and dragged him to the door of our cell and kicked him and whipped him and beat him for what seemed like hours.

"Hey man! He didn't do anything," Hajja Madeeha shouted. "It's not like he committed some big sin! The guy just wanted to go to the washroom. You can go to the washroom twenty times a day, but he's not allowed to be a human being!"

Shower time meant more torture for the men. The guards took the men out in groups. When the guards hit the shower doors with their batons twice that meant everybody out now. The poor men knew that they would only be allowed a few seconds in the shower, so they went into the showers with their clothes on and before they could wash anything the guards would bang on their doors. Some men chose not to shower at all. They chose safety over cleanliness.

Mandatory head shaving provided the guards with yet another way to torture and humiliate the men. A guard sat cross-legged on a chair. The men kneeled in front of him one by one. The guard grabbed their heads like an animal and shaved the men recklessly, slicing into their scalps, fracturing their sculls, and poking their eyes. The men had to remain completely silent and not let out a single peep or cry of pain. Any sound led to severe beatings.

The women were excused from the mandatory shaving rule – thank God. But the lack of water and the filth of the prison made long hair a new source of suffering. Our tiny heater could barely heat enough water for one of us to shower everyday.

Our shortage of clothing and the difficulty of washing them forced us to stay in the same clothes for a long time, even after a shower. Many times, we'd wash our clothes, hang them to dry on an elastic we removed from a piece of clothing and anxiously await for them to dry, with nothing else to wear. Often, partially dry was good enough. It seemed impossible to dry clothes in a tiny overstuffed cell. The water would condense from our clothes, drip on us and make our cell even more humid. But if we wanted clean clothes, we had no choice but to tolerate the dripping water and the sickening humidity.

## Blood, Lice and Tuberculosis

Prison policy included weekly inspections of cells. During his shift, Ibraheem examined the tiny window in our wall and tugged at the metal bars to ensure that no one had tampered with them.

"What do you think that we could have possibly done to them? Do you really think that us women could brake off metal bars?" Hajja Madeeha yelled.

"I have orders to follow."

The guards found many ways to infuriate us. The days they took our blankets to disinfect them, claiming to do it for the general health care of all the prisoners topped our list of irritants. We had no idea what they sprayed our blankets with, but when they brought them back they felt wet and smelled horrid. The smell of disinfectant drenched the air and suffocated us. But even more horrid than the smell of that disinfectant was the smell of the disinfectant they used to spray our cell after lice began to spread in the prison. Two months after our imprisonment, lice spread throughout the prison except for our cell, but that did not stop the guards from disinfecting our cell too, "just in case". We sat in the cell, begging them to let us out while they sprayed the cell, but they refused.

Whenever we thought that there could be no greater suffering than ours, we would hear stories about the male prisoners in Kafar Suseh Prison, stories that pushed our imaginations to darker limits. The guards dealt with the male prisoners' lice problem differently. They didn't only spray their cells. They called the men to the peepholes on the cell doors and one by one asked them to stick their heads out and nearly drowned them in insecticide.

After one year of suffering through all sorts of torture and of lacking basic nutritional and health needs, tuberculosis spread amongst the male prisoners. We listened to their violent coughing all night long. We watched the men through the cracks in our door as they went out to the *khat* with their arms around each other for support. Some of the men couldn't walk at all; their cellmates carried them to the washroom.

One night, it was my turn to take the garbage to the kitchen. Ibraheem opened the door for me and walked ahead of me to the kitchen. He stopped at the kitchen door, clutched a knife and glared at me.

"I swear to God it would not be a sin to stab this knife into your heart," he hissed.

I walked right past him into the kitchen and threw out the garbage. Hussain walked out of the kitchen. He didn't notice me. In his hands he held a bowl, just like the ones they served our meals in. The bowl brimmed with blood.

"Our buddy is dead," Hussain said to Ibraheem.

"To hell with him. Close the door of the solitary confinement cell he was in until we figure out what to do with his body."

Ibraheem took me back to the cell. A few minutes later, I peeked out of the peephole. Ibraheem and Hussain carried a dead body out of a cell. I told the women about what I saw in the kitchen. Hajja Madeeha said she had seen the guards carry a man out of a cell yesterday and put him in solitary confinement.

"He was so weak, they had to carry him," Hajja Madeeha said.

When one of the guards came to our cell, Hajja Madeeha had a hundred questions ready for him. She wanted to know who the man was, why he died and how he died. The guard grew sick of her pestering.

"He died of natural causes, okay? Of tuberculosis."

## The Villager

Watching guards carry corpses out of cells during the infectious outbreaks cut deeply into our hearts, but even more wounding was catching glimpses of the bodies of those who died from torture, although for them, death meant comfort.

One night, the guards turned off all of the lights and shut our peepholes. Only a dim hall light remained, but it was light enough for us to peek through a crack in the peephole and watch the guards carry out the body of a dead man, a man in a suit and tie, and throw him into a solitary confinement cell. This time not even Hajja Madeeha was able to extract answers from the guards, but chances are the man died from torture.

Another time, while we peeked out of the crack in the peephole, we witnessed the guards bring in a villager and strip him of all his clothes. Guards with whips and batons stood at either end of the hall. They whipped and beat the naked man. They shoved him to the other side of the hallway where another group of torturers awaited him. The man stumbled back and forth between the two ends of the hallway. The guards ordered him to put his hands on his head and walk slowly. Then they ordered him to run.

After exhausting him, the guards shoved the man into the showers. We continued to peek through the crack and although we couldn't see into the showers, we could hear what they were doing to him. The guards held the man under the shower and turned on the cold water. Then they turned off the cold water and turned on the hot water. Then cold. Then hot. Cold. Hot. And the shrieks grew louder each time.

## Mental Illness and a Cosmetic Touch-up

During the Hama massacre, which we of course had no idea about during our imprisonment at Kafar Suseh Prison, the officers pushed the torture sessions to new limits. My cellmates and I huddled in our cell, listened to sounds that came from the torture chamber and prayed for protection. The sounds went on and on and on and we couldn't bear it. Hajja Madeeha begged the guards to move us to another cell, one that was far away from the torture chamber. The guards refused.

Intensified torture meant more deaths. Officers dragged out dozens of bodies of men who were either dead or nearly dead. They wrapped the men in sheets and dumped their bodies God knows where. I will never forget the man they hauled out of the torture chamber and dumped onto the ground right in front of our cell to make room for the next victim. Bright red blood drenched the man from head to toe. His tongue hung out of his mouth. He begged the guards for a sip of water. The guards didn't budge. We filled a bowl with water from our washroom and spilled the water onto the ground at the door of our cell. The man licked the water like a starving dog.

The monstrous and continuous torture sessions drove many of

the prisoners to nervous breakdowns and hysteria. I remember one man, from the cell adjacent to ours, bursting into sudden laughing spells. He'd laugh and laugh and laugh for hours. A few days later, he'd fall into a crying spell and his sorrow would be contagious and would send the rest of us on crying spells of our own.

One day, guards barged into our cell and demanded to know whether we had any tranquilizers stashed in our cell. Hajja Madeeha took tranquilizers to steady her hands from the tremors she experienced as a side effect of prolonged electrocution.

"Why? Have one of the guards gone hysterical?" asked Hajja Madeeha in her usual sarcastic tone.

"No. There's a man, in a cell far from yours, who's gone hysterical. He cries all day and night. He's disturbing our sleep."

Sometime later, we witnessed yet another man plummet into hysteria. This one seemed to have lost his mind altogether. I watched guards pull him out of his cell, strip him, sit him at the top of the stairs and watch him for entertainment, like a good comedy. The man laughed and laughed and every time he calmed and tired of laughing, the guards provoked him into more laughter and exploded into their own wild roars, void of any sense of humanity or respect for the sick.

I will never forget the night the air force base in Damascus was bombed. That night officers knocked on our door and asked if we had any eyeliner, lipstick or any other cosmetic products. We looked at each other, confused.

"Hey man, does it look like we're coming from a wedding or something? Where on Earth are we going to get makeup in this place?" Hajja Madeeha snapped.

"You never know," he said.

A short while later, guards brought a man out from a cell and sat him down in front of our door. Torture marks covered his face and body. The guards handcuffed his hands and legs to a chair. They gathered around him and attempted to apply cosmetic products to cover up cuts and bruises. Somehow, Hajja Madeeha, through her special ways, found out about the airbase bombing. She also found out that the guards were preparing that prisoner for a television broadcast. The prisoner was to confess to the bombing on live television.

## Whitewashing the Prison

Torture in prison took many forms. Physical torture brought terrible pain, but it was temporary pain, pain that ended. The mental pain, the spiritual pain, and the anxiety, never end. We stared at the four walls that caged us and longed to step outside of them. We hung on to the hope that one day our suffering would end, but there were days when holding on to hope was hard.

The prisoners varied in their responses to our situation and the prison workers varied in their abilities to get to us. Abu Rami, the head guard during one of the shifts, was the master of this game. His preferred victims were Hajja Madeeha and Hajja Riyad. Many times, Abu Rami approached them with the promise of freedom. He invented release dates, ignited their longings and then relished in squashing their hopes. When the Hajjas caught on to his lies, he carelessly covered them up with more lies.

Abu Rami told Hajja Riyad that her release was coming soon and that the phrase, "knock on gas burner" was her signal to get ready for release and that she should sit tight and wait for the signal. One day, Abu Rami strolled by our cell and shouted, "knock on gas burner". Hajja Riyad pounced up, dashed for the door, pounded on it and called out to Abu Rami. When he didn't answer, she shouted out to the other guards and asked them where Abu Rami had gone, but no one cared to answer. For hours, Hajja Riyad lingered at the cell door, nervous and anxious and wondering what happened to her messenger. Nothing could distract her from her longings to step out of that door for good. Later in the day, Abu Rami returned.

"Tomorrow at twelve. It's confirmed," he told Hajja Riyad. "But before you leave, I want you to take this ball of yarn and knit me a sweater."

Hajja Riyad plucked the yarn from his hand and started knitting right away. She knitted through the night. Hajja Madeeha helped her knit and they managed to finish the sweater by dawn. Abu Rami showed up early in the morning, took the sweater and handed Hajja Riyad another ball of yarn.

"This time I want a vest," he said. "And it has to be ready before twelve."

Hajja Riyad and Hajja Madeeha knitted furiously and the vest was ready long before twelve. They sent the vest to Abu Rami with one of the guards. Hajja Madeeha helped Hajja Riyad pack her few belongings. The two of them then sat together and waited. They waited and waited and waited. Twelve o'clock came and passed and soon two o'clock passed and night fell; Abu Rami never came. Hajja Riyad and Hajja Madeeha realized they'd been used. They didn't know what to do with the rage they felt, but to raise their hands up to God and pray.

The game of false hopes continued. When the guards promised release, we knew they lied, but nonetheless we couldn't rid ourselves of that small sliver of hope that maybe, just maybe this time they were telling the truth. One time they told us that we were all going to be released at two o'clock that afternoon. We packed our few belongings and sat by the door and waited. Two o'clock passed. Night came. We lay to sleep, still suffering with the symptoms of hope.

In the morning, we confronted the guards. They told us there was a hold up and said it would be just a few more hours. They complained of too much paper work. They promised, "soon, soon". We waited another day and nothing happened. We confronted them again.

"Ya. Ya. You're not being released. The Ikhwan just bombed the air force in Damascus, so your release was cancelled. You're going to stay and suffer for the crimes of the Ikhwan. Every time they attack, you will pay."

We heard the guards chatting about whitewashing the prison.

"When?" Hajja Riyad jumped up and asked.

"In a couple of days," the guard replied.

When the guards said whitewashing, we thought they meant the release and pardon of all prisoners. Two days later, we watched as guards carried pails of paint and large brushes into the hallways. They smeared white paint over the blood stained walls, erasing evidence of the events that transpired in the hallways of Kafar Suseh Prison.

"Is this what you call whitewashing?" Hajja Riyad asked bitterly.

"Yes. Indeed we have now whitewashed the prison."

Hajja Riyad sat back down, slouched over and cried. The memories of our past pains and our tortured hopes flooded back to the rest of us and we all slouched over like Hajja Riyad and cried and cried and cried.

## Military Court

One day officers came to our cell, called out for Raghda and Lama and escorted them out of our cell. We figured they might have a visitor. Hours went by and Raghda and Lama did not return. We began to worry. Officers came back and called out for two more of our cellmates. Soon, the guards were escorting the sixth and seventh prisoner out of our cell and the rest of us decided we had to find out what was going on.

"When you come back, before they bring you into the cell, cough out loud if they had just taken you for a visit. Otherwise, don't do anything," we whispered to the seventh cellmate as she stepped out.

Later on, we heard her steps back down to the basement. She didn't cough. One hour later, they brought all seven women back to our

116

cell. Their faces looked pale and their eyes were full of fury.

"Military Court," they hissed through quivering lips.

After eight months at Kafar Suseh Prison, the government decided to present our cases to a military court. Solaiman Habeeb, an officer from the town of Kirdaha headed the military court trials. Because Habeeb was short, when he stood behind a table, all we could see of him was his thick head of hair and his shoulders.

Four officers attended the trials with Habeeb. They held each prisoner's file, announced the charges against her and read out her confessions. After reading out the files, the officers asked each prisoner whether she concurred and asked her to sign a document listing all the charges against her. The officers had no problem making the women sign; a few subtle threats was all it took.

Majida ignored the threats, denied the charges against her and insisted that her confessions were the result of torture.

"If you don't tell the truth, I'm going to throw you out the window, order your execution and deny you a single more breath of air," the officer shouted.

The next day the leader of the division, Khairbek, called for Majida.

"You told the officers of the court that you were tortured here. Who tortured you? Did anyone hit you? Did anyone really harm you?"

Khairbek himself had whipped and beat Majida.

"Who? Who was the one who tortured you?" Khairbek's face flared.

Majida froze.

"I don't know," she managed to whisper.

"No. Nobody tortured you. Nobody touched you. We have policies here. Nobody is allowed to touch anyone. But you, you're the one who is confused. I guess you were scared. But I don't understand why. Why were you scared?"

My other cellmates told me about how the officers at the military court not only threatened them, but mocked them with the same dirty language we'd grown accustomed to hearing from the guards. When Majida denied her relationship with Khalid Al-Sheik, a male prisoner, the officer who played judge at the trial shouted at her.

"Must I say aloud what Khalid Al-Sheik had to say about the colour of your legs?"

The four officers around him exploded into laughter. They laughed at Majida and teased her as she struggled not to breakdown.

Hajja Riyad came back from her trial with puffy eyes. She wiped away the tears on her face with her shaky hands.

"What happened?" we asked her.

Hajja Riyad told us that the officers yelled and shouted at her and told her she belonged in prison forever - that she deserved to stay in her cell for as long as the people of the cave.

"Oh Hajja, soon they will release you, but they're never going to let *me* out. I'll be stuck in here forever, just me and these four walls." Hajja Riyad sobbed on Hajja Madeeha's shoulder.

The officers put Hala on trial, like everybody else, although at the time she was still mentally ill and still out of touch with reality. Officers grabbed her by the arms and dragged her out of the cell. They brought Hala back to us filthy as a pig's pen. They had dragged her across the muddy grounds of the field where the military trials were held and mopped the filthy halls of Kafar Suseh Prison with her clothing.


# A Proposal to Marry and Another to Spy

After the military court trials of the seven inmates from our cell, the officers moved onto prisoners from other cells. Two months later, they returned to our cell with orders for the rest of us to be tried for being members of the Ikhwan. My court date arrived. Officers escorted me to the military court, read out the interrogation report and listed the charges against me.

"What's your relationship to Mukhlis Kanoot?" the presiding officer asked me.

"I don't know him."

"Didn't you two form a relationship through the organization?"

"Never."

"But he confessed to knowing you."

"That's not true."

I had never met Mukhlis Kanoot, but I did remember that he was a doctor and a friend of my brother's. *This must all be the work of Abdul-Kareem Rajab.* I looked up. Officers dragged my brother's friend across the floor. I saw bullet wounds on his body. Later I found out that he had attempted to escape, but officers had shot him down.

"Do you know her?" the judge asked.

"No."

"Get him out of here. It's time for him to meet his fate," said the officer who dragged him in.

A couple of officers grabbed him by the arms and hauled him out. Some time later, I heard about Mukhlis Kanoot's execution in Tadmur Prison.

"So, you do not accept the accusations against you?"

"No."

"Why not? Did anyone force those confessions out of you?"

"I never even confessed to any of these things, even though they beat me to near death."

The officer leaned forward. His eyes widened. "You mean they tortured you?"

"Yes. They tortured me. Don't you know that?"

"No. I don't know."

Abu Faris, the head of interrogations at Kafar Suseh Prison, who had escorted me to the trial, stood just outside the courtroom. The presiding officer, or so-called judge, called Abu Faris in.

119

"Listen. I want you to go easy on this girl and her friend Majida," the judge told Abu Faris.

The judge asked me to sign a new report, which he wrote and ordered officers to take me back to my cell. Four or five days later, the court called Majida and I back, separately. At court, the judge himself, Solaiman Habeeb, asked me to tell him about my life. I spoke about my life in general, explained to him that I wasn't a part of any organization and once again denied the accusations against me.

"Okay. I want to ask you a question," he said. "If we asked you to marry one of our men from the Ba'ath party, would you?"

"No!" I blurted out.

"Why not?"

"Because… umm… first of all, I would never marry without my parents' knowledge and consent. And second, I don't even want to get married now."

"Why not?"

"Because I want to continue my studies. I never thought about marriage."

"Ya right! I can swear that if I plucked out one of those men from the basement right now for you, you'd fall head over heals for him and marriage wouldn't be so out of question anymore."

"That's not true."

"Trust me. It is."

Habeeb dropped the marriage idea and turned his attention to a Kuwaiti newspaper he held in his hand.

"Look." He pointed to the newspaper. "Look at how the Ikhwan are exploiting you from the outside, in Kuwait, in Iraq… "

I leaned forward and squinted, but couldn't read the tiny print.

Habeeb looked down at the paper and pretended to read: "Heba, her husband and her children sit in the prisons of Syria. Majida and her children too are in prison, after Majida's husband was martyred."

Habeeb continued to make up exaggerated stories about how the

Ikhwan exploited us prisoners and used our tragedies to milk money from sympathisers.

"Well, thank God I don't know anything about what goes on outside," I said.

The "mercy session" ended without bringing an end to our uncertainties. We didn't know what would come of the trials, nor did we know which charges stuck and which didn't. Majida retuned to our cell shortly after me. Without a word, Majida withdrew under her blanket. We questioned her about her trial. She said nothing. In the middle of the night, Majida jolted up, turned to me with pain in her eyes and said, "I can't take this anymore. I'm going to explode."

"What happened?"

"Please. Please for God's sake, don't tell anyone, even if they ask you, don't say a word."

"What? What happened?"

"You know Abu Faris?"

I nodded.

"He made me an offer. He said he'd release me if… if…"

Majida winced.

"If what?"

"If I become an informant."

My eyes widened. I swallowed hard.

"I didn't know what to tell him, so he gave me two days to think about it."

I put my arms around Majida, squeezed her shoulder and told her not to worry.

"Don't even think about it. Don't believe a word they say. All they do is lie. He's lying to you. He just wants to see your reaction. He wants to know how you'd respond to such a proposal. He's playing with your mind, like they always do to us. Don't believe anything and don't worry."

Majida wanted to believe me, but I could tell that a part of her remained terrified. Days passed. Majida heard nothing from Abu Faris. No one spoke of the proposal again. Majida realized that the proposal was just another cruel joke. She let it go. Once again, the Mukhabarat showed us the stuff their hearts were made of and proved to us that their souls could sink lower than words could describe.

## Breathing Time

Eight months later, our circumstances deteriorated further. Officers shoved new prisoners into our cell. We slept shoulder to shoulder. We'd been begging and pleading for a long time for a breath of fresh air. After eight months of living in an underground cell, the officers granted us ten to thirty minutes of "breathing time" every few days. They took us out to a special field, reserved for this purpose, in the south end of the prison. The field was four or five steps below ground level and surrounded by big buildings and thick concrete walls. When we looked up, we could barely see the sky.

Somehow, we discovered that right after our "breathing time," the guards brought the men out to the same field. We figured out a way to communicate with the men. Hajja Riyad saw her brother's signature carved into the wall and soon after the rest of us began to notice other carvings on the wall. We realized some of the carvings were questions the male prisoners wanted to ask us. They wanted to know if certain women were in prison with us. We tried to answer their questions and engraved some names on the wall below their questions.

Hajja Riyad asked the men about her brother, if he was still at Kafar Suseh. The men wrote back: no. Hajja Riyad understood that probably meant the Mukhabarat had transferred her brother to Tadmur Prison. I asked the men about Khalid Al-Sheik, my brother's friend, the one the officers asked me about during my interrogation. The men wrote back: no. Below the "no," they carved a scull crossed with two bones. I figured that meant Khalid Al-Sheik was executed.

While Majida and I walked along the walls, during "breathing time," we caught sight of a man's head lathered with soap through a window in one of the buildings beside the field. The man pressed his face against the window, disappeared, appeared again, and then disappeared. We found out that that was the window of the male prisoners' showers and that the man was trying to communicate with us. He ducked every time one of the officers noticed him. From then on, whenever we noticed one of the men in the showers, one of us distracted the officer on duty and the rest of us tried to communicate with the prisoner. Mostly, we asked about other prisoners, probing for information about family members and relatives whom we thought might be at Kafar Suseh Prison.

One time, one of the men slipped us a hundred liras. The guards didn't notice. We weren't sure why the man slipped us the money. Our cellmate, who had taken the hundred liras added the money to the general fund we had created for our cell. Another time, another male prisoner threw us another hundred liras. The third time the men tried to give us money, the guards caught them and the men got hell for it. The entire south wing of the prison got hell for it. No one ever tried to slip us money again.


## Another Hunger Strike

Although the men never tried to slip us money again, the hell they saw for it didn't stop them from trying to communicate with us in other ways. That money incident led to a turning point for all of us. One time we were walking back to our cell after "breathing time" and we noticed two young kids, dressed in elegant, luxurious clothes.

"They're Khairbek's kids," the officers told us.

I wondered why Khairbek would bring his kids to the prison. When the kids saw us walking back to our cell, the little boy turned to his sister and grabbed her arm.

"Come here. Come here. The prisoners are coming," the little boy said.

The sight of young children reminded Um Mahmoud of her little ones, the little ones that she never managed to stop thinking about, worrying about and longing for. Um Mahmoud reached out to Khairbek's son, longing to feel a child in her arms. The little boy turned and ran away, terrified. When we got to our cell, Um Mahmoud exploded into sobs and soon every mother in our cell wept and wailed for her children. Even those of us who weren't mothers started to cry and the questions that had gnawed at us for months arose again. *Until When? How much longer?*

In desperation, one of the women suggested another hunger strike. We agreed we had to do something. Dinnertime approached and we gathered whatever food we could find, including some food that the men had secretly passed to us and some gifts of food that some of the women received from visitors. We divided the food between us and pledged to go on the hunger strike. When the guards opened the peephole to pass us our dinners, none of us got up to take the food.

"Why isn't anyone getting up?"

"We don't want your food or water," Hajja Madeeha said.

The guard lifted his brows.

"What? Take it easy now. What's the matter?"

"We don't want your food. We don't need it," Hajja Madeeha replied.

The guard closed the peephole and went to Abu Adil, the head guard, to inform him of the new strike. Abu Adil stomped to our cell and flung the peephole open.

"What's going on?" he shouted.

"Nothing," Hajja Madeeha said.

No one else dared to answer.

"Why won't you take your dinners then?"

Abu Adil called one of the guards. He told him to open our door, bring in our dinners and place them right beside us. The guard obeyed. Abu Adil looked down at us and said, "The one who eats is the one who helps herself." He left the cell and locked the door.

Half an hour later, Abu Adil came back, opened the peephole and asked, "Did you eat yet?"

No one answered. He peeked in and saw the food untouched. His face turned red.

"It's your choice," he hissed through clenched teeth.

The next day, we refused breakfast and lunch. High ranking officers came back and forth to our cell and told us that we were only harming ourselves and that no one cared if we starved to death. But they did care. They cared because Khairbek dangled promotions in front of officers, for the one who succeeded at ending our strike. Abu Shadi, the shift manager of the south wing, decided to give us a shot. He made small talk with us and pretended to be sweet and sympathetic.

"Either find a way for us to have visits, to see our kids and our families or end our imprisonment, even if it means execution."

"Trust me, if your families came here to see you, we'd never turn them away, but they're the ones who don't care to ask about you."

"That's because our families are terrified of even coming close to this place; just the name Kafar Suseh is enough to scare anyone off," Majida yelled back.

Our arguments went nowhere. The next day rolled around, with no sight of resolve. When the third day came around, things started happening. Abu Shadi gave up on his Mr. Nice guy approach. He opened our cell door and hollered, "All strikers, out!"

We all got up and marched out of our cell: Communists, Christians, Iraqi sympathisers, Ikhwan members and all. Abu Shadi glared at us.

"Nice." He shook his head. "You guys have a real multicultural

125

union going on here."

He led us to the interrogation room. Two officers entered our cell and searched every inch of it for any morsel of food we may have hidden. They found a few canned foods that the men had quietly passed to us. An officer ordered Moneera to open each can and dump its contents into the trash. He made us watch. The other officer wasted time by asking us useless questions.

"So what do you guys want again?"

"You know perfectly well what we want. We don't need to keep repeating ourselves."

After they searched our cell, they shoved us back in. Then, they cut our water supply. Real hunger and real thirst began to eat away at our feeble bodies and gnaw at our wilting patience.

## A Clove of Garlic

On day two of the hunger strike, reality hit. My frail body couldn't handle the starvation and thirst. I vomited blood. My ulcer made things worse.

Majida and I discovered a carton of eggs on a metal shelf in our cell. Sometimes, guards sold us things and I bought those eggs from a guard a while back. I thanked God for blinding the guards to those eggs. Hala, who also suffered from an ulcer, managed to sneak some food by the officers as well. She hid a bit of milk powder and some sugar.

Hala shared her sugar with the other women. They dissolved the sugar in a few drops of water and passed around a few spoonfuls to each woman every night. Majida, Hala and I were the only ones who knew about the carton of eggs and the milk powder. Hala and Majida decided to leave the milk and eggs for me, because of my deteriorating condition and managed to keep the food a secret. They feared that if the other women found out about the food, they would lose their will to continue

126

the strike and our efforts would go to waste. We had pledged that if one of us broke the strike, we would all end the strike.

Majida and Hala felt it was fair for me to break the strike secretly, because of how ill I had become. I licked milk powder and sucked raw eggs in secret. Majida left one egg a day for me in the washroom. My turn for the washroom always came after hers. She cracked the top of the egg for me, so that all I had to do was suck the egg out and dump the shells into the toilet. The other women didn't find out about our secret until we got to Katana Prison. In Katana, we confessed to sneaking the milk and eggs. My cellmates glared at me, their eyes full of rage. I felt like they were about to pounce and strangle me.

On day three of the hunger strike, we smelled garlic. The strong distinct smell of fresh garlic filled our cell. The women looked around and questioned each other. Everyone was a suspect. We sniffed around and traced the smell to Um Shaima's mouth. She swore that she had just found one small clove of garlic under her mattress, but the women wouldn't have it. They gave her hell for that clove of garlic, but decided not to let it break the strike. Nothing was going to stop us, not temptations, not threats, even though our bodies wilted and withered by the hour.

## The Strike Chief

The fourth day of the strike crawled by. Abu Adil opened our door early in the morning. We startled up.

"Who's the strike chief?" he yelled.

"We don't have a chief," we answered together.

"Who came up with the idea to strike?"

His voice sounded exceedingly violent.

"Nobody," we answered.

We were terrified of what would happen if one of us was singled out as the sole cause of this trouble.

"One of you must have been the first to say, come on girls, let's go on a hunger strike. I want to know who that person was now!"

We sat still and kept silent. He stared at our faces and examined them one by one. His eyes stopped at Um Shaima. He must have caught a look on her face. Or maybe he saw that she was the tallest and the largest one of us.

"Come here. You're the strike chief."

"Where are you going to take her?" Hajja Madeeha asked.

"I'm taking her to receive her punishment."

"No. I'm the strike chief," Majida jolted up and shouted. "Why are you taking Um Shaima?"

"Because she looks like she could have come up with this idea, but as long as you're willing to take the blame, you come with me."

Majida got up, slipped into her worn out shoes and walked out of the cell. I watched her pale yellow dress disappear behind our door, that pale yellow dress that was once bright green. Beneath that dress, I saw the bottoms of her pyjama pants, pants so big on her that they dragged on the floor as she shuffled away. On Majida's head was an old worn out cloth, wrapped around and around like a farmer. I watched Majida, her dress, her pants, and her scarf, disappear into the dark hallway. My stomach cramped. *What are they going to do to her?*

Abu Adil took Majida to the interrogation room in the basement.

"So, you're the strike chief?"

"No."

"So why did you lie then?"

"Because we don't have a strike chief or a cell chief or any chief, but you still wanted to pin the blame on Um Shaima."

Abu Adil's veins popped. His face turned scarlet.

"Well, you're the one who decided to take the blame for Um

Shaima, so you're going to take the beatings for her too."

Abu Adil grabbed Majida and pressed her into the torture wheel. The officers often used a wheel to torture prisoners. They curled the prisoners into the inside of the wheel and whipped them. Majida screamed and struggled to get out.

"So what if I don't want to eat? It's none of your business," she screamed and wiggled. "My body is my responsibility."

Madija managed to free herself from Abu Adil's grip. Abu Adil didn't try to catch her again. He let her go. God only knows why, but he let her go.

## Temptation and Threats

Majida escaped torture, but the male prisoners who declared a hunger strike in solidarity with us, weren't so lucky. News of our hunger strike leaked out to the men and they decided to band with us. The prison management quickly issued orders for the punishment of all male prisoners. Officers whipped the soles of every male prisoner's feet. The men abandoned the hunger strike.

On the fifth day of our strike, Khairbek himself came to our cell early in the morning, called for Aysha and escorted her to the interrogation room. Khairbek placed cheese and bread right in front of Aysha.

"Eat. Now. Right in front of my eyes."

Aysha refused. Khairbek exploded with foul language.

"You bitches definitely have some sort of connection to the outside and you want to take advantage of the events in Lebanon to further distress the government."

We had no idea what happened on the outside, not in Lebanon, not in Syria, not even in the cell next door. Khairbek insisted that we had connections. Khairbek hollered threats in Aysha's face. Aysha feared

129

torture. Aysha ate cheese. When she got back to our cell, she confessed and hell broke lose again, this time over a bite of cheese.

The next morning, Khairbek returned. He ordered each woman out, one at a time. He shoved food into each woman's mouth. The women bit down on their lips and when Khairbek managed to stuff a piece of food in, they refused to swallow. Then came Hala's turn. Hala had recovered from her mental illness. She clenched her jaw and sealed her lips. Khairbek rammed Hala to the ground, kicked her, slapped her and yelled at her like a man who'd lost all restrain.

"You're punishment will be unique, just for you. We're going to retry you in military court for what you did."

Khairbek was referring to the letter Hala wrote and tried to send to her mother with a Palestinian cellmate of ours whom the Mukhabarat had released. The letter found its way to Khairbek's office. Khairbek tried and tried to break our strike with threats and temptations, but none of us broke. I was the only one spared from Khairbek's fury. I was last in line, behind Hala. After Hala, Khairbek gave up and left.

The hunger strike put power into our hands. We felt that power and it reaffirmed our determination to hold on. Many officers, one after the other, approached us with all sorts of tricks and offers of special privileges, anything they could think of to break our collective will. First, they restored our water supply. Then, they brought in the most delicious of foods, foods we never dreamt of seeing in prison. Haitham brought us a big glass of thick creamy milk. It had been so long since we had seen such delicious food. Another officer brought us a bowlful of apricots and not just any old apricots, but the biggest, juiciest, sweetest smelling apricots I had ever seen. We defied temptation. We defied hunger.

Haitham came back to our cell and found the food untouched. Like all the rest, Haitham failed. Haitham's eyes grew wide with rage and he burst into a fit of foul language. He cursed religion. He cursed God. He ordered the food out. He kicked the plates of food in the hallway. Plates, cups, apricots and milk smashed against the walls.

After nearly a week into the strike, some of the women began fainting and falling to the ground. Others vomited repeatedly. Most of us had come into the strike anaemic and the starvation only aggravated our fragile health. Many of us could no longer get up, not even for prayer. We prayed lying down. We tied our blankets around our stomachs and pulled tightly to dim the pain. When the officers saw us in this state, they admitted defeat. Abu Shadi came to our cell looking serious and stern.

"Get up and state your demands."

We all lay there, too weak to move.

"I want… if we die, for all of us to be buried together," Raghda said.

"Your wish is my command," Abu Shadi scorned, "but don't you have any other demands?"

"I want to see my father… before I die. Even if it's just for two minutes," Majida whispered.

"Why?"

"To kiss his hands," Majida said, "and to make sure he is pleased with me."

"Ya, because you're such a good girl!" Abu Shadi snorted. "If you really were a good girl, you wouldn't be in this position."

Abu Shadi slammed the door and left. Moments later, he came back with boxes of 'Daleela,' feminine napkins, stacked in his arms.

"What are you doing? What are we supposed to do with all these boxes?" Hajja Madeeha asked.

"Didn't you guys put out a request for this stuff? See, we're fulfilling all of your demands."

We glared at Abu Shadi.

"What? We requested those when we first came here and we kept on requesting and requesting and requesting and now you bring them!" Hajja Madeeha yelled.

131

"I just received your request now."

We were so sick of their games.

"Forget it. We don't want them. We don't want anything from you. Just shut the door. Let us die. Then you can do whatever you wish with us," Hajja Madeeha said.

"No. No. Don't worry. You're not going to die. You're a like a cat. You've got nine lives."

Abu Shadi came in and out of our cell all day long, every time with a new attempt to break our strike and win whatever reward it was that Khairbek was offering. He came in and out of our cell so many times that we grew sicker of him than of starvation.

## Journey into the Unknown

The hunger strike continued. We woke up early on the seventh day to the sound of metal handcuffs banging on our door. Our weak and weary bodies startled in fear. I was in the washroom. I heard Abu Talal shout. He shouted my name. His voice mingled with the sound of metal on metal as he continued to bang the handcuffs against the cell door.

"Hurry! Hurry!" my cellmates said.

They could tell Abu Talal was losing his patience. *Abu Talal must be here to take me for execution.* I sat in the washroom, paralysed with fear. I couldn't get up. I couldn't answer. The women came into the washroom, lifted me up and walked me out to Abu Talal. I gazed at him in a daze. He slid handcuffs around my wrists.

"Just her? Alone? Take us too! Why is she the only one who deserves execution? We all deserve it. Come on. Take us. Give us rest from this life," Hajja Madeeha pleaded.

Abu Talal looked away from Hajja Madeeha and began to call out the names of my cellmates. The women stepped out into the hall and lifted their arms out for the handcuffs. Abu Talal stopped calling names.

Some of my cellmates remained in the cell. I noticed that all the women who stayed behind were non-Ikhwan. When the women realized that Abu Talal was not going to call them, they rushed to our sides, Moneera, the first of them.

"Wait! We want to go with them," Moneera shouted.

Abu Talal rammed her into the ground and yelled and swore at her. Moneera tumbled down. Abu Talal shoved the other cellmates who also implored to leave with us. We followed Abu Talal into the storage room, where they kept the prisoners' belongings. Abu Talal threw our belongings at us. Hajja Madeeha noticed that all of her gold, which they had confiscated upon her arrival, was gone. Hajja Madeeha questioned the officers about her belongings over and over again, but they ignored her pleas.

With our belongings in hand, we followed Abu Talal to an open field in front of the prison. I was the first one to step into the field. Abu Talal grabbed me and said, "Stand here." I turned and found myself in the middle of the field, the only woman, suddenly surrounded by a group of officers. Khairbek watched through his office window.

"Look up!" Abu Talal hollered.

"I don't want to look up." My head throbbed.

"Then I will rip your scarf off."

"Do what you wish."

"Do you not see that you are surrounded? If you do not end your hunger strike right now, I will humiliate you in front of all of these men."

"Do what you wish. What more can you possibly do, after all you've already done?"

Abu Talal exploded with angry insults. He cursed me. He cursed religion. I stood still. I looked down. I said nothing. Abu Talal turned and called out for Majida. He handcuffed Majida and me together.

"Do you know why all these officers are standing here?"

My body felt exhausted. My mind filled with worries.

"No. I don't know."

"We brought all these men out here to watch you, because you ladies have made spectacles of yourselves." Abu Talal shouted so that the other women could hear him. "And if you do not end your hunger strike right now, we are going to rip your scarves off your heads and humiliate you and you know exactly what I mean by humiliate."

Abu Talal grew wild with rage. Foam formed around his mouth.

"You daughter of an animal. You bitch. I swear to God, we will strip you naked and have you right here."

Abu Talal handcuffed each two women together and led us out two by two, into a car that awaited us in front of the prison. I was the first at the car, but I didn't have the courage to enter or the energy to even lift my foot up. I felt rough hands from behind push and shove me until Majida and I fell over into the car. The car looked like a cage, a real cage, with bars, a door and a lock. The rest of the women followed in, all out of breath, all on the verge of fainting. As we sat in the cage, any hope of freedom we ever had, died. They're either going to transport us to Tadmur Prison or to an open field for execution, I realized.

Some of the women became dizzy. Some blacked out. Hajja Madeeha materialized a lemon out of nowhere, peeled it with her fingers and wiped the women's faces with it. I heard the click of the car door locks and our journies into the unknown began.

## Part Three: October 1982 - November 1985
Katana Prison: A Slow Death

The car sped out of the prison grounds and onto the road, thrusting us from side to side at every turn. Our tired bodies crashed into each other and would have plunged out of the car if it weren't for the metal bars that contained us. Two heavily armed guards sat between us and the driver's seat. Two more armed guards sat between our firmly locked cage and the back door. Abu Talal sat next to the driver. Majida, Um Shaima, Hajja Madeeha, Hajja Riyad, Montaha, Eman, Raghad, Mona, Haleema, Um Mahmoud, Amal, and I sat in the cage.

I felt dizzy and nauseous. I looked around for an arm to grasp, for any support I could find. Most of my cellmates lay blacked out from the day's cocktail of hunger, exhaustion, fear and pain. I fought the dizziness. I struggled to think clearly. I wiggled my hands and tried to loosen them out of the handcuffs. The handcuffs tightened. I wiggled my hands again and tried to squeeze them out. The handcuffs dug further into my wrists. My fingertips turned blue. They numbed.

Just when I thought that we reached the peak of our tragedies, the driver slammed the brakes and the car stopped at a police checkpoint. A police officer approached the car, opened the back door and peered in. I thought he'd ask us to step out, but the officer quickly shut the door and the driver took off again. I caught a glimpse of the metal sign that arched over the police checkpoint. The sign read, "Katana Prison".

We waited in the cage at the back of the car for about fifteen minutes as the officers from Kafar Suseh and Katana Prison exchanged papers and whatever other information they needed to complete the transfer. An officer opened the back door and ordered us out. My cellmates and I stepped out of the cage like a bunch of zombies rising from the grave, barely aware of what was happening, barely strong enough to walk upright.

I pulled myself up and stepped out of the car, wavering with every step like the last lingering leaf in the autumn breeze. An officer grabbed my arm and held me up. My cellmates and I fell to the ground by the car and lay there in front of the prison entrance like beggars on the street. The officers from Katana Prison stared and whispered. Other prison workers gazed at us through windows. They examined us as if we were aliens from another universe. We were a sight to see, with our pale faces that hadn't seen the light of the sun in months and our worn out, discoloured, beggar like clothing, covered with patches and hanging off our bony bodies. We lay on the ground, each pair handcuffed together, so that even if we managed to find the strength to move, we couldn't.

Abu Talal had forgotten the keys to our handcuffs at Kafar Suseh. He left us there, lying on the pavement, handcuffed together and drove back for the keys. As soon as Abu Talal took off in his Mukhabarat vehicle, the officers from Katana Prison asked us to come inside and wait in a room, but none of us could move. The officers dragged us into the room and flung us onto couches. We waited for Abu Talal to return.

A desk, a few chairs and an arms cabinet decorated the room. Officers poked their heads through the door every now and then to check us out. The officers looked at us with wide sad eyes. Some of the officers chocked back tears. Moments later, the teary eyed officers wept out loud, sobbing and shaking. One of the officers, who looked in his fifties, grabbed our handcuffs and desperately tried to loosen them off our wrists. The handcuffs didn't budge. He tried to comfort us with gentle words as tears streamed down his cheeks and dripped from his chin.

"Don't worry my sisters, don't worry. Soon, we will take you inside and you will be able to live normally and start all over again."

He pointed out the window, sniffled and bit his lips, trying to restrain his free falling tears.

"Look," he said, "there are kids here and trees and other women. See over there, that's a woman from Hama. Her name is Ghazwa. And over there is …." he pointed out several other women. "God willing, you will feel better soon and get back to your lives."

Um Mahmoud looked out the window, saw a little boy and sighed deeply. She looked at the officer and said, "Do you think the sight of children here can replace the sight of our own children?"

"For God's sake… I swear to you that God willing, your children will come here and visit you and you will see them and be reassured."

The kind officer stepped out and came back with drinks. We couldn't believe what was happening. Two hours later, Abu Motee, the warden's assistant and Abu Talal walked into the room. Abu Talal unlocked our handcuffs one by one and without a word left with his officers.

Abu Motee saw the terror on our faces and tried to comfort us. He assured us that this place was different, that there was no torture here and that we didn't have to be scared anymore. We followed Abu Motee to our cells. He unlocked the door. Um Shaima stepped in first. The prisoners inside rushed to her, embraced her and literally carried her into the cell. Um Shaima pleaded with the women to put her down. She told them she could walk herself, but they couldn't hear her over all the excitement.

We found out that Abu Motee had notified our new cellmates of our coming. He had warned them that their new cellmates were victims of the Hama massacre and they were to expect us to be in terrible shape, with broken bones, gunshot wounds and various injuries. Abu Motee wasn't making things up or lying on purpose. That was truly what he figured after setting sight on a group of women who have been living in a basement for three years, a basement that resembled nothing of the outside world, except maybe a deep ditch dug for a grave.


## Court Charades:  Just Ten Years!

Katana Prison, an old stone building, similar in design to old Arabian homes, consisted of a large field bordered by several cells. Metal bars created a partition between the field and the cells and between each cell. One cell was assigned for political prisoners. The other cells were distributed according to the different cases and allegations against the prisoners. Two cells were allotted for murderers, one cell for drug users and another for prostitutes. There was a tiny fifth room that was more like a solitary confinement cell, where they had imprisoned Mahdi Ilwani's mother. Mahdi, one of the first men to carry out armed resistance against the government, was executed with a group of young men in 1979. They released Mahdi's mother shortly before our arrival at Katana Prison.

Although we were cell neighbours, interaction between the political prisoners and other prisoners was forbidden. When we first arrived, the guards allowed the political prisoners out of their cells to welcome us. We recognized many of the faces of the other political prisoners in Katana Prison, but they didn't recognize us. One of the prisoners, Sana, whom I went to university with, stood in front of me and gazed at my face.

"No, it's not possible," Sana said. "Is it really you? What happened to you? Did they dry you like a prune?"

Another prisoner I knew, Ghazwa, approached me, full of smiles and light hearted humour. Happiness filled our hearts and we felt as if we were visiting each other in our homes, dear and dignified. In the midst of hugs, kisses and tears, stories began to unravel...

Colonel Muwaffaq Al-Samman, the military leader of the town and the warden of Katana Prison opened the door of our cell. He greeted us, welcomed us to our new home, and told us that here, we were under his protection and that nothing bad would come to us. He assured us that the Mukhabarat were out of our lives and that our hunger strike was no longer necessary. He asked us to end the hunger strike and to be patient and persevere until God willed our freedom. An officer brought up a chair for the Colonel to sit in. The Colonel placed the chair in front of us and sat. A serious look came over his face as he took out a batch of papers. His eyes wandered.

"Listen to me now. I don't want any crying or wailing, okay? Just listen."

"Why? What's going on?" Hajja Madeeha asked.

"I received these documents stating each of your sentences and I want to read them to you."

Before we could say a word or even take a breath, he began to read our sentences.

"The National Security Court sentences the accused Heba Dabbagh to ten years of imprisonment and hard labour."

"Oh no! Dear God. No! Oh Heba," Hajja Riyad cried out.

Hajja Riyad grabbed me, held me tight and wailed.

"Oh God. No. Ten years!" Hajja Madeeha joined in.

But the shock over my ten year sentence wore off quickly as each one of the women remembered her own turn coming up and wondered how long her own sentence would be. The women refocused on the Colonel.

"The National Security Court sentences the accused Riyad D. to twenty years of imprisonment and hard labour."

"Hey buddy! I'm thinking maybe a fly was sitting on your paper and you accidentally saw an extra zero. Did you actually say twenty years? That's impossible," Hajja Riyad shouted.

The women quickly left my side to comfort Hajja Riyad. Her sentence was double mine.

The Colonel continued:

"Montaha J. - twenty years."

"Hajja Madeeha - ten years."

"Raghda K. and Mona A. - four years." Although Raghda and Mona's sentences were supposed to be four years, the government actually kept them for nine years with the rest of us.

"Um Shaima - four years."

"Aysha K. - Four years."

"Hooriya, Um Mahmoud - ten years."

"Mona F. and her sister - ten years."

"Majida L. - twenty years."

"Hala - ten years."

"Turfa - ten years."

When the Colonel finished reading out our sentences, he looked up and saw our miserable state with all the crying and tears, all on top of the condition we were already in because of the hunger strike.

"Don't take these as literal verdicts," he said with sympathy. "God willing you will leave here long before your sentences are over. Everybody who comes here always gets out."

The Colonel continued to comfort. He told us about our rights at Katana Prison and the new privileges we will have. He encouraged us to eat our breakfast and to try to fall back into a normal routine.

During the Colonel's little pep talk, our fellow inmates busied themselves with setting up a feast for us, a feast that spread from one end of the cell to the other. I gawked at the food. I turned to Majida and clutched her arm.

"Look: tomatoes, cucumbers, parsley and eggs!"

Although we hadn't swallowed a morsel of food for seven whole days, none of us got past the first bite. After one mouthful, our stomachs cramped. Even though we couldn't enjoy the feast, the strike was officially over. As we slowly regained our strength, we began to feel the thrill of victory. We knew that our hunger strike had not been in vain. We accomplished something, not much, but something.

We chatted with our new cellmates. They told us about the weekly visits that the warden allowed them. We smiled with excitement and anticipation at the thought of seeing our families. We awaited Friday, the appointed day for visitations, like a child awaits *Eid*. By Wednesday, we could do nothing but fantasize about our long awaited reunions with our loved ones.

# Hard Labour

Our rectangular cell, in the corner of the prison, was five metres wide. To get into the cell, you take one step down and then one step up. In the left corner was the washroom and on the right of the door were two windows that looked out onto the prison field. After the warden appointed us that cell and read out our sentences, he left for a while, and then returned with sponge mattresses, pillows and blankets for each of us. The mattresses, pillows and blankets looked old, over-used and filthy. The new inmates fought over the best and cleanest mattresses, pillows and blankets and raced to claim the best spots in the cell.

The cell was overcrowded as usual. I put an end to the battle between the women and lay my mattress near the cell door; half of it lay on the regular room level and the other half dangled down into the step. The chaos ended. The women settled down and organized a clean up of the room, to prepare it as our new living space. Some corners of the cell almost rotted away due to the aging structure. A huge chunk of our doorstep chipped off and posed a major slipping hazard. We asked the warden's assistant, Abu Motee, if he could bring us some cement to fix the step. He agreed.

Early next morning, Abu Motee stepped into our cell and called out for one of us to come out. Hajja Riyad was the first to answer. We heard Abu Motee say something to Hajja Riyad and the next thing we knew Hajja Riyad fainted and fell to the ground. Hajja Madeeha ran to her and splashed cold water on her face. Hajja Riyad's eyes fluttered open. She gripped Hajja Madeeha's arms.

"Oh Hajja, he wants to take me for hard labour. Please for God's sake, talk to him. Tell him I can't. My blood pressure will soar. I can't take it. It's too much," Hajja Riyad sobbed.

"What happened? Where are you taking her to?" Hajja Madeeha asked Abu Motee.

"I swear to God, I didn't do anything to her," Abu Motee

shouted. "All I did was say come here Hajja and take the cement."

Because of Hajja Riyad's bad hearing and her distress, she thought Abu Motee was calling her to serve the hard labour part of her sentence.

## Birth in Prison

Before we arrived at Katana Prison, the political prisoners' cell was already filled with inmates from many different cities: Ghazwa from Hama, Sana from Damascus, Um Mo'kal and her son, who was born in prison, also from Damascus, Um Haitham from Jisir Al-Shogoor, Um Abd Al-Basit and her daughter Aidah from Jisir, Saneeha and Fatima from Latakiya, and Um Mahmoud Kamil from Latakiya. Each woman sat shrouded in her own heartbreaking story of suffering and loss.

Ghazwa, a dentist, helped to purchase a hideout in Damascus for wanted members of the Ikhwan. Abdul-Kareem Rajab found out and informed the Mukhabarat. The Mukhabarat arrested her at her clinic in Sooran. At first, they took her to the political security branch in Hama, then to the Army Interrogation Unit in Damascus, where they detained her for 6-8 months. Then they transferred Ghazwa to Katana Prison, where she remained imprisoned with us until the end of our sentences.

As for Sana, someone used her identification to purchase a hideout. Sana never consented to the purchase; she didn't even know about it. The Mukhabarat discovered the house purchased under her name, arrested her and tossed her into prison.

Sana was born in 1960 and studied *Sharia* at university with us. The Army Interrogation Unit arrested her on the same day the Mukhabarat arrested me. During her interrogation, officers questioned Sana about me and asked her to show them to my apartment in Damascus. Sana led them to the apartment. The officers forced Sana to knock. My mother answered the door. My mother had come to visit me only to find a swarm of Mukhabarat officers lurking in my apartment. She didn't know I had been arrested the day before.

Quietly, my mother told Sana to go away, fearing the officers would arrest her. My mother didn't realize Sana was already in their custody. The Mukhabarat and the Army Interrogation Unit contacted each other and cleared up the fact that I was captured the day before. Since they no longer needed Sana to trap me, they sent her back to the Army Interrogation Unit.

Moteea, also known as Um Mo'kal, worked as a teacher, until the late 1970's, when the government identified her as being a part of a group of teachers whose loyalties were in question. The government transferred those teachers into various administrative jobs and forbade them from teaching. Um Mo'kal worked in a clinic as an administrative assistant. At the same time, the Mukhabarat also pursued her husband, but her husband fled the country before they could track him down. That's when they arrested Um Mo'kal as a hostage. But she wasn't enough to satisfy their rage at her husband's escape. Days later, they arrested his father as a second hostage.

Um Mo'kal was in her late thirties, a mother of four and about to give birth to her fifth child. They arrested her and kept her in a military clinic belonging to the national security division in Jisir. In a tiny room, in the military clinic, in the midst of all the fear and threats, Um Mo'kal felt the pangs of early labour. She banged on the door, shouted that she was in labour and shrieked in pain, but no one came.

Hours later, Um Mo'kal gave birth alone. She held her baby in her arms as he cried and cried and cried. The sound of the newborn's cries finally drew officers to her room. They allowed a nurse in to see her, but there was little left for the nurse to do. The officers transferred Um Mo'kal and her baby to the The Military Interrogation Unit in Damascus, where she stayed for months, before they brought her to Katana Prison. When we arrived at Katana Prison, we met Um Mo'kal and her son, who had just turned eight months. Haleema, another prisoner, suggested the name Mo'kal, after Mo'kal bin Yasar, a companion of the Prophet Mohammad, and because Mo'kal means imprisoned.

Um Mo'kal suffered everyday as she watched her baby grow up between four walls, his future unknown to her, just like her own, except for the certainty of a life confined to prisons, cells, and solitary confinement. She watched Mo'kal in the arms of the other inmates. She watched the women use her child to satisfy their own cravings for their children. She watched how her son served as their entertainment, a tool to fill time and to relieve them from their boring routines. What hurt Um Mo'kal the most was when the other inmates did with her son what they pleased and taught him what they pleased, with no regard for what she wanted for her son.

Um Mo'kal held her son tight and kept him by her side as much as she could, but he was a child and he needed to explore. Um Mo'kal's inability to keep her son under constant supervision and to monitor everything the other inmates said to him cost her dearly. One of Mo'kal's first phrases was, "Damn Asad". Every time Mo'kal heard the president's name or saw his picture, he automatically blurted out, "Damn Asad".

One time, Mo'kal fell severely ill. He cried and cried and cried until the guards got fed up and took him to the military clinic. Mo'kal saw a picture of the president hanging in the clinic and in spite of his illness managed to cry out, "Damn Asad" within earshot of several people. His mother didn't know about his new favourite phrase yet. She stood shocked and shaken. Somehow, she managed to squirm out of getting into too much trouble.

When officers took Um Mo'kal to her military court trial, she had to take her son with her. Mo'kal noticed a statue of the president in a corner of the room. As he and his mother stood in front of the court officials, Mo'kal stretched his neck, spat on the statue and said, "Damn Asad".

The court official instantly ordered Um Mo'kal and her son to be put in solitary confinement for chastisement. Mo'kal burst into tears and shouted even louder, "Damn Asad! Damn Asad!" Every time his mother tried to shut him up or cover his mouth, he yelled louder, "Damn Asad!"

## Causing Disturbance

One of the other women, imprisoned in Katana Prison before us, was Um Haitham, mother of four, also from Jisir. Her husband hid several wanted men in their house. The government ambushed her house. A gunfire exchange took place. Some men were killed, some escaped and Abu Haitham and his wife were arrested and put through horrendous torture. Um Haitham feels certain that they executed her husband. They decided to keep her in jail with the charge of causing disturbance, the same charge they indicted Um Mo'kal, Um Abd Al-Basit and her daughter Aida with in military court. They held all of them in prison until the end of 1985.

Sameeha and Fatima, cousins from Maraj Khoka in Latakiya, left the city for the mountains with a group of relatives on the run from the Mukhabarat. Fatima was fifteen. Sameeha was sixteen. Another girl, Ghaniya, went with them. She was eighteen. In the mountains, the three girls cooked and cared for the wanted men. Soon the government caught onto them, thanks to a snitch. They ambushed the group and a struggle followed resulting in the death of Ghaniya and several men. The rest of the group including Sameeha and Fatima were arrested.

At first the Mukhabarat took Sameeha and Fatima to Sheik Hasan Prison in Damascus. They tortured them for three days, before they transferred them to Katana Prison. The Mukhabarat refused to return Ghaniya's body to her family and claimed to have buried her themselves. All of the men who were arrested with Sameeha and Fatima were sent to Tadmur Prison.

Another of our cellmates, Um Mahmoud Kamil, was also from Latakiya. She was in her fifties, a grandmother and mother of four or five children. The Mukhabarat arrested her just days before me and accused her of aiding wanted men in their escape from the country. They claimed that she facilitated their attainment of travel documents through her relatives. They imprisoned Um Mahmoud Kamil in Kafar Suseh Prison before we got there, but quickly transferred her to Katana Prison. She told us how they tortured and beat her with no regard for her old age. She stayed at Katana Prison with us for the entire length of our imprisonment.

## Double Agent

Asmaa Faisal, wife of Riyad Al-Turk, a well-known communist leader, was also our inmate. She was a doctor in her fifties. She'd been in jail about three years before we got to Katana Prison. They released her a few months after our arrival. Although we lived with her for a short while, she left a good impression on us, with her kind treatment.

Ameera, who was in Katana Prison with Asmaa before our arrival, was the opposite of Asmaa. She was a Kurdish woman, from Damascus, in her mid-forties. She was married to an Iraqi and worked with him in the Iraqi embassy. The Mukhabarat accused her of working as a double agent. Ameera spied for Syria and Iraq. The Syrian government imprisoned her. The Iraqi government ordered her execution in her absence. Her husband divorced her. She remained in Katana Prison after our release. She never bored of hurting us, creating problems for us and talking badly about the Ikhwan.

"You will see, soon, all of the prisoners will be released, except the Ikhwan. You poor things will have to sit and watch the rest of us be set free," she told us over and over again always speaking loud enough for all of us to hear. In the end, we were released and she was the poor thing who had to sit and watch us walk free. They released her a year or two after us.

## Victims

Life in Katana definitely differed from life in Kafar Suseh. The new privileges and improvements were a blessing, but prison, no matter with how many privileges, is still prison just as handcuffs, even if made of gold, are still handcuffs. Prison makes you forget the feel of freedom and gives you nothing to look forward to, so when you think about the future all you envision is more problems, more pain and more suffering. We had no choice but to adapt and survive. Every time we felt the walls closing in on us, we sought new ways to vent, to breathe and to keep alive.

At first, we didn't mix with the prisoners from the other cells, the non-political prisoners. Our doors opened to the field at different times. One group went out in the morning and the other in the evening and the next day they reversed. Later, we began to speak to them from behind bars. We listened to their stories to kill time and entertain ourselves. We counselled them and advised them. Many of them were victims of bad parenting, miserable childhoods, or unfortunate circumstances.

We got to know one of the non-political prisoners, a young girl who listened to us and let us help her through some sad circumstances and a dismal future. The young girl's troubles started when she got into a disagreement with her family. Her parents kicked her out of the house and told her never to come back. The young girl had no one to turn to. The only person in the world who held out a hand to her was a woman who ran a whorehouse. The woman took her in and dragged her into a life that led her to jail.

My inmates and I felt sorry for the young girl; we felt that it was the faults of others, not her own, that forced her into that kind of a life. We contacted one of the social workers that conducted research at our prison. Contact with the social workers or with law students who studied the cases of non-political prisoners was forbidden, but somehow we managed to contact one of them. We relayed to her the young girl's story and the social worker seemed touched and took it upon herself to help the young girl. The social worker helped the young girl through her trials and even introduced her to a man whom she later married.

## The *Kirwana*

A description of Katana Prison would not be complete without a description of our meals. Our main meals came from Kala Prison in enormous metal pots and trays, but our servings, which we called the *Kirwana*, always arrived just after we reached the brink of starvation.

This is how it worked: an officer drove the prisoners who had trials to their court hearings and on his way back, stopped by Kala Prison to pick up our food. When the food arrived, the guards plonked it in the prison field and opened the cell doors. The prisoners stampeded out into the field to grab their shares. Arguments and fights erupted the minute the doors opened. "She has more! She has less! We want this! We don't want that..." The arguments and fights led to bad feelings and spoiled appetites. When things became completely out of control, the warden appointed Ghazwa as the official food distributor. Poor Ghazwa held the responsibility of dividing the food between the prisoners, until the day she was released.

That's *how* we got our meals in Katana Prison. Now I'll tell you the story of *what* our meals consisted of. Many times, after we got hold of our shares, we turned our spoons in our bowls and watched cockroaches float to the top. Sometimes, the cockroaches didn't float to the top; sometimes they ended up between our teeth. We became accustomed to the footprints of officers who stomped on our food before they brought it to us. Other times, the driver arrived earlier than expected and dumped our food trays at the front door of the prison. Dogs and cats rushed to the food and ate much of it before the warden could notice the early delivery.

We secretly asked one of the female guards to buy something for us to eat when she went for lunch. Sometime later, this became allowed and we no longer had to ask the guards in secret. Um Deebo, one of the female guards, regularly brought food to the prison and sold it to us at ridiculous prices.

Water was another problem. The taps in our cells provided little water and so we took turns receiving water from a central tap in the prison. The guards extended hoses to each cell from that central tap. Every hour, the water switched from one cell to the next. Each cell could manipulate the amount of water the next cell could receive. If one cell used too much water, then the next cell would end up with a drizzle. Water became yet another source of tension between the prisoners.

When the Mukhabarat headquarters finally decided to allow television into the prisons, it was only for the purpose of educating the prisoners about the revolution of the Ba'ath party, and keeping us up to date on their glorious accomplishments. The television was no exception when it came to the long list of things the prisoners argued about.

Hajja Riyad insisted that everybody keep perfectly quiet during news broadcasts. She was afraid to miss a word. She worried she'd miss an announcement about a general pardon for political prisoners that the government may decide to broadcast. In 1985, the year of President Hafiz Al-Asad's Bay'it Al-Abad, a pardon was indeed announced, but it was only for the men who had apposed mandatory military service. The minute Hajja Riyad heard the word "pardon" on the television, she went into shock and shouted hysterically, "Thank God! Thank God! I'm going to see my mother."

When we heard the details of the pardon, we fell silent. Hajja

Riyad took it the worst. She spent days weeping and grieving.

## The Fires

I'll never forget the fires in Katana Prison that added more chaos and suffering to our already arduous lives. A fire once broke out in the washroom of the torture room, burning to death a woman named Fatima. Fatima was charged with the murder of her husband. The fire spread from the washroom to the rest of the cell until it reached the rest of the inmates.

Majida and I sat next to our window at the time, a window that looked into the torture room. It was just after sunset. Majida and I sat together and recited from the Quran. The women in the torture room glimpsed me through the window and I saw their lips move, calling out to me, begging me for help. We were locked in and couldn't do anything to help them. We yelled out to Um Deebo, our guard, but she ignored our pleas as usual. After "breathing time" in the field, the guards locked our doors and ignored all of our calls.

The fire spread into the field. Smoke filled the air. Flames rose so high, that they touched the electricity wires above the field. The flames quickly drew closer and closer to the gas tanks in the kitchen. Finally Um Deebo noticed the fire and rang the alarm. Officers swarmed around in the dark and tried to determine the source of the fire. They found nothing.

In the midst of the chaos, one of the inmates noticed that the fire had engulfed Fatima, one of the prisoners. The inmate grabbed a blanket and flapped it furiously at Fatima, but to no avail; the fire ate away at Fatima's skin. Fatima lay in a coma for about a week, moaning all day and all night, before she died. We listened to her moans all night. We smelled her burnt skin. We saw the puss and mucus that erupted all over her body.

The second fire I remember was in our cell. The gas tank that heated the water we bathed in blew up and ignited with fire while one of the women was in the washroom. Instead of opening the door, the woman accidentally locked herself in. She sat in the corner of the washroom and watched the fire between her and the door grow. We broke the washroom lock. Majida rushed into the washroom, grabbed the gas tank, engulfed in flames, ignored her burning hands and threw the tank into the step at our cell door, saving the woman's life.

## God Have Mercy

The privileges we received in Katana Prison were uncountable compared to life in Kafar Suseh Prison. The greatest privilege was our right to visitations. For some time, they even allowed us to write and receive letters. I wrote to my brother in Aleppo and to my aunt and even to Um Shaima in Saudi Arabia. They all wrote back. The letter writing privilege lasted for two or three months. Strict restrictions on letters, books and any literature were re-instated after that, but the weekly visits on Fridays continued.

Families of the prisoners gathered from all over the country. They gathered in front of the prison from dawn, waiting for visitation to begin. They waited for hours at the front door of Katana Prison before the officer in charge allowed them in. The officer drove the visitors to the visitation hall, searched them and whatever gifts they may have brought for the prisoners and then brought the prisoners out to the visitation hall. Like the prisoners, the visitors too sat behind bars. Between the prisoners and the visitors was a hallway patrolled by officers. The officers listened to conversations and jumped in whenever they pleased.

Our first Friday at Katana was full of excitement. We asked the women who were here before us, and who already had visitors, to

151

ask their families to contact our families, so they could know we were here and that they could come visit us. When Gazwa's family came to see her, I begged them to contact my family, desperate for a chance to see them on the following Friday. I didn't know that my family was murdered eight months ago in the Hama massacre. Gazwa's family knew. Gazwa's mother was also murdered in the Hama massacre. The following week, Gazwa's family came back and told me that they could not contact my family. The city had changed, they claimed, and they no longer knew where to find my parents. They told me about what happened in Hama, but no one mentioned my family.

During the next visit, Sana's family came. I begged them to go to my aunt's house in Damascus and inform her of my transfer to Katana Prison. Sana's relatives visited my aunt. She told them about my family, but they couldn't bring themselves to tell me the news. They claimed they couldn't find my aunt. The next time they visited, they told me they actually visited my aunt, but that she was sick and they couldn't ask her about my family. I began to sense something horribly wrong. After Sana's family left, I confronted her.

"Come here. I need to talk to you," I said. "Your mother visited my aunt and my aunt told her something about my family. What did she tell her? Did my father die?"

Sana remained silent.

"God have mercy on him," she whispered.

"God have mercy on him," I repeated. "If he really is dead, then yes, may God have mercy on him."

"Just like that? You say: God have mercy on him?"

I felt as if the pains of prison had made other pains more bearable.

"Yes. God have mercy on him. What can I do for him if he is dead? If I bang my head against that wall, will he come back?"

Tears streamed down Sana's face. I could tell there was more to the story.

"Did anyone else die?"

Sana nodded.

"My mother? Is she dead too?"

"God have mercy on her."

"Dear God! Then where are my brothers and sisters?"

Sana sobbed.

"They went with your mother. She couldn't leave them behind, so she took them with her."

"Have you gone mad? Are you kidding? All of my brothers and sisters dead?"

"Yes. All of them. God have mercy on them all. Isn't that better than one of them being left behind, left for you to worry about?"

*I must be asleep. I must be having a nightmare.*

"That's enough. Don't tell me more."

I had no will to listen to another word. I did not even care to know the details.

My aunt and uncle came to visit the next week, my aunt shrouded in black.

"Why are you wearing all black?" I asked.

"Oh, just because," she said. "I feel like wearing black today."

"Has Grandma passed away?"

"No."

"Then why are you wearing black?" I demanded.

My uncle winked at me, motioning to me to change the subject, but I couldn't. I couldn't let it go.

"Why are you winking at me? What's going on?"

He didn't want to repeat the story in front of my aunt who was already traumatized.

"Nothing. Nothing is going on."

"So why are you wearing black? It makes me feel anxious."

My aunt smiled at me, a sad, sorrowful smile.

"How can you ask that question?" my uncle blurted out. "Don't

153

you know the news?"

The news that Sana relayed to me came flashing back, as if I had forgotten and just now remembered.

"Yes. I know that my family is dead, but I'm asking her why *she* is wearing black?"

It didn't occur to me at the time, that my aunt was mourning my family, that she was in full black because her brother and his family were murdered. My uncle realized that I had lost it and tried to explain things to me slowly.

"She's mourning your family's death. Do you understand?"

"If you're going to come visit me in all black next time, then don't come, because a martyr is alive not dead and if you want to mourn them because they are alive, then don't come and visit me."

## Grey with Agony

My aunt didn't take the visit very well, but I took it even worse. My aunt burst into tears and my uncle hurried to comfort her and calm her down, but he couldn't do so for a long while, not until my aunt began to comprehend the state I was in and understand why I was behaving like I was out of my mind. Next time my aunt came to visit, she didn't wear black.

I never found out the details of my family's murders until later, when Majida's mother told me. Majida's father came to visit one Friday. Majida didn't recognize him. His hair had turned grey; his face had wrinkled and he sat in a wheelchair, a wheelchair he needed ever since he heard the news of his daughter's arrest. When Majida realized it really was her father standing right there in front of her, she jumped up and down, ecstatic. She got tongue-tied. Words wouldn't come out. It took her several minutes to get a hold of herself and speak.

"I didn't recognize you," she apologized. "You're grey."

"You my dear daughter are the one who made my hair turn grey."

Majida's father was a supporter of the Ba'ath party and an opposer of the Ikhwan. Majida thought he might have turned against her too, but her father burst into tears at the sight of her.

"Look, I came here to visit you my dear daughter with my head held high and dignified. Praise be to God."

The next visit, Majida's mother came. Majida and I both erupted with indescribable joy and excitement. The first thing Majida's mother told me was that my brother Warif had been killed. She told me the story from the beginning.

After my mother's release from prison, the Mukhabarat created a trap at my family's house. They figured that my brothers would surely come to greet my mother after her release and the Mukhabarat would be there ready to capture them. But none of them turned up.

The Mukhabarat then went after my father. Every once in a while, they took my father out to the park along the Assey River in front of our house and tortured him in public. They beat him. They burned his beard. They dragged him along the streets to humiliate him and to make an example of him for the people. My mother would come out and yell at them and pray to God to punish them.

"Hand your sons over and we'll leave your husband alone and give you your daughter back," their leader shouted back at her.

"First bring me my daughter. I want to see her with my two eyes and hold her in my two arms, before I tell you where the rest of my children are. But as long as she is not right here in front of my eyes, you will not take anything else from me. You would have to kill me first." My mother challenged them as usual.

The second calamity happened when my brother Warif was murdered in Aleppo. He was eighteen. He stayed at a hideout, a house full of wanted men in Aleppo. The Mukhabarat found the hideout, ambushed it and shot the men. This happened sixteen days before they murdered the rest of my family. Although my mother was distraught when she found out about Warif's murder, she hid the news from my father, whose health couldn't handle another blow. My mother went to visit Majida's mother, took Warif's picture with her, looked at it and cried and cried and cried and let it all out before she went back home to my father.

My mother continuously struggled to visit me in prison. Her own horrible memories of Kafar Suseh didn't stop her from coming to the prison with Majida's mother, meeting with Khairbek once again, and begging him for a glimpse of me.

"Sorry. No one here by that name," was all Khairbek replied.

Majida's mother told me that my mom went crazy with rage at Khairbek. She left his office and stood at the window of our old cell that looked out onto the prison field. She begged one of the officers to please just give her a tiny sign, anything to let her know whether I was still here or not. She got nothing. She left devastated and shattered, without seeing me, without even finding out whether I was there or not, whether I was dead or alive. Things never got better. Nothing changed, until the Hama massacre.

## Hama, Cut off From the World

We were still in Kafar Suseh Prison when the events in Hama began to unravel in February 1982. In our encapsulated lives, we knew nothing of what was going on in the world. Some news did leak into the prison, but Khairbek warned everyone with severe punishment if anyone even hinted to me about my family's murders. In Katana Prison, I heard bits of information about the horrifying events that took place in my hometown. Majida's mother filled me in on the rest of the story, in particular, what happened to my family.

Majida's mother told me that she had seen in her dream my

young sisters and brothers all sleeping together in one bed. The bed was sinking in a flood and although my siblings were drowning, they were still moving around alive in pure water and then my mother came in and threw herself into my aunt's lap and split in two. When Majida's mother woke up that morning, she felt a wrenching feeling that my family was in danger. She sprung from bed, woke her husband up and begged him to go check on my family and to try to bring them back to Majida's family's house.

Majida's family had moved from the town of Tawafira, where we were neighbours for a long time, to a suburb close to the city of Homs. It was a long drive between our two houses now. Majida's father left right after dawn prayer. When he neared the city of Hama, he found it surrounded by police and blocked off from all directions. He went back home, sparing himself from the horror that was about to take place. Inside the city, people were dying on the streets by the hundreds.

During the massacre, my aunt tried to get into Hama, desperate to help my family escape. Everybody tried to stop her from her suicidal mission, but no one could, not even her husband. She insisted on trying. She managed to get in and made it all the way to the street where my family lived, but there, she found army officials who forced her back. My father's body had been lying on the street for four days by then. Nobody had the courage to even lift his corpse off the street.

## A Piece of Bread

The story of my family's murder began when a group of Ikhwan members grouped together and sought refuge in our neighbourhood. The police weren't able to infiltrate their stronghold. The government ordered the neighbourhood sealed off and prohibited any supplies, electricity or water from coming into the entire town. The blockade lasted for seven days, until not a shred of food or a drop of water

157

remained in my parents' house.

My father went out and asked the first officer he saw for something to sustain the children with. My uncle, who watched from his window in a nearby building, told me that the officer shouted at my father and ordered him to go back to wherever he came from. My little brothers and sisters cried and cried in hunger. My father could not bear it. He went out again and told the guards that all he wanted was a piece of bread for the children.

"Go back into your house before I shoot you and drop you to the ground," the officer shouted.

But that only kept my father back for a short while, before he went back out for a third time and begged the officers for a piece of bread to keep the children from dying. This time the officers responded with gunshots and my father rushed back towards the front door, but not in time. My uncle screamed and fainted at the sight of my father's dead body. His daughter in–law ran to help him up. Other officers heard the commotion and threw a torch at our house to see what was going on. The officers forced their way into the house, grabbed my mother and the children as human shields and spread throughout the house.

During those short moments, as my father dropped dead at our doorstep, my brother Mahir heard the gunshots from the basement, where my family had gathered for safety, and stepped out to see what had happened. When Mahir saw his father dead on the porch, he ran back into the house, up to his room and grabbed the gun that the Mukhabarat themselves had given to him. The Mukhabarat had passed around guns to kids as young as Mahir, who was barely thirteen, entrusting them to defend the revolution. Mahir charged out of our house and fired back at the officers that had killed his father. He killed several officers before they shot him dead.

Khairbek relayed this story to Majida and my other cellmates.

"We gave him the weapon to protect us with it, but he used it against us. They're all traitors. That's why we killed every last one of them, even tore the young ones to pieces because they are the seed of Ikhwan and their fate can only be Ikhwan," Khairbek told my cellmates.

My mother ran out of the house shouting at the officers, crying, and praying to God to punish them. That's when they shot her, right at our front door, just like my father. With my father, brother and mother lying dead on the porch, the officers marched into the house to finish off the others. Five of my brothers and sisters huddled in the basement: Yasir who was four, Kamar who was five, Rana who was six, Safa who was seven and in her first year of school and Dilal who was twenty years old. The officers killed them all.

I had three brothers left. Safwan was long out of the country. Ghassan and Samir were still hiding in Aleppo. My family's corpses were gathered along with the bodies of the other dead in the city and dumped into a mass grave just days before the murders and destruction ended, the curfew was lifted and people felt safe enough to come out of hiding. My aunt and uncle drove to Hama to see what had become of my family and found nothing but my mother's scarf at the front door in the middle of a pool of blood. In the basement, they found blood splattered on the walls and ceiling, but no bodies.

## Hurry to Jihad

Amir, my fourteen-year-old brother, was also killed in the massacre, far from home on Azar Street. My mother had sent Amir to stay with my grandmother who lived with my uncle who was away in Saudi Arabia. My mother worried that if the Mukhabarat came into my uncle's house and found only an old woman, they would rob the place, as they commonly did. The Mukhabarat did come to my uncle's house and did much worse than what my mother feared.

The officers found my uncle's lute and sat to play it, while other

159

officers ransacked every other room in the house. They laughed wildly as they turned everything upside down and inside out. They had no one to answer to, no one to stop them. Amir hid under the bed. The officers ordered my grandmother to get up and dance. My nearly seventy year old grandmother got up and danced for them. She danced for fear that they might find Amir. She danced for fear that they might demand more than a dance. The officers stole what they wanted, destroyed what they left and then took off.

Amir came out from under the bed. He heard the *muathin* call out from the mosque, "Hurry to *jihad*". Amir took off his watch. He made *wudu*. He prayed his final prayer, the prayer of a martyr. He gave his watch to my grandmother.

"Take this watch in memory of me. Give it to my mother. Pray for me."

Amir ran out of the house. My grandmother called out and shouted for him to come back, but Amir didn't come back. She watched him run into Taweel Plaza, where the Ikhwan had grouped. He left the plaza only once, to knock on the door of a nearby house. He stood barefoot, in torn clothes and asked for any bit of food or clothing the woman could give him. He told her his friends were dying of cold and hunger. The woman only had daughters and didn't know what she could give him. She gathered some old jackets and big sweaters, some food and other supplies and sent him away.

The next day Amir's friends found his dead body on Azar Street. They lifted his corpse and buried him in a place piled with the ruins of a mosque the Mukhabarat had demolished. After the Mukhabarat left the city, they dug up his body once again and buried him in a proper graveyard. I never found out exactly which graveyard that was, because the man who buried him ended up dead as well.

That's how I found out about the murders of my parents and my five sisters and brother. My cellmates knew all along, but they decided not to tell me. Somehow, the news didn't shock me. It didn't traumatize me, like everybody thought it would. I never felt sad for my family. I only felt sad for myself, for my loss. My family, they were in a better place now.


## Pain Killer Needles

Days passed. Life in Katana Prison fell into the same dull and all too familiar routine and I felt like a huge, heavy stone was parked on my chest. I fell prey to a new set of diseases, one after the other, diseases that I had never encountered before. My illnesses drove me right into the hands of a malicious doctor, a product of the Ba'ath Party.

Dr. Sameer was an intern at the prison, originally only treating the non-political prisoners, but when the number of political prisoners and their illnesses shot up, he began to spend some time every now and then to see only those whose conditions were very serious. But Dr. Sameer's visits were useless. The most he ever did was hand the prisoners a few painkillers that never worked. Dr. Sameer didn't behave like a professional doctor. He behaved like a Mukhabarat officer. Whenever we complained of anything, Dr. Sameer replied to us like a robot: "There is nothing wrong with you." We grew so weary of hearing that reply again and again that we no longer even went to him with our medical problems.

For the first few months, while I still had the ulcer, the one I had inherited from Kafar Suseh Prison, I requested to see Dr. Sameer. I felt desperate. The pain was unbearable. I was trying to explain to Dr. Sameer what was wrong and what I felt, when he interrupted me and said, "There is no medicine for these symptoms. You will have to find a way to treat yourself."

Thank God that one of my cellmates had a relative who was an experienced doctor and who visited her once in a while. He treated us secretly and slipped us medication. Due to his help, my ulcer improved and the pain began to recede, but not long after, new pains began to plaque me. I started feeling pain at the beginning of every menstrual cycle, pain so bad that I caved in and requested another appointment with Dr. Sameer. I begged and pleaded for painkillers.

A few days later, Dr. Sameer called Hajja Madeeha and told her that he had called on a group of doctors to discuss my symptoms and come up with possible treatments and they had come to a decision. I received a package of needles. I had already injected myself with two doses of the medication before my cellmate had a chance to ask her relative about the needles. Her relative asked to see the needles. My cellmate took one with her during visitation and showed it to him.

"These needles are not painkillers. They're fertility drugs," he cried out.

He marched off in a rage straight into the warden, Colonel Muwaffaq Al-Samman's, office. After that incident, we never saw or heard of Dr. Sameer again, but nobody investigated his crimes or questioned him on what he did to me, nor did anybody care to replace him with another doctor.

## Urine or Blood

I don't know what became of Dr. Sameer, but I do know that my pain didn't go away and my suffering didn't end. I began to feel other symptoms in other parts of my body. The pain flared up and I fought it; but the pain fought back harder and won. I couldn't bear it anymore. I found out that I had a kidney infection. I saw blood in my urine. I vomited continuously. I rushed to the washroom many times a day with diarrhoea.

The environment I lived in worsened my condition. I spent the month of Ramadan in the year of 84, in a dire state. I couldn't fast a single day in Ramadan. I couldn't even pray. My cellmates couldn't sleep due to my constant cries of pain. I became so weak that I couldn't even get up to use the washroom. My cellmates carried me to the washroom.

At the same time as my kidney infection, a flea infestation spread throughout the prison, and so when my infection pains settled for a moment, the fleas took over the job of tormenting me. There was never a lack of things tormenting me in Katana Prison. Every new source of torment brought a new taste of torture. Majida, God bless her, stayed up many nights, sitting by my pillow, plucking away at the fleas. She did the best she could. After sometime, when I had neared death, Colonel Muwaffaq Al-Samman, the warden, took notice and ordered that I be taken to a specialist, on his responsibility. They took me in a police car and they drove around in the town of Katana until they found a kidney specialist. The specialist examined me and handed me painkillers. She told the officers that I needed to get some tests done. I gave a urine sample. The officer handed the sample to a lab worker.

"Is this urine or blood?" asked the lab worker.

When the results came back, the doctor prescribed six needles every day. Um Mo'kal injected me with the needles and even after my sides were filled with needle pricks, I felt no improvement. The prison management sent a letter to the national security branch in Kafar Suseh explaining my situation and requesting permission to take me to Mowasa Hospital. An initial agreement arrived, but it was dependant on the doctor's diagnosis in the hospital.

The next day, officers carried me into a police car. I faded in and out of consciousness. At the hospital, groups of students surrounded me, eager to learn from my case. A doctor emerged from the crowd. She took off my coat and examined me quickly. She gave me an injection for the pain. After that, I no longer felt anything.

When I regained consciousness, I found myself back in the cell with my cellmates hovering over me. *They're watching me take my last breaths.* The painkillers wore off quickly and the pain came back full force. Two or three days later, they took me back to the hospital. The same thing happened over and over again, from the cell to the hospital and from the hospital back to the cell. I gained nothing from these trips but exhaustion and more injections in my arms.

The last time they took me to the hospital, my cellmate told her doctor relative, and I found him there at the hospital waiting for me with my brother, Ghassan, and my cousin who was an intern at that same hospital. They took me up to the top floor in the hospital, where better care was offered. The doctors took more tests and the results came back quickly.

During my stay at the hospital, a strange thing happened. A doctor stepped into my room and rushed to my side. He bent down and whispered.

"Aren't you Safwan Dabbagh's sister?"

"Yes."

"What happened to him?" He quivered. "And why are you in prison?

He didn't wait for me to answer.

"It's okay. God will help," he whispered.

His eyes swelled with tears.

The doctor examined me and spoke softly, explaining to me that Safwan and him used to be friends at university. He said he'd do his best to keep me in the hospital for as long as possible so that I could get the treatment I needed. He passed my diagnosis to the hospital manager. The hospital manager agreed to keep me in the hospital as long as he had the permission of the national security office. The officer in charge of guarding me politely asked me to wait by the hospital entrance with my brother while he went to get permission from Kala Prison to keep me in the hospital.

# An Opportunity for Escape

A police car passed by as my brother and I waited at the entrance. I felt weak. I couldn't see the steps in front of me. My head spun. Everything started to spin. My brother threw his arms around me and guided me down the steps like a blind person. We sat on two chairs outside the hospital, alone and unguarded.

"What if I help you escape right now," my brother whispered.

In the state I was in, escape sounded meaningless. Freedom sounded meaningless.

"I don't want to escape. They'll catch us at the border, send us back and our problems will only double."

A couple of minutes later, the police car passed by again. An officer poked his head out the window and asked us if we wanted to come with him instead of sitting and waiting. We agreed. The police car travelled through the neighbourhoods of Damascus, heading towards Kala Prison, which was located in the midst of the old neighbourhoods of Damascus. I watched people from the window, buying, selling and busy with life. I saw students, labourers, workers and businessmen. They swirled around in the cycle of life, working to secure their daily bread, all of them too busy with life to take notice of what went on around them, blind and deaf to their surroundings, blind and deaf to the oppression in their country.

When we got to Kala Prison, one of the officers quickly hopped out of the car and hurried into the prison office to get the approval I needed to stay at the hospital. He returned a moment later, his eyes lowered and sad. The request was denied.

I was so used to disappointment that I didn't even care. I felt nothing. They drove me back to Katana Prison, back to my cellmates, back to our sad and sorrowful lives. My cellmate's doctor relative came to visit more and more often and brought medicine for me. My condition improved bit by bit. After one month, I began to go the washroom alone, but I didn't regain my normal strength for two more years. I spent those two years unable to move around, wash my own clothes or even bathe myself, constantly depending on the kindness of others. My cellmates grabbed every opportunity they could to provide me with nourishing food and anything else to help bring me back.

## The Lost Child

Prison life brings days pregnant with secrets and futures wrapped in riddles that cannot be unravelled until an appointed day. Prison life also mixes suffering with strange stories and creates distinctive environments that condition the prisoners to expect anything at anytime and to get used to encounters with all sorts of oddities. Without warning and beyond expectations, a story unravelled around us, a story of a lost boy, whom the police found in a Damascus neighbourhood.

The sight of the little boy pained our hearts. A little lost boy, barely six years old, imprisoned against his will, in a cell filled with prostitutes. The police who found him lost in Damascus locked him up with the prostitutes while they waited to hear from his parents. Five months passed and the police heard nothing. No parents. No relatives. What made the sad situation even worse was that the little boy was mute. He couldn't even tell us his own name.

The guards and his cellmates began to call him Ahmad. Ahmad's cellmates soon discovered that Ahmad made a useful and obedient servant. They ordered him around, yelled at him, and even hit him. One evening, in Ramadan, after breaking our fasts, I sat by the window and munched on a sweet. The guards had left the cell doors open for airing, as they usually did after *iftar*. I turned from the window and found myself nose to nose with Ahmad. Ahmad stared with eyes wide open and focused directly at the sweet in my hand. He stretched out his hand and said, "Give me one."

I couldn't believe my ears at first. For months, Ahmad never spoke a single word and I just couldn't believe that all of sudden he was actually speaking.

"Girls! Girls! Ahmad spoke!" I shouted.

When we told the guards that Ahmad spoke, they seemed touched and told us to keep Ahmad in our cell.

"Maybe Ahmad didn't like the atmosphere in the other cell," the guard suggested.

We huddled around Ahmad, hugged him and welcomed him into our group and Ahmad started to speak.

Hajja Madeeha asked him for his name.

"Ahmad Badr Al-Deen," he said.

"Where are you from?"

"From Hama."

The women lifted their brows at his answer.

"What brought you to Damascus then?"

Ahmad's lips quivered. His eyes watered.

"They gathered me with all the other kids that were left in Hama after what happened there and then they put me in Al-Umawi mosque and I didn't know where to go after that."

"And where is your family?" Hajja Madeeha asked.

Ahmad's tears turned to sobs.

"They died," he whimpered.

"How?"

"My mom sent me to get my dad from his shop and I ran to his shop and went in and then I saw that a wall fell on my dad and he was dead and there was blood everywhere. So I went back home crying and I wanted to tell my mom about what happened to my dad, but when I got home, my mom was dead."

Ahmad's expression turned from grief to worry. He turned to Hajja Madeeha.

"Don't tell anyone. If I hear anyone say my name, then that

167

means you told them. Please don't tell anyone."

As the little boy told his tale and unravelled the mystery that had kept all of us curious for months, we ached for him. Ahmad gained a special place in our hearts. My cellmates and I showered him with privileges and special treatment. One day, as I sat sewing with a small manual sewing machine that Raghda's family had struggled to bring for us, Ahmad came up to me.

"For God's sake, get that machine out of my face," Ahmad shrieked. "I don't like to watch anyone sew."

"Why?"

Ahmad started to cry. Hajja Madeeha put her arms around him and gently asked him why he hated to watch anyone sew.

"Because," he blurted, "because my mom used to sew. She was a tailor and she had a machine just like the one Heba has and my mom used to wear prayer clothes just like hers too and sit and sew just like that."

One time, one of my cellmates called out for Aysha. Ahmad ran to Hajja Madeeha and said, "Please for God's sake, tell them not to call her Aysha."

"What would you like us to call her?"

"Call her the one who wears glasses."

"Why?"

"Because my mom's name is Aysha."

Hajja Madeeha took the opportunity to ask him some more questions.

"What does your dad do?"

"He owned a Quran library."

"Where?"

Ahmad described his dad's shop to us, down to every last detail and our hearts melted for him even more. Ahmad became our new cellmate and we watched him bloom and flourish like no other child we'd ever seen. Ahmad was a genius. He learned every recipe, every sewing pattern; every thing we did, Ahmad watched and learned. Ahmad recited the *athan* for us and recited the Quran beautifully as well. Sometimes after prayer, Ahmad would raise his hands in prayer and say, "Oh God please send down a bomb on Tadmur Prison."

The warden, Colonel Muwaffaq Al-Samman, heard about the little boy and came to see him. Ahmad won the Colonel's heart instantly and the Colonel began to take him home and bathe him and spoil him. The warden had a boy and a girl around Ahmad's age, and he began to take Ahmad with his kids to swimming pools and other places. He even appointed a private driver to drive Ahmad between the Colonel's home and the prison.

Once Colonel Al-Samman took Ahmad to the store where he bought his household needs. Ahmad learned his way to the store and started to go there alone and take things from the store and tell the clerk to put it on the Colonel's account. Ahmad put his purchases in a box, took them to the train station and sold them. When Colonel Al-Samman came looking for Ahmad, he always found him with us and when Ahmad left us, we always assumed that he was with Colonel Al-Samman. Neither of us really knew where Ahmad was.

At the end of the month, Colonel Al-Samman got the huge bill. He had no idea where it came from. He inquired about the bill at the store and the clerk told him that Ahmad had been buying things and charging them to his account. Colonel Al-Samman did nothing.

## Two Personalities and Two Slaps

Ahmad's reputation flourished and spread even amongst our families. Whenever our relatives visited, they remembered Ahmad with gifts, and when visitation time ended, they argued over who would get to take Ahmad home for a visit. Ahmad became the centre of the entire prison's attention. Guards, prisoners and their relatives all spoiled Ahmad to ridiculous extents, and moulded him into the kind of kid whose nose dripped with blood or who dropped to the ground unconscious at the sound of a request.

Ahmad began to love some of the women in our cell and hate others. He never hesitated to create enmity between cellmates. We watched with wonder his amazing talents unfold and take shape. Once, Aysha did something that displeased Ahmad. Ahmad hollered for a guard to rush to our cell.

"She yelled at me," he told the guard and pointed.

The guard looked at Ahmad with sympathetic eyes. He glared at Aysha.

"If this happens again, I'm going to cut off your visitation rights."

I remembered a while back Aysha telling us that she had a feeling about this boy, that he seemed to have two personalities and that something was not right with him. Ahmad's alter personality didn't surface until one time when he was scheduled to visit Hajja Madeeha's family in Homs. Hajja Madeeha dressed him in his new shoes and sat him in her lap and waited for visitation time.

"Sameer Jaffan," one of the officers called out from behind our cell door.

Ahmad's nose began to gush blood. Ahmad blacked out.

"Who were you calling?" Hajja Madeeha called out to the guard, confused at what had just happened.

"Didn't you see how your buddy just fell to the ground?" the guard asked.

"Why?"

"His name is not Ahmad. His real name is Sameer Jaffan. Didn't you see his picture a while back all over the news on television?"

We remembered that we had seen a broadcast about a lost boy and they showed his picture on the news. It didn't occur to any of us that the lost boy could be our Ahmad. We remembered that when that

170

broadcast had aired, Ahmad ran to the television and turned it off. We thought he was just playing. My cellmates and I stared at the guard. We felt shocked and confused.

We washed the blood that streamed from Ahmad's nose and splashed cool water on his face. An old man stood behind the bars of our door cell, cried and banged his head against the bars. The man was Ahmad's father. The officer came in and took Ahmad to the Colonel's office.

"Who taught you to say that your name is Ahmad and to claim that your parents died in Hama?" the Colonel asked.

"Heba," Ahmad replied.

"Are you sure it was Heba?"

"Yes. Otherwise how would I know what to say? She's the one who told me say this and do that."

The Colonel called me to his office and began to yell and shout at me without an explanation.

"May God not bless you! Do you know that you are destroying the country's reputation? You wicked, ill-natured... I thought you were different."

Hajja Madeeha had accompanied me to the Colonel's office.

"Take it easy buddy. Tell us what happened," she pleaded.

"She," he said pointing at me, "wants to destroy the country's reputation. She is a wicked... hateful... vengeful..."

"Why are you saying all this?"

"Because she is the one who taught that boy to recite all those lies."

"Let me tell you, all the girls bent over backwards to please him, except her. She's the only one who didn't give him any special treatment."

The Colonel ordered me back to my cell. I felt more shocked and more confused. Hajja Madeeha tried to calm my fears as we shambled back to our cell. We passed an officer on our way back. Hajja Madeeha stopped and asked him to please explain to us what was going on.

"This kid, God damn him, has been playing all of us, from the youngest to the oldest. He's been claiming to be an orphan while knowing that his family was out there looking for him the whole time. His poor mother and his poor father told us that every once in while he pulls a stunt like this. He runs away from home and starts deceiving people with wild, crazy lies."

The Colonel took the boy into the interrogation room with his father and asked him again who had really taught him to say all those lies. The boy admitted that he had invented all of his own lies and that I had nothing to do with it. The Colonel swung his arm back and slapped the boy, a slap so hard it could have killed him. Then he pulled his arm back again and slapped the boy's other cheek. The boy sat still and said nothing. He left the prison with his parents, dragging his feet one at a time down the prison hallways. I watched him shuffle away. Half of me tried to comprehend what had just happened and the other half felt like I had just returned from the cinema.

## Release

Months and years passed and it was the year 1984 and we still sat withering away in Katana Prison and we no longer cared to keep count of the days or months. In prison, each day dragged by so slowly, so painfully that it felt like a hundred days.

On one of those days, Abu Motee, the warden's assistant, came into our cell and began to shout out names, "Eman T., Eman K., Aysha, Haleema..."

The women looked up in wonder.

"Come on. Get your selves ready for release."

The women stared, their faces blank. His words didn't register. They figured that he'd either spoken wrong, or they'd heard wrong.

"I said get yourselves ready for release."

The women trembled.

"We won't leave without everybody else," Um Shaima and Eman said. Their eyes brimmed with tears.

Eman came up to where I lay on my mattress, still sick, and sat on her knees at my head. Tears rolled down her face.

"I won't leave unless you let Heba leave with me."

"You're more than welcomed to stay here even though we've received orders for your release. Or if you want, you can sit at the front door of the prison and wait for Heba there."

"No. I won't leave. I won't leave her."

"How can I leave while you're still here?" Um Shaima cried at my side.

The warden grabbed Eman and Um Shaima and dragged them out. Eman and Um Shaima lunged out for anything they could clutch, the wire mesh, the bars on the door, anything. Other officers helped the warden pull Um Shaima and Eman out. Um Shaima and Eman wailed. They kicked and swung their arms until they found themselves standing outside the prison.

Later, we found out that the officers had taken them to the national security division first and from there released them. I never saw either of them again. The release of those women and the release of Sana a few weeks later, because of the *haraka tas'heehiya*, President Hafiz Al-Asad's correctional movement, enlivened our hopes. The doors of freedom were finally cracking open and we couldn't help but hope for our turns.

Days passed and proved us wrong and our hopes submerged once again. New prisoners poured into our cell, one group after the other, each one of them digging deeper into our wounds, making us feel more and more sure that our lives were destined to end between these four walls, in this cell, in this prison.

# In His Seventies and They Burned His Beard

Um Khalid, Omaiya, and Um Zohair had spent one whole year in the Military Interrogation Prison in Damascus, before they were brought to Katana Prison in 1984. Both women had suffered severely and lost many loved ones.

Omaiya was the daughter of a famous sheik in Damascus, Sheik Ahmad. The Mukhabarat imprisoned three of the sheik's sons: Alaa, Mostafa and the eldest, Shihab. From what we heard, Shihab was later executed in Tadmur Prison. The Mukhabarat imprisoned every member of Sheik Ahmad's family at least once and most likely twice or three times, including one of the sheik's granddaughters, Shaima, who was two years old.

I remember Officer Abdul-Aziz Thalja saying during my interrogation: "Listen, you know that so called Sheik Ahmad? I burned his beard with fire. The Mukhabarat arrested him the first time and then released him. Then, after two of the sheik's sons were murdered, the Mukhabarat arrested him again.

Omaiya grieved twice: once for her brothers' deaths and another time for her husband's. The Mukhabarat arrested her husband, Salih, a doctor from Aleppo, one year before our arrest. They accused him of associating with the Ikhwan and funding the resistance movement. The Mukhabarat also arrested Omaiya's sixteen year old son along with his father, but later released the son on the condition that he would cooperate with them. When he got out, Omaiya found a way to secretly send her son to Turkey and save him from falling into Mukhabarat cluches. The Mukhabarat arrested her instead.

Omaiya stayed in the Military Interrogation Prison for one year before they transferred her to Katana Prison, where they held her for another year. Major interventions by some of her close friends with important connections led to her early release. I still remember when Omaiya first walked into our cell. She looked at me and gasped.

"You're here," she said. "They didn't throw you out of a plane?"

I raised my eyebrows.

"What? What do you mean?"

"I swear to God, we heard that they threw you out of a plane and we cried for you. Oh, how we cried for you."

Um Zohair, who was in her forties, had suffered many losses too. Her brothers were one of the first to be murdered by the government for partaking in the resistance movement. Mukhabarat officers shot her brothers during a confrontation. Being one of the first families to suffer such losses for the cause brought Um Zohair's family a sort of fame as their reputation spread in the city. Um Zohair decided to go for *hajj* that year. On her return, she was greeted with the Mukhabarat at her door, ready to arrest her for no clear reason. She spent a year in the Military Interrogation Prison before they transferred her with Omaiya to Katana Prison. They were both released in 1985.

## Fruitless Years

Ibtisam married a medical intern in Latakiya. Three days into their marriage, the Mukhabarat arrested her husband and his brother for reasons Ibtisam knew nothing about. Ibtisam and her family worked tirelessly and spent large sums of money until they found a connection, someone who could set her up with a visit with her husband in Tadmur Prison. Ibtisam got five minutes. Five minutes wasn't even enough time for her to catch her breath after she saw what Tadmur Prison did to a man.

One month after that visit, Ibtisam found herself handcuffed and transported to a military interrogation unit in Latakiya and then to the military headquarters in Damascus. They locked her up for seven or eight months at headquarters, before they transferred her to Katana Prison.

Ibtisam arrived a few weeks after Omaiya's group and spent several fruitless years here with us, never knowing what her crime had been. She heard nothing about her husband during her entire imprisonment. Last she heard was that he had caught tuberculosis and was transferred from a joint cell in Tadmur Prison to an undisclosed location.

## Just Got Here Yesterday

Barely a few weeks after Ibtisam joined us, yet another prisoner arrived, Amal, from the political prison in Hama. During the Hama massacre, Amal had left to The United Arab Emirates, where her brothers lived. In 1985, she returned to Syria to visit her family and her hometown. Mukhabarat agents met her at the airport, arrested her and transported her to the political prison in Hama, where they tortured her severely. They tried everything to make Amal confess association with the Ikhwan and spill information about her brothers, who were "wanted criminals". The Mukhabarat squeezed for every last detail about her brothers' whereabouts and activities.

My aunt's husband told me that he was in that same political prison in Hama, at the same time as Amal. He told me how he and all the other men could never sleep because of the sounds that rang throughout the prison while they interrogated Amal. The Mukhabarat transferred Amal to Katana Prison, where they held her for five more years, before releasing her.

When the committee in charge of our affairs, headed by Hasan Al-Khaleel, met with us during the last while of our imprisonment, Officer Al-Khaleel looked down at Ibtisam with disgust and said: "You just got here yesterday and you want to leave with them?"

# The Old Child

A few more weeks passed. A few more guests arrived and joined our weary journey. This time, we got two sisters from Aleppo. The first one, Ragheeda, was a religion teacher. The second one, Aysha, was an English teacher. Their stories began when Ragheeda's husband, an engineer, became wanted by the government. Ragheeda lost contact with him. They had two sons and one daughter. Ragheeda got word that her husband was killed in Damascus. Ragheeda searched for a way to support her family and found nothing but an offer to teach in a school in Saudi Arabia. Aysha and her husband accompanied Ragheeda to Saudi Arabia. They lived there for several years before they decided to come back to Syria to visit their family, their country and to attend their niece's wedding.

The two families packed their pick-up truck with their belongings, gifts for their relatives and all sorts of lavish clothes and accessories for the bride. At the Syrian border at Daraa, customs officers stopped them and asked them what they were bringing into Syria. The customs agent disappeared for a few minutes and retuned with the news that they were wanted by the national security branch of the Mukhabarat. The customs agents kept the car and all that was in it and escorted the two families to Kafar Suseh Prison. At the prison, the agents contacted relatives to pick up the children, Aysha's nine and Ragheeda's three. Aysha was seven months pregnant with her tenth child, but that didn't stop the interrogators from torturing her severely. They tortured Ragheeda as well. They tortured her for information about her husband, the husband they had themselves murdered years ago.

The interrogators accused the sisters of taking part of organized government opposition activities. About two months later, they transferred them to Katana Prison. When she arrived at Katana Prison, Aysha was nine months pregnant and by some miracle, her baby had survived the torture sessions. When Aysha's labour pains began, we

177

begged the warden to allow a midwife from the other joint cell to spend the night in our cell. He agreed without knowing the reason for our request. Aysha suffered through the pains of labour until dawn, when she gave birth to a girl. She named her Tasneem. I remember the morning Tasneem was born was also the morning of *Eid Al-Kabeer*.

The first time I looked at Taseem, I felt as if the hair on my head stood up at sight of her frail body and wrinkled face. She looked like an old woman, ready to die. Aysha stayed with us while Ragheeda was released before our transfer to Dooma Prison. They released Aysha's husband several months after us. Aysha and her husband worked tirelessly, contacting every connection they had, to get their car and belongings back, but they got nothing – not even a reply.

## The Mysterious Communist

From among the newcomers during that time in Katana Prison was a lady from Altal, Hind Kahoji, cousin of Fadya Lathkani, a leader in the communist organization who was imprisoned with us in Kafar Suseh Prison. Hind was an engineer, married and barely past thirty. Her husband was most likely in prison too. They put her in the other joint cell and we never found out much about her. She was mysterious and kept to herself. They released her a few months after us with a large group of other communists.

## The Prisoners from Tadmur

Tadmur Prison was like a locked up grave; inside was death and outside was life. When a group of women from Tadmur Prison were transferred to Katana, we felt it was a miracle. We quickly found out that the primary reason for their transfer was the spread of scabies and tuberculosis in Tadmur Prison. The other reason was that the government had just completed the construction of a new prison called Saednaya and celebrated its grand opening for the service of the nation. Now, the Mukhabarat wanted to sort out their prisoners. They executed those on death row and transferred those they wanted to keep to various other prisons. Five women from Tadmur Prison were chosen to be transferred to Katana Prison and they became our new cellmates.

## Um Hassan's Tragedy

Three of the newcomers came from the same family. Khadija, who we also called Um Hassan, was in her fifties. She arrived with her two daughters Salwa and Yusra. Um Hassan's husband hid a group of wanted men in his house in Hama, before the massacre. He took a liking to two of the men and offered his two daughters in marriage to them.

When the Syrian army invaded Hama, the family fled to a nearby town, like thousands of other Hama residents, but Um Hassan's daughter, Yusra refused to flee from danger without her husband who had stayed behind in one of the Ikhwan bases in Hama with other wanted Ikhwan members. The Syrian soldiers discovered the base and ambushed it. The Ikhwan put up a resistance long enough for Yusra's husband to escape.

Abu Khalid, Yusra's husband's friend, who was paralysed in more than half his body was shot and killed. Khalid's wife, Laila, was also shot during the fire exchange, and so was their three-week old daughter. After the ambush, the soldiers captured Yusra and Laila. They tore the newborn out of Laila's arms, dragged Laila away and left the wounded baby to take her last breaths alone.

Yursa quickly gave into the monstrous interrogators, confessed her family's whereabouts and led the police to the town where her family hid. Um Hassan and Salwa were arrested, but her father managed to escape. Um Hassan's sister and her husband also happened to be visiting and the Mukhabarat arrested them along with the rest of the family. People say that Um Hasan's sister and her husband drank poison in their cells before their interrogation began. As for Um Hassan, the officers caught her attempting to swallow the poison and took it out of her mouth before she could swallow it.

Um Hassan sat in her cell, her thoughts scattered between her own grim condition, the death of her sister and brother in-law, and the fate of her seven nephews and nieces, who were now orphans with no one to care for them. But most of all, she thought about her children. She thought about Fawaz, who had barely turned three. She thought about her daughters Amal and Narjas and she thought about her eldest son, Ghazwan, who had just entered grade six.

Just when it seemed like the situation couldn't get worse, Um Hassan's husband was caught, arrested and imprisoned in 1985. Ghazwan, her eldest son, quit school and got a job fixing cars at an auto shop, so he could support himself and his brothers and sisters. Um Hassan's husband was eventually released. He returned to his children, but only to die a few days later due to the severe torture he endured.

Um Hassan's worries caught up with her sanity. She broke down repeatedly. She screamed in our faces and grabbed whatever objects she could get her hands on and threw them in all directions. Her worst days were the days her kids came to visit her. They would shamble in, the older ones taking turns to carry the younger ones and they would stand behind the glass window and stare at their mother. Their visits brought her such pain. When they left, the pain would rise and intensify and Um Hassan didn't know how to deal with it. She sobbed and screamed and slapped her face, as if physical pain could somehow dull the pain in her heart. Um Hassan went on like that for days and days after those visits.

When Um Hassan was released with her two daughters, she found her gold jewellery at the prison security deposit stolen. When she went home, she found her house in Hama demolished. The Mukhabarat claimed that her home was an Ikhwan hideout. Um Hassan left the suffering of prison life only to enter a new life of suffering as she tried to survive with her kids in a tiny mud house with two tiny rooms, no bigger than a prison cell. When it rained, the roof of the house became saturated and heavy and many times the roof caved in and they would suddenly find themselves drenched in an avalanche of mud.

Um Hassan's seven nieces and nephew's luck wasn't any better. They found no refuge, except with some runaway Syrian families in Amman who felt sorry for them and took them in. The youngest child, who was disabled, soon died because of the lack of care and medical attention. The families who cared for the rest of the children married off the two eldest girls before their twelfth birthdays.

## The Seyloon

The tragedies of Um Hassan's family didn't end there. After the political security division finished with their interrogation, they sent Um Hassan and her two daughters, along with their family friend Laila, to Tadmur Prison. By then, the family had confessed to aiding wanted men and providing them with a hideout. In Tadmur Prison, they watched guards round up groups of prisoners for execution every single day and wondered when their turn would come.

Salwa was pregnant and her due date crept closer and closer. Her cellmates had no way to help her during her terrible labour. They didn't even have anything for the newborn to wear. God sent some mercy to them in the form of Raghda. Raghda was a midwife from Hama who was thrown into their cell just days before Salwa's first pangs of labour. During her labour, Salwa moaned and groaned quietly through clenched teeth. The women did everything they could to keep her from screaming aloud. They worried about the guards hearing her. They worried about punishment.

Hours and hours later, the baby was born and the women could no longer keep the birth a secret. The newborn's cries rang out throughout the prison. Guards barged in to investigate. The women told them that Salwa had just given birth. One of the guards, with a touch of humanity left in him, handed the women an empty metal can and some matches. The women tore pieces of their clothing, lit the burner, heated water in the metal can and bathed the baby. Salwa told us that her cellmates later cut the umbilical cord with a slice of metal from the can the guard gave them.

One of the inmates with Salwa, Um Tony, was a Christian woman who the Mukhabarat had accused of selling fake passports to wanted criminals. After her imprisonment, she turned into an informer, like Fadya Lathkani had. She told on the guard who had helped the women with the empty metal can and matches. The warden, Faisal Ghanim, showed up to deal with the situation. He swore and cursed and threatened the women. He grabbed Aida, one of the inmates, dragged her into the hall, ripped off her headscarf, stomped on it like an animal, and spurted out a continuous flow of foul language.

When Faisal calmed down, he ordered the punishment of the entire cell. All of the women were to be transferred into the Seyloon. The Seyloon was a large and damp grave with no light and no air for breath. It was home to mounds of cockroaches and spiders and all sorts of other creepy insects. Baby Samya was only twenty days old. She was not spared from the suffering of the Seyloon. Samya developed chronic asthma that stuck with her into her adulthood.

I remember when the inmates from Tadmur Prison arrived at Katana, after two years in Tadmur and several weeks in a prison in Homs. The guards stopped them in front of our cell, searched them and confiscated their belongings. Little Samya took the opportunity to sneak away. She ran between the legs of the officers and into our cell. I ran to catch her, excited at the sight of a baby. I grabbed her and lifted her up into the air. My heart leapt into my throat. I felt that little Samya was going to fly out of my arms. She was that tiny, that light.

## Nerve Infection

Um Hassan and her daughters, along with Raghda and Mona joined us. Eleven women had been imprisoned in Tadmur Prison. Five of them were transferred to Katana. The remaining six, Aysha, Nadia, Aida, Salsabeela, Laila and Um Tony each suffered different fates. Aysha and Aida were transferred to Aleppo Prison where we met them near the end of our prison term. Salsabeela was transferred with Um Hassan's group to Homs Prison at first, but the Mukhabarat forgot her there, as we found out later. They didn't realize that she was missing until years later.

The Mukhabarat released Laila, Nadia and Um Tony from Tadmur Prison. They released Laila due to major interventions and connections. As for Nadia, she had become so sick and so close to death that they saw no point in keeping her any longer. Um Tony had done such a good job of informing in prison that they set her free and hired her as a professional informant.

Raghda and Mona were close friends, both from Hama. Raghda was a midwife and Mona was a graduate of the Islamic Jurisprudence College and a religion teacher. Mona and her husband had helped secure a hideout for wanted men. The Mukhabarat caught them after the Hama massacre. The men in the hideout and Mona's husband escaped and poor Mona was the only one they caught and imprisoned.

In the national security branch in Hama, they tortured her severely to get her to confess association with the Ikhwan and to tell them where her husband and the other men hid. They electrocuted Mona repeatedly, so many times that she ended up with a nerve infection in her legs. Mona couldn't sleep, except with a fan blowing air directly at her legs.

After her interrogation, they sent Mona to Tadmur Prison, along with Raghda, who they had arrested in the hospital where she worked as a midwife. Raghda never told us about her torture. We never learned of her story. She was quiet and mostly kept to herself. She complained only to God and trusted only him with all her worries and pains.

## The Forgotten Prisoner

Those were the five women who came from Tadmur to Katana Prison. During the end of our prison terms, we chanced to meet three of the other six Tadmur inmates: Aida, Aysha and Salasabeela. We never saw the final three, but we did hear their stories.

Aida was an engineer working in Aleppo. When she found out that her name had turned up on the government's list of wanted criminals, she tried to escape. She was an only child and her father feared for her and sent her to Damascus to live with some friends until things settled down. A while later, she felt it was safe to return to Aleppo. But the situation was far from safe. The Mukhabarat were after her again.

The Mukhabarat tracked Aida down, arrested her and charged her with the help of the informer, Samih Kiyalee. We heard that she was tortured severely in the secret police division, mostly by Omar Hameeda and Mostafa Al-Tajir. Aida never spoke much about her suffering. We happened to meet briefly in the military interrogation prison in Damascus, shortly before our release. That's also when I met Aysha. Aysha was a teacher who was arrested around the same time as Aida, but I never learned the details of her arrest and imprisonment.

Salsabeela was an elderly religion teacher from Hama, probably in her sixties. She was arrested because of her brother's links to the Ikhwan. They arrested her son along with her. He was only sixteen. I heard about Salsabeela's torture, but not from her. I only met her in the last few weeks of our imprisonment, during which she didn't talk much. They had forgotten her in Hama Prison after they transferred her from

Tadmur Prison. When they decided to release us, they read out her name along with ours and were confused when she didn't turn up.

"Do you know Salsabeela? Do you know where she ended up?" the leader of the division asked in his desperation to locate her.

"Yes. She was in Hama Prison and she's probably still there," one of the women answered.

They looked for her in Hama Prison and indeed found her there alone and forgotten in solitary confinement. After her release, Salsabeela went home, but only to find her house taken over by government officials. Until today, Salsabeela is not allowed to leave Syria, even though her husband and children live in Saudi Arabia. As for her brother, whom they arrested with her, she never heard of him again.


## On a Wooden Board

Nadia was one of the three women released straight from Tadmur Prison. She was an architect and one of Aida's close friends. Her husband hid wanted men in their home. The Mukhabarat found out about the hideout and ambushed the apartment. The idea of being captured by the notorious Mukhabarat terrified her. Nadia heard Mukhabarat officers force their way into her apartment. She ran to the balcony and looked around. There was no escape. She lifted her legs over the railings of her third floor apartment balcony and jumped.

Nadia survived the fall, but suffered countless broken bones all over her body. Passer-bys thought a car had struck her and called the police. The police arrived and asked what happened. Unable to think clearly, Nadia told them that Ikhwan members had come to her door and forced their way in and that she jumped off the balcony to save herself from them.

The police called for backup. A fire exchange took place between the Mukhabarat inside the apartment and the police outside the building. Each group thought that the other was Ikhwan. Eventually, they realized their mistake, but not before several policemen were shot and injured.

The Mukhabarat's wrath for Nadia ignited. They dragged her to prison and threw her into a cell with no treatment and no painkillers. Nadia lay on a wooden board. She couldn't move, due to a major break in her hip. Her crushed bones began to decay.

Nadia discovered that she was three months pregnant with her dead husband's baby, but soon she began to bleed profusely and miscarried. Nadia's condition worsened day by day and deteriorated so quickly that the authorities had no choice but to release her about seven or eight months after her detainment. They decided that she was more trouble than she was worth.

## Singing a Love Song

A month or so passed and the new prisoners began to blend in with the old ones and we all learned how to share the tiny space we had, but before we knew it, even more prisoners poured in from different places. Three of the new prisoners were: Sameera, Najwa, and Najah, who liked to be called Um Zohair. The Mukhabarat transferred Um Zohair from a political security prison in Hama. She had passed through the national security prison in Kafar Suseh as well. Najwa came from Al-Maslamiya Prison in Aleppo and also passed through Kafar Suseh Prison before she arrived here. Sameera was transferred directly from the national security prison in Hama.

The new stories of the three prisoners opened our eyes to the new chapters of oppression and monstrosity that governed our country and its people. The most minor of political cases in Syria received treatment almost as severe as the major criminal cases. Sameera, who was only in her twenties, had three children; the youngest was an eight month old.

186

Her husband was killed in the Hama massacre. Sameera never found out how, but the people who had given her the news of his death told her that they found her husband's corpse in *Sahat Al-Assey* in Hama, with his name burned into his body.

Sameera's husband was a construction worker. After the Hama massacre, someone informed the Mukhabarat of a hideout in Sameera's home. The Mukhabarat ambushed her house and indeed found a secret room that her husband had built, where members of the Ikhwan hid. Sameera knew nothing of the hideout. The Mukhabarat found the secret room empty, except for some books, but that didn't stop them from getting a head start on Sameera's torture.

The officers tied Sameera to her bed and blindfolded her. Some of the officers beat her, some yelled at her to name the men she hid in the secret room and one officer sang. He sang an old Arabic love song.

The Mukhabarat took Sameera to the national security division, where the torture and interrogation continued. They got nothing from her. She knew nothing. They had no reason to hold on to her, but they did hold on to her for years and didn't release her until the time I was released.

Um Zohair was an older lady in her fifties. She had gone to Amman with her husband to seek treatment for his heart condition. Her husband needed surgery that he couldn't get in Syria. The sixty five year old man was too weak to recover from the surgery and passed away in Amman. After the funeral, Um Zohair returned to Syria. The informants in Syria flared and became a lot more active after the Hama massacre. They spread rumours about Um Zohair. They said that she had brought back money with her for the Ikhwan and that on her way to Amman, she transported letters to criminals who had fled from Syria. The national security division in Hama ordered her arrest.

The allegations against Um Zohair were ludicrous and baseless, but the Mukhabarat harboured a grudge against her family and so her innocence made no difference. At the beginning of the Hama massacre, the Mukhabarat took revenge on every wanted man who fled from their capture by arresting their fathers and brothers. They hounded the rich and honoured families of the country. That's when the Mukhabarat arrested Um Zohair's three brothers, along with a whole group of innocent men. They whipped and cursed the men all the way to *Sook Attaweel*, a market place in the city. In the market place, they told the men to turn around and go back home. It's over, they told them. No explanations. The men turned and started to walk away. The officers pulled out their guns and shot several rounds of bullets until each of the men fell to the ground.

One of Um Zohair's brothers was hit only in his foot. He was one of the first to fall to the ground. One by one, the other men toppled on top of him as bullets pierced their bodies. When there were no more men standing, the officers left. Um Zohair's brother pulled himself out of the pile of dead bodies and crawled home. He stayed home long enough for his family to nurse his wounds and then fled the country, never to return again.

## Supplication as Sustenance

All prisoners suffer bitterly, but some suffering can be unbearably bitter, beyond help, beyond resolution, leaving a person with nowhere to turn, but God. Like the story of Hala, whom only God was able to save, and the story of Najwa, who suffered from severe psychological regression that she never really recovered from until the last days of her imprisonment.

Najwa was an honour student in her second year of medical school in Aleppo. She was engaged to a young man who the Mukhabarat began to pursue just like thousands of other men in Syria. When her fiancé disappeared, Najwa travelled to Jordan to search for him. Her father travelled with her, but only after much convincing and begging.

188

On their way back to Syria, the police arrested them both. They charged them with being messengers for the Ikhwan. Her mother ended up alone with no one to help her raise and support her three young children. She had to take them out of school and send the eldest, who was in grade six or seven, to work in a chocolate factory. In the midst of her suffering, the mother began to bleed severely. The doctors said they had to perform a hysterectomy.

Najwa, a sensitive soul, found out about her mother's condition and grew worried and upset for her mother and siblings. She also worried about her father who had disappeared into the prison system for years and her family couldn't find a clue about his whereabouts or condition. Najwa began to feel that all her family's tragedies were her fault. Her guilt spread like a disease and tormented her incessantly. Her transfers from one horrible prison to another and from one monstrous interrogator to the other, pushed her further into a downward spiral that soon took her sanity.

When the Mukhabarat transferred Najwa from Aleppo to Katana Prison, she had already entered the first stages of her mental illness. She always looked dazed and behaved strangely. After our transfer to Dooma Prison, her condition deteriorated. It became so bad that we all lived in constant anxiety for her.

Najwa's mattress was beside Majida's and Majida's mattress was beside mine. When Najwa felt her illness coming on, she'd warn us: "Oh girls. Oh Heba. Look. Don't leave anything in front of me. No needles. No scissors. No knives. No forks. No spoons. No piece of metal…"

Najwa's illness got worse and worse and soon she couldn't sleep at all. She walked back and forth across our cell, stepping between our mattresses. Soon the illness permeated into her religious beliefs. She began to exaggerate her *hijab*. She wanted to cover her body more and more. She asked me to lengthen the sleeves of all her clothes, although they were already longer than need be. Her mother brought her bars of soap. Najwa dug through the bars of soap with her fingers, dug and dug until her fingers poked through to the other side.

"Look," she'd say after she was done digging through the soap, "anything people do inspires God's word. Look, even this soap makes us proclaim that there is no God but Allah…"

At bed time, Najwa went to her mattress like the rest of us, but she stayed awake, with her eyes wide open. In the middle of the night, she got up, stumbled over Majida, came over to my mattress and poked my legs to wake me.

"Come. Stay up with me."

The sight of Najwa's face inches from mine in the middle of the night petrified me, but I felt sorry for her, so I often got up and stayed up the rest of the night with her. Sometimes, she asked me to sit with her in her mattress and she would sit so close to me and ask me to join her in supplication all night. Najwa spent days in this state, without food or drink.

"Don't you get hungry?" I asked her.

"Their sustenance is praising God and supplication," she said as if quoting from some place.

I sat next to her and chanted along prayers nervously. In the morning, she went around the cell and passed out all of her belongings to the other girls, leaving nothing for herself, but the clothes on her body. She gave most of her belongings to a non-political prisoner who had the same mental illness as her and who had escaped from a mental institute.

Sometimes Najwa seemed to improve, but then her illness would rebound. Her condition fluctuated, but mostly went downhill. Sometimes it got so bad that her behaviour became too strange and too painful to watch. And worse yet, it even seemed to be rubbing off on those closest to her, those who slept next to her, Majida and me. We'd find ourselves waking up in the middle of night, against our will, and breaking down in gushes of sobs. Majida began to have constant nightmares. I listened to her scream and cry out for help in her sleep.

Najwa's mother seemed to catch the mental illness as well. Even after Najwa and her father were released from prison, Najwa's mother still suffered from memory loss and loss of awareness of what she was doing. She wandered in the streets and visited people she knew and stayed at their houses for days without telling her family. They would search for her in hospitals and police stations.

When they finally decided to pardon the political prisoners, Najwa was among the last to be released. It was as if they wanted to suck the last bit of sanity out of her before letting her go. She was also the only one who was released in Damascus. They refused to take her to her city, as they did for every other prisoner.

Those were the prisoners who suffered along with me for years and years. There were others who joined us only briefly and then were quickly released. From among them were a group of women from a village near Hama, a mother, her three daughters in-law and their small children. One of the daughters' husband was wanted by the government. He decided that the best thing to do was get his whole family out of Syria, but the Mukhabarat arrested every last one of them at the border. The women and children spent a year cooped up with us in our cell. We were so crowded at that time that we sat on top of each other. The women and children were released one year later, but they never heard of the husband again.

Another prisoner who joined us for a short time and who was one of the very few non-political prisoners was, Georgina Rizk's sister. Georgina Rizk was Lebanon's beauty queen. Her sister was accused of murdering her own husband. The police seemed to fear that her husband's family (Al-Jindi family) would try to avenge his murder by attempting to kill her, so they beefed up the prison security and put her in our cell. She shared our cell for one year, after which she was pronounced innocent and released. Every time she left the prison for her trial, she borrowed black clothing from us and shrouded herself in them, covering even her hair. She wanted everyone to see that she was mourning her husband's death. She treated us well and we reciprocated this treatment. She seemed understanding and compassionate about our situation. After her release, we never heard from her again.

## The Management and Exploitation Committee

The lives of the non-political prisoners ran parallel to ours. They shared our cell, our condition, our suffering, but they had fewer restrictions and more releases. They viewed us with respect, because we were imprisoned for our opinions and principals and not because of any crime we committed. The guards hated us for that. The guards viewed us with the same hate and disgust as the government. They went out of their way to make our lives as difficult as possible. They ignored our requests and exploited us every opportunity they had.

Exploitation was all we found after meeting the prison management committee, which was in charge of all political prisoners, in charge of rehabilitating them so that they could once again become good citizens. When we issued a request in the year 1984 for permission to write our school exams, the committee took up the issue and promised us to seriously consider our request and to bring it up with higher management. They told us to start studying while we waited for the response. We studied and eagerly prepared for our exams. Soon the committee informed us that our request was denied. Abu Samir, the head of the committee, suggested that they provide us with work we could do from prison, for pay. We agreed.

Officers brought piles of beads and thread to our cell. We sat and pushed thread through the beads for hours. It was tedious work. Soon the guards came to collect. They gathered up our colourful creations and walked out without leaving a penny behind. We wondered what they planned to do with our creations. We refused to do anymore work for them.

## A Marriage Proposal

Time passed in Katana Prison and we were still prisoners behind the same bars, between the same walls and trapped within the same boring routine every single dreadful day. Visitations often brought bits of consolation, until one day a visitation brought new fear and terror to my life. During the end of 1985, my aunt from my mother's side visited me in Katana Prison for the first time after years of sending my greetings to her and pleading with her to visit me.

When I saw my aunt that day through the mesh of wire, I exploded with sobs. I felt as if I was seeing my mother in front of my eyes and for the first time, I felt the pain of losing her burn within me. An uneasy feeling overtook me as my aunt began to speak. I felt puzzled by the strange things she said. She spoke for hours and I quickly felt more and more uncomfortable.

My aunt explained that she had not visited me before because my brother had warned her not to. She decided to visit me now, because she had found a connection, someone who was working on getting me out and that the only condition for my release was that I leave the prison a married woman. I was shocked at the nature of the condition, considering my situation and the shape I was in. When I told my aunt that the condition did not make sense, she simply repeated the offer. I felt that marriage was completely out of the question for me and I couldn't make sense of the connection between marriage and release.

My aunt left me, but not before reminding me that she would be waiting anxiously for my reply. The next day held yet more surprises for me. My aunt's son requested to visit me. I went out to speak to him. He told me that he was serving his mandatory duty in the army and that he had managed to get transferred to Katana just for me, to be close to me.

He began to shamelessly flirt. I got up and shambled back to my cell in disappointment. Two or three days later, my cousin requested to meet with me again.

"If he comes again, don't even open the door for him because I don't want such a visit," I told the guard right in front of my cousin.

For some reason, at the end of the week, my cousin appeared again, this time with my aunt by his side and an engagement ring in his hand. I decided to switch my tone of voice and resort to blatant honesty.

"Who told you that I agreed to this proposal? I don't want to get married. I don't want to be released. What do you think of that?"

"Why not? Does my son not appeal to you?"

"No. You're son is wonderful, but I don't want to marry him."

"Fine. Don't agree to the engagement, but keep the ring."

She tossed the ring over to me and walked away. I called the guard to take the ring back to her, but she had already left. The next day, my cousin showed up, by himself this time. He begged me for a tiny note or anything he could take to my brother Safwan, who was still out of the country, so that he could get my brother's approval to the engagement. I immediately began to see the signs of a conspiracy clarifying - a conspiracy that I later became certain of. The Mukhabarat were behind the whole game, and my own aunt was involved. I discovered that my aunt and cousin had direct involvement with the Mukhabarat. The clever plot was a trap for my brother Safwan and I was the bait. I would be released in Turkey, and of course, Safwan would come to meet me and fall right into the hands of the Mukhabarat. One week later, they sent a third person to work on me.

It was the day before *Eid Al-Adha*. This time they sent Husni Ibraheem Basha, my brother Ghassan's brother in-law. It was his first visit. I was surprised to see him. I remembered hearing that he was an informant for the Mukhabarat. He recited the same offer to me.

"Listen. We're pulling some major strings for you here. If you

194

cooperate, you will be in Turkey on the fourth day of *Eid*."

"And why would they take me directly out of Syria? I don't want that. I want to stay in my country."

"That's the condition."

"What will I do in Turkey?"

"You can go to your brother."

With those words, my suspicions crystallized and I realized where this was all going. Soon Husni left and I was back in my cell behind locked doors. Sunset was approaching and my cellmates scurried around preparing for *iftar*. The cell door opened. A guard stepped in. It was one of the kinder guards. He looked around the cell. His gaze stopped on me. He turned to leave, but then lingered in the doorway. We realized that he had something to say, but was hesitating.

"What's going on buddy? Tell me. Is something up?" Hajja Madeeha asked.

The guard called her out into the hallway.

"Some men from the national security office came for Heba," he said anxiously, his voice teetering.

Hajja Madeeha turned to me.

"So, tell us brother, why are they here? Heba's faith is strong and she is not afraid."

Hajja Madeeha stepped back into the cell.

"Get up buddy. Get yourself ready. Come on girls, pack Heba's stuff. Pack her a toothbrush and a prayer rug."

"Why? What's going on?"

"It's okay. Don't worry. The police are here for you. We're used to this by now."

I felt my heart leap. All the horrible possibilities raced through my mind. I fumbled with the little bag that the girls packed for me, unable to hold it steadily. I followed the guard out of the cell. He broke down in tears. Fear clenched my body.

I ended up in the warden's office. A man in civilian clothing awaited me. It was General Omar, head of The Military Interrogation Prison.

"Are you Heba?"

"Yes."

"Please come with me."

"Is something going on?"

"No. Just a little trip."

"I know all about your little trips," I said and flung my palms at him, "five minutes that turn to five years!"

## Part Four:  August 1985 - October 1985

Military Interrogation Prison:  In the Depth of the Unknown

The Mukhabarat vehicle accelerated over the bumpy road. My legs jerked up and down involuntarily. I pressed my palms against my legs. I didn't want anyone to see how nervous I really was. The car sped. I felt like we were flying over the road. The driver swerved. My head flung and banged the top of the car.

Another Mukhabarat vehicle took us over. Cars and pedestrians dashed out of the way when they saw the flashing lights and heard the blaring sirens. Another Mukhabarat vehicle tailed us. The drivers pressed down on the accelerators and the engines roared. I looked out the window. I saw Jadeedah Artuze, a well-known site for military executions. *They must be taking me for execution.*

The Mukhabarat vehicles whizzed past the military site and continued on and on, until the sun set, the sky darkened and we arrived at a military interrogation unit in the town of Miza. Wide open gates greeted us and the three Mukhabarat vehicles sped right in. Once again, I felt severed from the outside world.

The vehicles screeched and stopped in front of the entrance of the building. An officer approached me, blindfolded me and handcuffed my arms behind my back. He led me into the building.

"Even for my first interrogation, they didn't blindfold me or handcuff me," I said.

"The rules are different here." The officer grabbed my shoulders and shoved me forward.

He pushed me up a long flight of stairs. Then he took me back down a flight of stairs and then back up. We continued climbing up and down stairs, until I lost all sense of direction. I felt exhausted and scared. I hadn't eaten a thing after breakfast. We stepped into a long hallway. The officer turned me to the wall and told me to wait. About five minutes later, the door in front of me opened.

"Tell her to come in."

I stepped into the room. *I wonder what kind of room I'm in.* An officer led me to a chair and sat me down. The blindfold slipped and I saw the shadow of a table in front of me and a man sitting behind it.

"What do you see in front of you?"

"Nothing."

The man speaking to me was Kamil Yusif, the head of the Military Interrogation Unit. He feared greatly for his own safety and took great measures to ensure it was never compromised. He was Christian and didn't have a big tribe backing him up like most of the Alawi division heads. No one ever saw Kamil Yusif's face.

"Where's the other one?" he asked the officer.

*I wonder who they're talking about.*

"He's downstairs in the solitary confinement cell number 24, sir."

A pang of terror shot through me. *They must have caught my brother. They must be interrogating him right now.*

"What is his condition?"

"He is sitting on the ground, his legs and arms handcuffed to the back and he is blindfolded, sir."

He was trying to intimidate me and it was working.

"Now, Miss Heba, look here. If you tell us the truth, there is hope that you will be released. If you lie, you will never be released."

"Good. That's better."

"And why is that?"

"Because I'm not going to have any information about anything you ask me. I've been in prison for the last five years and as you know, no news comes into prison and none gets out. We don't even watch television."

"Don't you interact with any of the other prisoners?"

"No."

"Why not? Are you any different from them?"

"No, but God gave each person their own nature and my nature is quiet. I don't like to talk."

"Not even to the non-political prisoners?"

"I don't talk to them at all."

"Why? Are they a different species?"

"No, but that's just my nature. I don't even like to talk to my friends who are in the cell with me."

"No, no. You will tell us exactly who is the keeper of your secrets."

"I don't have a keeper of secrets. I don't need one. What big secret do I have to keep anyways?"

"Yes you do have a secret. Don't think that I don't know anything about you prisoners. Granted, we placed you in a city prison, but I still know everything about you."

"Then who do you think is the keeper of my secrets, since you're so clever?"

"Majida."

When I heard her name, I remembered how my cousin used to get annoyed of Majida. When my cousin visited me in prison, Majida would stand by my side, encourage me to refuse him and sometimes even scold him herself and ask him to leave me alone and go away. He would get really agitated just at the sight of her. *He must have been the one who told them that Majida was the keeper of my secrets. He must have told them bad things about me too.*

"She is not the keeper of my secrets or anything. She just happens to sit beside me. I don't talk to her anymore than I talk to those who sit far from me, especially because she was my friend at university. Anyways, what is this big secret that you think I am keeping from you?"

"I don't know. You're the one who will tell me."

"I don't have any secrets. Why don't you just take me back to prison? I'd rather stay there all my life than listen to people speak lies about me."

"Okay. Then tell me who comes to visit you?"

"My aunt's daughter and maybe once a year my aunt and uncle come to visit me."

I knew they knew about my aunt's daughter. They knew she visited me and they knew that she went to medical school in Damascus.

"That's it? No one else?"

"No one else."

"What about Husni? Didn't he visit you?"

At that time, their entire plot had not completely clarified in my mind and I hadn't yet figured out each person's involvement and intention and so I didn't want to mention Husni's name, fearing that I might harm him and he had visited me only that one time.

"Oh, I forgot him. I guess because he only visited me that one time."

"Okay. I will give you a paper to write down all of your visitors, and without lying."

"God willing, I will not lie."

"Take her to the other room," he told the officer.

In the other room, the officer unlocked my handcuffs, handed me a paper and a pen, lifted my blindfold and left. I wrote down the same things I already told Kamil Yusuf. Ten minutes later, the officer returned, replaced my blindfold and handcuffs and took me back to Kamil Yusuf's office.

"You have nothing else to tell us?"

"No."

"Take her to a solitary confinement cell."

The officer grabbed me again and led me down some steps. We exited through a door on the ground floor, got into a car and drove in circles around the building. Then the officer took me back into the building and down a long flight of stairs into the basement.

# *Eid* in a Grave

The stairs were made of stones, stones so old and worn out by all of the feet that had trampled over them that they were full of cracks and holes. In the basement, they took me first to a room, where they confiscated my comb, the bit of money I had and my watch. I took one last glance at my watch before they snatched it away and saw that half the night had passed. They dropped my belongings into a large envelope and labelled it with my name and conviction: Heba Dabbagh, Ikhwan.

We entered another small room. The officer sat me down on a chair and walked out.

"Can I lift the blindfold now?"

"No."

"But I can barely breathe."

"What does a blindfold have to do with your breathing?"

"It does have to do with it. It's a psychological thing."

He left without answering me. Another officer came in. I asked him the same question. He told me I could loosen the blindfold a bit if I really did feel like it was constricting my breath, but I couldn't take it off.

It was the middle of the night and I was exhausted, but I couldn't sleep. The insomnia I felt when I was first imprisoned five years ago returned. I sat on the chair in the tiny room cloaked in fear and sorrow and wondered what lay ahead. I sensed the guards going back and forth in the hallways, celebrating *Eid*, just like the guards in Kafar Suseh Prison celebrated *Eid*, with loud laughter and dirty language. I felt like their voices slammed into my ears and vibrated in my head.

The same questions swirled in my mind again and again. *Why did they bring me here all by myself after all these years? Why are they asking me the same old questions? What will they do to me?*

In the morning, when a new day had begun, I asked to go to the washroom. The guards let me use their washroom. The door was cut several inches off the ground and they sat right in front of it. I felt uncomfortable. The discomfort turned to fear and I couldn't go. I opened the door.

"I don't need to go anymore."

The guards led me back to the same chair and I sat there until the early evening. I felt invisible to all the prison workers who passed by. They didn't speak a word to me or acknowledge my existence with even a morsel of food. In the early evening, an officer came and took me down the crooked hallways to the solitary confinement cell they had appointed for me. I saw a group of prisoners, miserably dressed, being examined by a doctor, who seemed a prisoner himself. He took blood from their arms. I wondered what was wrong with them. As we passed the prisoners, the guard shouted, "Faces to the wall." The prisoners' faces turned to the wall immediately, just as the guard cracked his whip in the air. Before I could grasp what was going on, I found myself in front of a solitary confinement cell. The officer pulled the heavy door open.

"Am I going to stay here?"

"Yes. This is the best solitary confinement cell we have. Top rank," he smirked. "You should thank God for it."

"What?"

"Yes. This cell is brand new. No one has been in it yet. So thank your lord and get yourself in."

He threw two blankets in, locked the heavy metal door and left. I looked into the meter-and-half by meter-and-half cell and felt myself pushed into the process of slow suffocation. The walls looked thick, and I could touch the ceiling with my hands. In the middle of the ceiling was a small vent for air, but it wasn't working and there was no other vent or window in the cell. Over the door was a thick peephole covered with two layers of wiring. Behind the peephole was a dim light that through all those layers seemed to light nothing but itself.

When the guard locked the door, I felt as if he had just buried me alive and left. I felt death at my door. My throat tightened. I couldn't breathe.

That was one of my lowest moments. I couldn't go on. I lost sense of what was happening. I forgot why I was there, why I was all alone in a dark grave. I felt tired, so very very tired. My body, my mind, my spirit, all tired. I let the fatigue take over and cloud everything and I felt my muscles become limp and I let all the thoughts and worries swirling in my head slip away until I no longer felt anything.

The next thing I knew, the cell door opened. I squinted at the darkness. Someone poked me with a stick.

"Get up. Get up."

*Is it the angel of death?*

I tried to remember what had happened. I realized that night must have passed and that it was morning and probably time to go out to the *khat*. I figured I must have fainted. I didn't know what I was feeling anymore. Did I feel angry? Sad? Scared? Or maybe I felt all of these. I lost sense of time and place. I no longer had my watch and I couldn't tell night from day. When the guard called me again, I pushed myself up, trembling. I felt confused. I followed the guard to the washroom. The washroom was huge and filthy.

I washed my face. The cool water brought some sense back to me. I shuffled back to my cell. A guard brought me food. I turned away. No appetite. He left and locked the door. I sat on the floor and felt the ground around me like a blind person. I heard a loud roar from behind the wall. The sound shook me to my core. I convulsed like a person possessed, until I realized that it was the sound of the vent starting up.

Five minutes later, the noise died down and the silence returned. Then it started up again, a rambunctious rumbling that sounded like a monster, a monster imprisoned like me, roaring and lamenting. The roaring and rumbling continued, on and off, on and off, blasting sounds into my ears every few minutes, puncturing them, until the blasts seemed to turn into a constant buzzing sound. In the darkness of the cell, my senses seemed to slip and I fell into a semi-conscious state. I awoke the next morning to the sound of the customary chanting of *Eid*.

## *Eid* Chanting from the Cell of Riyad Al-Turk

The sound of *Eid* chanting on the radio rung out from my neighbouring cell, where they kept the leader of the communist opposition, Riyad Al-Turk. The radio was one of the few exceptions they made for him during his ten year stay in solitary confinement. There were four solitary confinement cells in the hallway; each two faced each other. My cell was the first on the left. The cell across from me belonged to Riyad Al-Turk.

A few days later, guards brought a new prisoner to the cell on my left. I caught a glimpse of the young man only once while the door to my cell was open for airing. A guard stopped in front of his cell with dinner and the prisoner stuck his upper body out of the cell and took the food. The only thing I knew about him was that he often asked the guards to let him out for *wudu*.

Riyad Al-Turk enjoyed many privileges other prisoners in the Military Interrogation Unit never dreamed of. Every once in while, he received visitors. The guards even allowed him to cook his own meals. Sometimes, he cooked for the guards too and even washed the dishes. After being neighbours for a while, Riyad began to send me bits of his special dishes. I didn't eat any of them. I always returned his food with the guard who brought it. He also sent me tissues, tea and other such items. One time, while my cell door was open, I saw him. I think he requested from the guards to let him see me and they indulged him. He walked by my cell I caught a glimpse of him too, but he didn't stop to say anything.

It was the morning of *Eid* and I had awakened to the sound of the *Eid* chanting, which was usually the promise of new things and happy times, but for me the joyous chanting brought only dread. As hard as I tried to keep it together, I erupted into sobs. Everyone on the outside was alive and celebrating with the spirit of *Eid*, but not me; *Eid* brought me no joy, held no meaning. I couldn't even tell night from day.

The cell door opened. An officer stood in front of me, his stature short, his moustache long. The sight of him filled me with discomfort.

"What's your name?" he asked.

"Why?"

"I want to know, because there was another girl here who looked a lot like you. Maybe it was you. Have you been here before?"

"No."

My friend Ibtisam, who had come to Katana Prison a few months ago, had passed through this prison and I guessed he had mistaken me for her. I asked him the name of the girl he had seen here. It was Ibtisam.

"And what's your name?" he asked.

*He just wants to fool around.* I frowned.

"Why do you need to know my name? If you want to know it, go and look for it in your files."

He left for a while and then came back with Omar, the warden, by his side, and several other officers standing behind them. One of the officers held a bowl of burgul in his hands. The officer placed the bowl on the floor. Omar pushed it towards me with his foot.

"Stand up," Omar said.

"I can't."

"What's your name?"

"Didn't you get that last night?"

"Answer me, you rude bitch."

He continued to curse and yell and with every utterance from his mouth I grew angrier and angrier.

"Can I know why you put me here?" I hollered.

"Tomorrow you will find out for yourself."

"But I didn't do anything."

"If you really didn't do anything, then you will be released tomorrow," he spoke coldly.

"Please, just tell me what I am accused of and how long I have to stay here."

*I'm going to go crazy. I cannot stay here for another minute.*

"Don't you know yourself? Don't you know that you are a criminal?"

His words felt like the lid of a pressure cooker, leaving no escape for the fury bubbling in my heart. I bit down on my lips to keep myself from exploding into a fit that I knew would bring no good. He slammed the door shut and continued his rounds of *Eid* greetings. I felt a nervous breakdown coming on. I looked around for comfort, for anything to help me hold on to my sanity. I sobbed. My body trembled. I sobbed and sobbed and trembled, all alone in a dark grave and I called out in complete surrender to my only hope – God.

A moment later, my cell door opened. A guard stood at the door.

"Don't be scared my sister. You can consider me your brother. Tell me, how often would you like me to open your door and check on you?"

I squinted at the guard. I couldn't believe what I was hearing.

"If it was my choice, I'd want the door open all the time. Otherwise, I can't breathe and the vent in here is useless. It just hums in my ears all day but brings no air."

"Okay, anything for you. I'll keep your door open all night, but if anyone asks you, don't tell them who opened it."

"Here take this." He handed me a lira. "If you ever need anything during my shift just knock once and I'll be right here."

And so this guard, whom I will call "S," walked away and left the cell door open, a window, it felt like, between God's mercy and me. S checked up on me during all of his shifts. He always left my door open and asked me if I needed anything. When they came around with cups of milk for him and all the other guards, he saved his cup for me. He left it at my door. I never asked anything of any other guard again. I waited for his shifts, knocked once like he told me to and asked him for food if I was hungry or to go to the washroom when I needed it. When I grew to really trust him and knew that he was a moral person, I asked him for a comb and a nail clipper.

"You don't have a comb?"

"They took it from me."

"Write a letter to the warden."

I sent the petition to the warden and they brought me a comb, but it was so filthy that it seemed as if it had been used by a hundred prisoners before me. I tried everything to clean it, but too much dirt and filth clung to its teeth that nothing could get it clean. I sent another petition, but this time it was refused.

Ten days at the Military Interrogation Unit passed and I still had not had a chance to shower or comb my hair, which sat day and night under my scarf. I feared lice. I worked up the courage to ask S if I could take a shower and if he could bring me a comb and a nail clipper. He apologized and told me that what I had requested was forbidden here. But later on he brought me a small men's comb from Riyad Al-Turk and a nail clipper too, all under his own personal responsibility. He also brought me a bar of soap and plastic slippers.

Two nights later, S knocked on my door and asked me to follow him to the washroom. The washroom was in the middle of a long silent hallway lined with cells. I felt terrified. At the door of the washroom, stood another officer, Yaseen. S ordered Yaseen to shut the door behind me, sit in front of it and not let anyone in until I was done. I stepped past the metal door and found a series of sinks and toilets. Beside them stood three showers covered with doors several inches short of the floor.

I stepped into the shower, but I had a feeling that Yaseen was going to follow me in and so I did not take off any of my clothes. I heard steps. I looked under the door and saw Yaseen's shoes. I opened the door and ran out into the hallway.

"Where to? Where are you going?"

"I want to talk to the warden right now! What were you doing in there you disgusting…"

Yaseen ran after me and called out my name.

"Come back here. You're breaking prison rules."

I ran back to my cell.

"Bring me the warden so that I don't have to break prison rules," I shouted even louder.

S heard my shouts, rushed over and asked what happened. I told him everything.

"Instead of guarding her, like I told you to, this is what you do, you idiot!" he shouted furiously at Yaseen.

"You can blame me this time my sister, but do go back and shower," S said apologetically.

I followed him back to the washroom, stepped inside and locked the door. I stood in the shower for a long time, unable to take my clothes off, before I felt sure that it was safe. I turned the water on and showered. When I got out, I found Yaseen sitting in his chair as if nothing had happened. He gawked at me.

"Don't you want to take a look at that beautiful face in the mirror? I have one if you want…"

"May God punish you," I muttered.

I scuffed back to my cell. There was nowhere else to go, nowhere but that tiny grave, where all I could do was sit and count the days of my life slip away. *Why am I here? When will I get out?*

A couple of weeks into my imprisonment at the Military Interrogation Unit, the heat in the basement rose and the smell of rot mixed with sweat suffocated us. The warden showed up. He called me out, blindfolded me, handcuffed my arms behind my back and led me through a series of stuffy, maze-like hallways. I couldn't breathe. I asked him to please move the blindfold, just so I could breathe for a second.

"Even if you really are dying, I will not take the blindfold off. Those are the rules."

I gasped for air. I began to feel faint. The officer presented me to Kamal Yusuf in blindfolds and handcuffs.

"Do you have anything to tell us?" Kamal asked.

"No." I raised my brows. "Why would I?"

He didn't bother to answer my question.

"Take her back."

They took me back to solitary confinement. I spent twenty days in that cell, without sun or moon. The only sense of day or night I got was from the guards' shift changes and from the London broadcast that I overheard every afternoon from, Riyad Al-Turk's cell.

## Ups and Downs

God's mercy overpowers all else. Only a few days later, God sent me another touch of his mercy, a kind soldier performing his mandatory military duty. He treated me well, just like S had. He brought me things I needed and let me out to the washroom more often so that I could wash and drink whenever I wanted. When I told him that the vent in my cell wasn't working, he fiddled with it for hours until it rumbled back on. When I went to the washroom, he would call on another guard to mop my cell, tidy it up, air out the blanket and do everything he could to make it better for me.

But this one soldier was the exception. Rudeness, immorality and indecency were the rule at the Military Interrogation Unit. The other officers consistently carried sticks or whips or some other torture tool. Omar, the warden, always carried handcuffs and blindfolds. But thankfully, I never heard sounds of torture, because I think the interrogation room was far away from my cell.

209

One day, one of the officers brought me the last couple of bites of his falafel sandwich.

"Aren't you hungry?" he asked.

"No, but before you ask me anything else, I want to ask you how much longer I have to sit here?"

"I don't know. I swear. That's not my job."

"Fine. I'll put my trust in God."

The officer stepped close to me and crouched down. He wore a thin white *jilabiya*, so sheer I could see his body.

"Would you want to get out of here, if someone could get you out?"

"No."

"Strange. I haven't met anyone else who enjoyed sitting in solitary confinement."

"I thank God for whatever he gives me."

"I swear, I am shocked. Why did they bring you here after five years in prison? Do you know why?"

"No. I don't know why. It's God's will."

"Okay. Well, if they release you right now, and I swear you're like a sister to me, and I'm just a soldier who lives all alone and you know what the life of a soldier is like... I have a two-bedroom apartment in Muhajireen. I would give you one room and sleep in the other."

"And why would you do that?" I snapped. I wanted to shut him up and end his transparent game.

"The word is, you have no one out there."

"Who told you that?"

"Your family died in Hama."

"Just because I no longer have my family, it doesn't mean I no longer have God. I'll always have God."

The officer frowned and got up.

"So you don't want out?"

"No."

He left my cell, slammed the door shut and tinkered with the electrical switches that controlled the light bulb in my cell. My cell went dark. Something told me that he had messed with the light switches so that he could come back into my cell unseen. I had just received dinner a short while ago in a heavy plastic bowl. I dumped the food out and held the bowl up in the dark.

"Who's there?" I called out.

No answer. I heard my cell door slowly creek open and I sensed someone creep into my cell. I shoved the plate into his face as hard as I could.

"I swear to God if you don't get out of here, I'm going to scream so loud for all the guards to come."

"Why? I just want to come in and fix your light."

"And how do you know that my light burned? You're the one who fooled around with it until it burned out, you idiot."

I called out to S. I yelled and screamed and hit the door with my plastic plate. A few guards ran to my cell and asked what was going on.

"This despicable man fooled around with the electrical switches until he burned the light bulb in my cell and then he claimed he wanted to come into my cell in the dark to see what happened."

They grabbed his arms, forced him out of the cell and cursed at him all the way down the hall. They replaced my light bulb with the light bulb from the cell next to mine and left my poor neighbour in darkness.

## Failed Connections

On that same day, they had collected the blankets from all of the cells for sterilization. I didn't know where they took them to be sterilized, but they piled them back up in the hallway a short while later and began to redistribute them back among the prisoners.

"I'm going to let you out now to pick whatever blanket you want," one of the guards on duty told me.

I chose a blanket and turned back to my cell. The guard followed me.

"I want to tell you something. God willing, you will be released soon, because they don't bring anyone here unless they're about to be released. And I heard that you had some connections that have succeeded in obtaining an order for your release."

"God willing…"

"But, don't tell anyone. If they find out that I told you, they will ruin me."

"I won't tell. May God reward you."

In the morning, the kind guard's shift was over and another guard took over. He was short and had a long moustache and deep-set eyes that I had grown accustomed to seeing, but something about the look on his face that day sent shivers of repulsion through my body.

"Why are you crying?"

"What?" I startled. "I'm not crying. Why did you open the door suddenly without giving me any warning?"

"I was just passing by and I wanted to see if anyone had bothered you."

"No. I'm fine, thank you. Please just shut the door. I don't want to see anybody."

"I swear, I just wanted to check up on you," he said and took slow steps towards me. "I'm worried about you. My heart aches for you…"

I was huddled in the corner of the cell. I jumped up, shoved the guard and tried to pull the door shut. He grabbed my hand. I pushed him again with all my strength. He stumbled back. I grabbed the door, pulled it hard and screamed.

"If you don't leave, I'm going to scream so loud that every

worker in here is going to come running."

The guard with the deep-set eyes left. Before I could catch my breath, he returned.

"Come on. Get ready. This is your last day here. They're releasing you today," he said.

I didn't know whether to believe him or not, but I gathered what few belongings I had. My only clothes were the ones I was wearing. I stepped out of the cell, turned and saw the guard standing beside my door. He pinned me against the wall and tried to wrap his arms around my neck. I felt fear and rage. I shoved the guard away, ran down the hallway and shouted and cursed at him.

"I just wanted to have a cup of tea with you," he said and ran after me. "It's still hot if you want…"

At the end of the hallway, the guard with the deep-set eyes caught up with me, pushed me through the door and left. On the other side of the door was another guard, one of lower rank. His name was Jalal. Jalal asked me to sit down.

"You have a connection from the Military Interrogation Unit that has ordered your release, but the national security division, who arrested you in the first place, refuted that decision." Jalal paused for a second. "So you're going back to Katana Prison."

Before I could say a word, another officer grabbed my arm and led me into a room, the same room in the basement where they held me when I first arrived. I sat there through the afternoon and well into the night. At about ten or eleven that night, officers led me out into a car, handed me back my belongings and drove me back to Katana Prison.

Later, I realized that they really were about to release me, as a part of their grand plans to use me as bait for my brother, but for some reason they sensed that their plans were going to fail and sent me back to Katana Prison.

# Malicious Rumours

I returned to Katana Prison the same way I left, in a Mukhabarat vehicle that sped so fast that it seemed to jump along the road in the middle of the night, practically running over anything in its way. When we got to Katana Prison and officers handed me over to the guards, my old friends sensed my arrival and fell into hysterics: shouting and calling out for me and pressing their bodies against the windows, like birds in a cage, fluttering on top of each other. They didn't calm down until the guard threatened to take me to another cell. They stepped away from the window, but I could still see the love and longing in their eyes. I walked through a fence towards the cellblock. Some of my former cellmates called out to me from another cell.

"Come here. Come to us."

The women pleaded with the guard to open up for them and let them greet me. He gave in to their pleas and opened up the doors to both cells. He let us all meet together and we had a beautiful gathering that I will never forget. I still remember how Mo'kal and Samya, the young children who shared our cell, grabbed their diapers and pulled them over their heads, mimicking the women who wrapped scarves around their heads. They all ran to me and hugged and kissed me.

The only damper on that bright gathering was when my cellmates told me about the rumours that Amira Zarkali, one of our cellmates, and Um Jameel, the female guard, had circulated about me after I left. Um Jameel constantly cooked up new ways to make us suffer. The two of them claimed that I had managed to make contact with the Ikhwan on the outside and that I received letters and money from them. This sent my cellmates into a fit of panic as they worried what would become of me after such accusations. They never dreamt I'd come back to them alive and safe, but it was God's will that I return.

# The Blue Cow

Back at Katana, the suffering decreased compared to solitary confinement in the Military Interrogation Unit, but it certainly didn't end. The only thing that brought any novelty to our lives was saying good-bye to a group of cellmates being released. The group included Um Mo'kal, Um Haitham, Um Abd Al-Basit, and her daughter, Aida. A few months after, Um Khalid and Um Zohair gained their freedom as well. They were all released in the same manner. Officers read their names out in the morning and gave them a bit of time to gather their belongings. Then they took them to a military interrogation unit from where they would be released.

It was a very emotional time for me when I watched Mo'kal and his mother walk out of our cell, Mo'kal, who was born and grew up in prison until the age of five. I remember the first time he stepped off prison grounds, when my brother Ghassan, during one of his visits, took him for an outing with the permission of the warden. When he came back, Mo'kal was all worked up and he went on and on to his mother about his day in the world of a free person.

"Mama. Mama. I saw someone walking on four legs!"

We asked my brother what Mo'kal meant. My brother laughed and told us that Mo'kal had seen a donkey. Ghasan also told us that while Mo'kal was walking, he had stepped on a rock and the rock had rolled under his foot and Mo'kal had exploded into sobs. And when Mo'kal heard the warden start his motorcycle, he grabbed Ghassan's leg and held on to it with such fright.

When Mo'kal turned three, they sent him to his grandparents' house in the country, so that he could meet his siblings and begin to get used to life outside of prison. But his grandmother and siblings couldn't handle what they saw of him. Mo'kal would gather stones and throw them at his siblings, sometimes cutting them badly, but Mo'kal never meant to hurt anyone. He simply didn't understand that stones could

215

hurt people.

When we asked Mo'kal what he saw at his grandmother's house, Mo'kal said, "I saw a blue cow pee milk." After prodding him for a while, we realized that he had seen a man milking a cow and that he called the cow blue because he barely knew a thing about colours.

Mo'kal's release was emotional, but so was his coming back for a visit a few months later with his mother. The girls all gathered around him and waited to hear his famous phrase, "Damn Asad," but he didn't say it. His mother was anxious to show us how freedom had changed Mo'kal.

"Tell them what you learned in school, *habeebi*..." Mo'kal's mother told him, so Mo'kal would tell us about all the new things he'd learned. And so this child who spent the first five years of his life behind bars began to sing songs of praise about the revolution and its leader, President Hafiz Al-Asad.

His mother said that when she told Mo'kal they were going to come visit us at Katana Prison, he burst into tears. When she asked him why, he said, because when he got there Abu Mostafa would make him go back in the cell and lock the door. Mo'kal refused to step into our cell. Even after assurances from his mother and Abu Mostafa himself, Mo'kal still took stiff baby steps towards us, his face tight with tension. After tasting the pleasures of freedom and returning to see us still locked up behind bars, Mo'kal gazed at us with pity and sadness in his eyes. During the entire visit, Mo'kal repeatedly glanced at the cell door, terrified that it would close on him once again.

## Part Five: November 1985 - October 1989

Dooma Prison:  The Battle against Time

Several more weeks passed by in Katana Prison and my cellmates and
I did everything we could to pass the dreary days, to push along every
dreadful minute. The more time that passed, the more hopeless we felt
and the more certain we grew that this journey of ours was without an
end. We saw no light that could end the darkness that encompassed our
lives.

News filtered into our cell about the possibility of our transfer
to another prison. The prison workers hinted that we should reduce the
amount of stuff we kept and prepare for the possibility of moving soon,
but we had long ago erased the words "release" and "freedom" or even
"transfer" from our vocabularies. We continued to live in our tiny cell,
which seemed to be getting tighter and tighter.

One cold November morning, the warden and a group of officers
barged into our cell and told us to get ready for transfer on the following
day. The first question that sprung to our minds was, "where to?"

"To Dooma Prison," they said.

"Why?"

The guards explained that the prison here was overcrowded
and that the government just finished building this new prison in Adra.
They transferred Dooma's prisoners to the new prison in Adra, so that
we could be transferred to Dooma Prison. They also told us that Katana
Prison would be transformed into a detention centre. But other rumours
floated around, rumours that I didn't pay attention to until after our
release, rumours that placed me as the cause of the transfer. The rumour
had it that my brothers intended to rescue me, but that Ghassan's wife
had ratted them out and so the Mukhabarat decided to transfer us all.

The rumour didn't surprise me. Many things led me to be certain
that my brother's wife indeed was an informant, just as other relatives
of mine and many men and women of my country had all turned into

217

informants in greed for the benefits such positions held. Sometimes, the only benefit informants found was a subdued fear of the Mukhabarat and a tragic safety in feeling that they were on the same side as the force bringing so much fear and torment to so many.

The transfer date was set and we scurried around gathering what little belongings we had accumulated over the years. The next morning, guards positioned themselves on the roof of the prison, all over the prison grounds and at every door and entrance. A big truck drove up to the prison. Officers packed our belongings and our gallons of gasoline that we had purchased for the heater in the washroom. The truck brimmed with bags and jars. They handcuffed us and led us onto a bus, two by two. Armed officers sat at the front and back doors of the bus. We were on our way to our new home, twenty of us bound for Dooma Prison. The driver took the road out of the city. One police car sped ahead of us and two more trailed behind for security.

Dark clouds covered the sky and blocked the sun, turning the daylight into depressing darkness and adding more grimness to the day. By the time we arrived, we were exhausted and starved. We found our belongings dumped carelessly in a hallway in the prison. Many of our things were missing or broken. Our gallons of gasoline, which were most dear to us, for we had fought long and hard for permission to purchase them, were missing. We questioned the officers; they pretended to know nothing. Some of them made promises to help us recover our missing belongings, but they recovered nothing.

Guards guided us to our new home. They allotted two cells for us political prisoner. The arguments ignited instantly over who got which cell and over who got which spot in each cell, but the fighting was in vain for the prison administration had already allotted our spots long before we arrived.

# Our New Abode

Dooma Prison looked most like the old Arab style homes with stone walls. In the middle of the structure was a water fountain surrounded by plants. A large, open space spread between the fountain and the cells that outlined the building. There was a kitchen, a washroom, a medical supplies room and a room we called, *Nadwat Al-Sijin*, where we could buy necessities. There were three solitary confinement cells and six joint cells. The first joint cell on the right held the prostitutes, the second held murder convicts. The first cell on the left was for drug users and traffickers and the second for thieves. In between them was a room formerly for literacy training, but that program was scrapped and so it became a general room.

The two rooms in the middle of the prison were allocated for the political prisoners. The one on the left was long and narrow and held my allotted spot. Large shelves bordered the right and left sides of the room, with mattresses piled high on top of them. Below the shelves were small storage closets for the inmates' belongings.


# Spy of All Times

A surprise awaited us in Dooma Prison. During our last few days in Katana Prison, Officer Mufiq Al-Samman was transferred. Someone set him up to look like he was working with the Ikhwan. But our comfort at seeing a familiar face in Dooma Prison didn't last long. The warden, who was not higher up than Mufiq Al-Samman, but who was a Durzi from the Sabi family, was ready to give us a taste of his poison. Less than a week after our arrival at Dooma Prison, he issued strict orders that took away many of the crucial rights we used to have.

Warden Sabi approached us during one of our "breathing times" outdoors and told us to bring out our gas burners because those were now prohibited. We had no choice but to obey, so we went back to our cells and brought out our burners, but then we decided to protest and we refused to go back to our cells. The warden negotiated with us and in the end allowed us to take our burners back to our cells.

A few days later, Warden Sabi barged into our cell for a surprise inspection. His men confiscated our gas burners and our metal and glass utensils and equipment. They locked our doors indefinitely and said they would teach us a lesson never to refuse to return to our cells or protest again. There was nothing we could do but write to the head of the prison, Mufiq Al-Samman. We sent the letter through one of the guards, relaying all that had occurred. Mufiq Al-Samman intervened and we got all of our belongings back, but the warden refused to give up his efforts to make our lives miserable. He planted a spy amongst us, Amira Zarkali, who broke every vow of silence to us and who cunningly dragged out all of the information the warden requested.

Warden Sabi came up with yet a new order, even more harsh than the previous ones. He forbade all visits for political prisoners still awaiting the rulings of their military court trials: this included most of my cellmates. Many of them had completed their trials but still did not know their rulings. The court officers told them that the rulings were classified.

The spirit of resistance stirred anew and those prisoners affected by the new order decided to go on a hunger strike until the decision was reversed. There were twenty of them, each of whom was registered under the Ikhwan. We found out that the communist prisoners were exempt from the new order even if they hadn't received rulings yet. The rest of us who had already received our rulings did not participate in the hunger strike for fear that they would take away our right to visitations. We couldn't risk our only connection to our families and the outside world. Nonetheless, the warden issued an order forbidding us from coming close to the mesh wiring that stood between us and our visitors. They didn't want word of the new inhumane rules in Dooma Prison to slip out.

The hunger strike lasted about twenty two days. By the end of it, the strikers were dying. We carried them to the washroom, changed their clothing and cleaned their spaces. They were completely unable to move. We grew exhausted of caring for the strikers. We may as well have been on the hunger strike ourselves, especially since we ate as little as possible out of respect for their feelings. Some of the strikers began to have high blood pressure. Others suffered convulsions. The warden sent them to the prison doctor who looked after the guards and administrators. We carried the women to him one by one, wrapped in blankets, like corpses.

## Poison and Blood

After nearly a month under Warden Sabi's ruthless orders, someone higher up issued an order for his transfer. We didn't know who or why. What we did know was that the order did not bring us any relief, nor did it end our troubles with wardens. In Sabi's place, they appointed Imad, an Ismaili officer from Al-Silmiya. Imad was no less hateful than Sabi. When Imad got into the mood for evil, his face looked venomous. But we didn't give Imad much leeway. We simply refused to sit down and take any more oppression. We decided to face up to him. With an air of carelessness and overblown pride, he tried to subject us to the oppressive ways he was used to treating political prisoners.

Imad walked into our cell one morning, stood in front of one of my cellmates, his chosen victim for the day, and ordered her around and beat her into obedience. My cellmate swung her arm back and slapped him hard across his face. Imad stepped back, shocked and deflated. He shrouded his shock with boisterous threats of punishment. We all began to shout back at him that he had no right or authority to punish us and we accused him of being the man behind our forbidden visitations.

Imad knew he was losing control. He recognized the danger of the situation. Some of the inmates on the hunger strike truly were but breaths from death. Imad backed off. He also promised to write to management concerning the need for rulings in our cases and to ask about some of the rights that had been taken away from us.

Our families proved to be quicker than Imad in reaching management. They succeeded at reinstating our most cherished right: visitations. The strikers ended the hunger strike. Some of the other pressures and restrictions eased a little as well, but not completely. Imad did what he could to disturb visitation times. He didn't allow our family members to come in until two or three in the afternoon. Majida's mother told us about the many, many times she stood in front of the prison doors and kissed the ground and offered to kiss Officer Imad's feet. She begged and begged for him to let her in to see her daughter and give her some things, but Imad refused. When she gave up hope of seeing her daughter, she scribbled a few words onto a paper, hoping to comfort her daughter with them until she was allowed to visit. She begged Imad to take the paper to Majida. Imad took the paper, held it out in front of Majida's mother's face, ripped it to pieces, threw it on the floor and stomped on it.

## From Politics to Economy

One of the first new inmates to join us in Dooma Prison was a Palestinian in her thirties named Jameela Al-Batsh. She was studying in Syria, when the police arrested her, along with a group of communists. Among the charges against them were the bombings of a tourist hotel in Aleppo and an embassy in Damascus. Jameela was convicted in 1979 and sentenced by the National Security Court to life imprisonment. After seven years in Aleppo's Al-Maslamiya Prison, they transferred her to Dooma Prison around the time of our arrival there in 1986 and released her only two years after our release. Even though she spent two years with us, she quietly kept to herself and didn't mix with others, not even with the other communist inmates.

A few weeks later, a French literature student from Damascus named Hilal, arrived. Hilal was accused of hurting the economy. Her father was a big currency exchange businessman in Damascus. The government pursued him after they instilled major restrictions on currency exchange. Hilal's father fled Syria.

Soon after, Hilal's father sent her seven and a half million liras from Jordan and asked his daughter to give them to another currency exchanger within Syria. When Hilal arrived at the exchanger's house, she found Mukhabarat officers everywhere. They were there to arrest members of the Ikhwan for distributing banned publications. The Mukhabarat mistook her for one of the Ikhwan and arrested her along with them. When they searched her car and found millions of liras, they forgot all about the Ikhwan and the publications and took off with her, the car and the money. The Mukhabarat didn't return the money until after her release three years later.

## A Hostage for Cowards

Days passed and soon we had a new guest, Azeeza Jallood. She was the wife of a military officer, Ibraheem Al-Yusuf. Azeeza was the first person arrested after the Madfaiya incident, where a group of armed oppositionists infiltrated an army base and killed a large group of Alawi soldiers. The Mukhabarat tortured her severely. Then, they released her and used her as bait to capture her husband. They didn't succeed, so back to prison she went. A short while later, they found her pregnant. The Mukhabarat were infuriated. They accused her of knowing where her husband was and meeting him behind their backs. Omar Hameeda beat her on her belly and hollered out to the foetus like a possessed man,

"Down. Come down and swear to God that you are with the Ba'ath."

God protected Azeeza's baby. The Mukhabarat released her after imprisoning her in a military camp and torturing her there as well. After her release, she gave birth to her baby, Ismael, before the Mukhabarat arrested her one last time, along with little Ismael, who was no more than a month or two old. They left her and Ismael alone in a solitary confinement cell in Al-Maslamiya Prison for four years.

Azeeza lived through a nightmare unlike any other. One time during her imprisonment, some of the male inmates decided to hold a mutiny. They created a stronghold in one of the joint cells in protest against the torture, terrorizing, and inhumane treatment. They burned their mattresses and refused to obey orders from the Mukhabarat to evacuate the cell.

The prison officials thought that armed members of the Ikhwan had seeped into the prison as participants in the mutiny and didn't dare come close to the cell. They pulled Azeeza out of her solitary confinement cell and used her as a hostage. They threatened to kill Azeeza if the men didn't surrender. Azeeza lived in this state of terror for two days, until the Mukhabarat called in a sniper, who shot the male prisoners dead one by one, right in front of Azeeza's eyes, until there were no men left standing in the cell.

When they transferred Azeeza to Damascus, her family was finally able to take baby Ismael to live with his siblings. Azeeza's children all stayed with her parents since her husband's entire family was in prison. Azeeza stayed in the military interrogation prison for eight months before they transferred her to Dooma Prison where we met her and shared a cell with her until our release. Even though they read Azeeza's name among those who were pardoned, they took her back to Al-Maslamiya Prison and imprisoned her for another two years in solitary confinement and under harsh conditions. They refused Azeeza any visitation rights. Azeeza suffered a nervous breakdown. Sometime later, they allowed Azeeza's son to visit her, but continued the prohibition for all other family members.

Azeeza lived in constant fear for her children, especially after hearing threats from officer Hasan Khaleel, the head of the committee, who met us before our release. Khaleel said to her, his words full of hate, "The families of the people your husband killed have not forgotten about their revenge. There is a fire in the hearts, a fire that still burns strong, and they are ready any minute to take action on that fire, to take their revenge. You shouldn't live close to your children. You should stay far, far away from them so that you do not feed them your malice and criminality."

That was why Azeeza worried constantly about her children. She worried about where to hide them from the Alawis. God protected Azeeza's children. Ismael came to visit us in Dooma Prison with his grandfather when he was about seven or eight years old. Ismael was very intelligent. When he came into our cell, we offered him some breakfast. I wanted to put some money in his pocket for *Eid*, but he looked at me with teary eyes and said, "We on the outside can get money, but you guys in here can't get anything." He swore he would not take a penny from me.

## In Bed with the Communists

There were twenty-four inmates in my cell on the day that fourteen new prisoners, all communists, arrived. The warden ordered us to take them in, and each Ikhwan prisoner was to split her mattress with one of the new communist prisoners. The newcomers were arrested as a group when the Mukhabarat uncovered their involvement in organized armed opposition against the government.

The new inmates told us that they were coming from a military interrogation unit where they were severely tortured, men and women alike. They told us about their many friends who were now half paralyzed because of the torture. The Mukhabarat sat some of the prisoners on a torture chair. Then they turned on the power and the chair slowly folded in on itself. The person sitting in the chair bent with the pressure, chest against thighs, until the spinal cord snapped.

We felt for our new inmates and did our best to make them feel welcomed despite their different political outlooks. But soon it became harder and harder to keep up the niceties as the number of communists in our cell grew to nearly thirty. Most of them felt no need to keep up a pretence of cooperation and mutual respect. They labelled us the enemy and frowned at us with scorn and contempt. Making the situation worse, many of the new inmates did not concern themselves with cleanliness, whether it was bodily cleanliness or the cleanliness of where they sat and slept.

When my friends and I awoke for nightly prayers, we needed to fold our mattress and the mattress of whoever lay beside us in order for us to have space for at least two of us to pray at a time. With a communist inmate sharing each of our mattresses, our nightly prayers became a difficult feat.

Soon, we ran out of patience with our new inmates. Many of them allowed themselves to get so filthy that a nauseating stench wafted from their bodies whenever one of them moved or turned over. We agreed to divide the cell in half and gathered ourselves on one side. They happily agreed to the deal, but every night, fights broke out between them over mattresses and spaces. Majida and I always waited until all the fighting ended and everyone settled down. Only then did we lay our mattress down in whatever spot remained. Sometimes the fights between them got so bad that one would turn over the others' mattress or kick away her belongings. All the shouting and banging eventually brought officers into our cell, but even then, the fights didn't end.

# The Cell

The communists enjoyed the new arrangement of the divided cell and began to hold meetings they called the "cell". They kept us up many nights with endless chatter on the virtues of Marx and Lennon. One night, I was sick with typhoid fever. The communist inmates were in the middle of one of their "cell" meetings. I moaned and moaned in pain. The communists grew restless of my disruptions. One of them, a doctor named Tamadur Abdullah, suggested they give me painkillers. They went to the prison nurse, came back with a needle and Tamadur injected me with the medicine. Within seconds, my jaw went numb and I couldn't move the lower part of my face or utter a word. Minutes later, I lost consciousness. My friends panicked and began to swear and curse at Tamadur.

"Why didn't you tell us that you wanted to kill her just for the sake of your damn meeting?" Hajja Madeeha yelled.

As the days passed, the tension between the communists and us grew. The tight space and the misery of the situation only added to the tension. Many of our discussions with them led to fights, often ending with them shouting threats, "One day soon, when we take over the government, we will hang all of you in Marja Square in the middle of Damascus."

# The Daily Pilgrimage

Execution would have been a blessing compared to the tedious prison life, devoid of purpose or hope. The constantly increasing number of communists, the cramped cell and the exceeding strictness of the prison management sucked us of all patience. Chaos took over. Arguments and fights became the norm. Many times, the water cut off and each of us waited up to a month for a turn to shower.

Visitation times became erratic. Often the management refused visitations for everybody or delayed the admittance of visitors until nearly the end of visitation time. The guards searched the food the visitors brought for us, turning it over in their hands and poking their fingers into it, until we were too disgusted to want it anymore.

We grew so upset and distressed with the situation that we created a means to vent, a sort of pretend pilgrimage to take our minds off our troubles. There was a fountain in the middle of the field where they took us for "breathing time". We decided this fountain would be our *Ka'bah*. Every morning during "breathing time," we circled our *Ka'bah* and recited the special prayers of pilgrimage. One time, an officer found us in the middle of our ritual.

"What is going on?" he asked, his eyebrows raised in confusion.

We were all very involved in our circling and prayers and barely noticed him.

"We are performing pilgrimage," one of the women answered.

"Dear God! You're all going to end up in the Ibn Seena Mental Hospital."

## Reemi

My memories of Dooma Prison, like my memories of the other prisons, are etched in my heart. Reemi is one of those unforgettable milestones of my time in Dooma. Reemi is a calm tiny kitten. He was a gift from a family member of one of the non-political prisoners. My friends and I bought Reemi from her and raised him.

Reemi was wonderfully clean and intelligent. If we needed something from one of the other cells, we tied a little paper around his neck and sent him to fetch it for us. He would go to the next cell and come back with what we wanted. During visitations, he'd help us take the things our family brought us from the visitation room to the cell, carrying them in his mouth. He slept at our feet every night like a trustworthy guard.

One time the head of the Damascus police force arrived to search our cell. He caught sight of Reemi. He burst into a fit shouting that animals were forbidden in this place. He called one of the officers and told him to put Reemi in a bag and throw him out somewhere outside of Damascus. The officer obeyed. He took Reemi from us and we fell into depression over missing him. We felt we'd lost a family member.

Three days later, in the early dawn, we saw Reemi trying to sneak back into our cell, his fur filthy and in a miserable state. When we saw him, joy filled our hearts and we ran to him, like a mother would run to her missing child. After our release, one of my former cellmates returned to Dooma Prison just to pick up Reemi and take him to her home in Aleppo.

## Part Six:  December 1989

Release


Four more years passed, four more years slashed from our lives, four more meaningless, purposeless years. Winter arrived once again in Dooma Prison, but the seasons, like the years, slipped away with little regard. During these stagnant times, a series of events began to unravel and cut through the silence.

One cold October day in 1989, the guards called out to Azeeza and Ghazwa to gather their belongings and prepare to leave, with no mention of where or why. The guards refused to answer our questions. We thought maybe they were reinvestigating Azeeza and Ghazwa's cases or taking them to court and that they would return to us within days. But a whole week passed without news of them. A guard came in once again and called out for Um Hassan and her two daughters Salwa and Yusra. Um Hassan and her daughters left with the Mukhabarat officers. Days and weeks passed and we didn't hear a thing about them either.


## A Dream and Glad Tidings


During those years, I continuously dreamt of my mother. Every night, I saw her pregnant and in labour, but unable to deliver. One night, I saw her in labour, but this time, she was able to deliver. I told Hajja Madeeha about my dream.

"It's a sign that you will be released soon," she declared.

As Hajja Madeeha said this, the warden walked into our cell that early morning and read out twelve names: Madija, Um Yasir, Lama, Raghda, Montaha, Hala, Najwa, Madeeha, Riyad and Heba. He followed the list of names with one word: "release".

They had promised us pardon and release many times, but never kept their word. The news didn't move us. Majida and I were sitting in a corner reciting from the Quran when the officer shouted at us to get up and get a move on. We sat still.

"Stop lying to us. We don't need more lies," we told him.

The guard swore to us that he was telling the truth today and showed us the list of names printed on an official document. Even as he insisted, we couldn't bring ourselves to believe him. We stayed sitting in our corner.

"Fine, I will bring in the Mukhabarat task force that came to take you so you will believe me."

The guard did indeed bring in the task force and only then did we believe him and burst into a noisy fuss of tears, laughter and kisses. We gathered our belongings. Majida and I dumped our things into one big bag without thinking and dragged it behind us, spilling out some of our things onto the ground, but we didn't care a bit. We felt overwhelmed, unable to absorb the events unfolding around us, still in a state of disbelief. The whole prison seemed in an uproar at the news of our release. The non-political prisoners congratulated us on our way out and called out to each other, "The political prisoners are being released. The political prisoners are being released."

Some of the kinder guards and officers approached us and asked whether the news was true. They congratulated us warmly with tears running down their cheeks. I don't even remember how we eventually got to the vehicles outside or what the vehicles looked like or the exact chain of events, but I will never forget how our beloved kitten Reemi followed us out with tears streaming down his furry cheeks. We rode in the vehicles until we found ourselves at the doorsteps of the Military Interrogation Unit and everything felt like a strange dream.

# We are Here

From the doorsteps of the interrogation unit to the reception room, officers guided us, still handcuffed. We had to check in our belongings and fill out the necessary paperwork. Then they took us down those ugly stairs that we knew well enough from our previous visit and into the basement where they put us in a joint cell, in the north side of the Military Interrogation Unit. As we walked down the hallways, we heard the voices of our former cellmates who left before us. They banged on their cell doors and called out, "We are here. We are here." The officers yelled at us to shut up. We didn't care. We shouted out greetings and congratulations to each other. Eventually, we found ourselves in a small cell, all fourteen of us, with no space for breath. We knocked on the door and complained.

"This cell that you claim doesn't fit all of you fit ninety two men before you," said the guard.

We stared at the guard in shock. How could this cell possibly fit ninety two people? As we looked up at the high ceiling, we noticed carvings of mosques with signatures below them, a trademark of the Ikhwan prisoners. We couldn't fathom how the prisoners could have reached such a high ceiling, but we began to understand as we thought about what it would be like to have ninety two men stuffed into this cell.

"Now we get it buddy," said Hajja Madeeha to the guard. "You stuffed ninety two men in here by piling them one on top of the other until they reached the ceiling."

# Only Kidding

One night passed, then two, then three and four and we all huddled against the cell door ready for that second when the door would open for good, continuously telling ourselves that it must be any minute now. As the days passed, we began to question and wonder whether our hopes were but a mirage, as all our hopes before had been. We teetered between holding firm to our dreams of freedom and completely suppressing them, until the joy and excitement withered away, our expectations died and we fell back into tedious prison routine. Being directly under Mukhabarat watch and feeling the terror of their presence made our situation even more miserable.

Our days in the Military Interrogation Unit, as we found out later, were a period of chastisement. Officers spoke to us harshly and enforced rules so strict that they outdid even the days of Kafar Suseh Prison. The guards brought food that was barely enough for half of us. They kept our cell door locked at all times. "Breathing time" happened only according to the mood of the guard on duty, and he decided for how long, ten or fifteen minutes if we were lucky. We spent "breathing time" in a small indoor field surrounded by high walls. But the hunger, anxiety and closed doors didn't do to us what the cries for help and screaming of prisoners in the torture chamber did.

When the guards felt like taking the men out for "breathing time," they took them out running into the field barefoot, regardless of the extreme cold. They ran around chased by sticks and cables like a herd of sheep. Their faces looked so pale, so yellow that they seemed luminous from afar.

I remember one time when one of the male prisoners from a neighbouring cell took a few seconds too long in the shower. The guard on duty dragged him out of the shower and beat him continuously with whips and cables. Then the guard began to order him around.

"Pick up the slipper with your mouth," he hollered.

The poor prisoner had no choice but to bite down on the slipper and pick it up.

"Crawl with it in your mouth all the way to the toilets."

The toilets in the Military Interrogation Unit were in a state so appalling that one could not bring themselves to look at them or go anywhere near them. The man crawled behind the guard all the way to the toilets, which consisted of holes in the ground overflowing with filth. The guard stomped on the prisoner's head and submerged it into the hole. The guard ordered the man to pick up the slipper with his mouth again, told him to crawl in a different direction and whipped him with every step. The prisoner screamed and screamed and begged and begged for the guard to stop. We couldn't bear it.

"Are you human? Is there no mercy in your heart?" Hajja Madeeha shouted.

Then all of us began to call out.

"Please if you won't have mercy on him, then at least have mercy on us and torture him somewhere else," we pleaded.

"What? What's the matter?" asked the guard, with a silly smile on his face. "We're just kidding around."

One time, the guards walked by our cell while passing out food. At the Military Interrogation Unit, the peepholes were at the bottom of the door. One guard placed a plate of food in front of our door and another guard opened the peephole for us to reach out and take the plate. That day, Azeeza pleaded with us to ask the guard if he knew anything about her husband's family, if they were in the Military Interrogation Unit as well. It was my turn to bring in the plate that day. I poked my head out of the peephole and looked up at the guard.

"Have you heard of the Yusuf family?"

"Yes, they brought all of them to the south wing..." the guard whispered.

Before he could finish his sentence, the officer behind him grabbed him, pushed him down and beat him right in front of our door. The guard begged and screamed for the officer to stop.

"It's not my fault," he screamed. "She spoke to me... I didn't talk to her... I didn't talk to her..."

"It really isn't his fault," Hajja Madeeha shouted, hoping to distract the officer from the beating if only for a second. "This low life here asked him about the food, just about the food."

But the officer didn't turn to her or pause for a second. He continued beating and whipping the guard until he had his fill.


## The Leader had no Idea

More days passed. We began to sense serious hints of release coming soon. They brought us out to the offices in the basement and asked us to fill out forms detailing everything about our lives. They took pictures of us in many different positions, holding a board with numbers on it. Fifteen days later, they officially informed us of our release.

"Buddy, why did you remember us now, after all these years? What's the occasion?" Hajja Madeeha asked.

"Well, it seems the leader didn't know about you ladies."

"Oh, so now he knows that we exist?"

"Yes."

"Nine years of our lives passed and your leader didn't know about us?"

"Yes, I swear. If only he had known about you before, he would have let you out long ago. As soon as he found out, he ordered us to let you out."

"Why are we still here then?"

He told Hajja Madeeha that Syria was now mourning, in solidarity with Lebanon, the assassination of Lebanon's president, Rene Muawad. They had been ordered to lower the flags and close all official government departments. And so they made us wait another two or three weeks, during which time we met twice with a newly formed committee, put together especially for us. The committee's job was to inform us of our release and bid us farewell with no hard feelings. The committee was headed by Officer Hasan Al-Khaleel, along with Kamal

Yusuf, the head of the unit, and other officers. When it was my turn to meet with the committee, I met with Kamal Yusuf in a blindfold, as did the others.

"Don't think that the fact that we are releasing you means you can feel free to do as you please. I have Mukhabarat watching you from within your own family."

"I never did anything wrong to begin with," I said.

He instantly began to curse and swear at me and call me a criminal, too stubborn to confess. He also informed me of my duty to report any wanted criminals who contacted me, or who I might come across. Kamal Yusuf emphasized this to Azeeza even more stringently and threatened her children's safety again. When Kamal Yusuf met with Amal he said, "Why do you want to leave so soon? You just got here yesterday."

The purpose of the committee was to emphasize to us that we did not deserve our freedom and to remind us that we were still convicted criminals and our release was solely due to the kindness of the president and his generous pardon.


## Rehab and Repair

Among the façade of kindnesses that the Mukhabarat poured upon us before our release was a program of rehab and repair carried out by the same officers whose job it was to torture. The program was put together for Samia, Salwa's daughter, who was born in Tadmur Prison and raised in the prisons of Homs, Katana and Dooma. She had ended up in the Military Interrogation Unit at an age when she should have entered school, although she looked barely a year or two old. Samia was a shock for anyone who set sight on her, due to her frailty and pale skin.

The Mukhabarat wanted to do everything they could to hide any evidence of their abuse and criminal behaviour. They didn't want to let

Samia out into the world, where all comers and goers could see her in a state that screamed of their crimes. And so they began this rehab and repair program. They took Samia and her mother out to a field outside the basement and let her acquaint herself with the real world. They fed her extra and handed her sweets and even brought her some toys to recapture what bit of her lost childhood they could salvage.

One day, Kamal Yusuf, the head of the unit was coming back to his office. His car stopped near the field. His driver came out, opened the door for him, carried his briefcase and followed him to his office. Kamal Yusuf glimpsed Samia on his way. He called out to her, took her into his office and played and chatted with her. When she came back, she told her mom, "Mama, when I grow up, I want to be a colonel."

"Why?" her mother asked.

"So I can have a car and a driver who will drive me around and carry my bag and walk me to my office, an office just like Colonel Kamal's."

"How will it be like his office?"

"It will have a rug on the floor and nice lights and pretty things we don't have in here."

Samia, copying the inmates around her, engraved her name into the walls and it broke my heart when I read what she wrote below her name. Samia wrote: I was born in Tamdur Prison and I lived in Katana Prison and Dooma Prison and... Samia listed all the prisons she had lived in and all the dates.


## The Drunken Colonel

The powerful head of the Military Interrogation Unit, Kamal Yusuf, turned into a silly fool when night fell and the time for his drink arrived. In his half conscious drunken state, he often called on poor Ghazwa, brought her into his office and chatted with her, his speech a slur of meaningless mumbles. Other times, he'd come down to the basement, stand in front of the cell door and speak to her through the peephole. Most of the time, Ghazwa didn't know what to say and sat in terrified silence.

One night, it was past 1:00 am and we were asleep in our cell, when we suddenly felt the peephole fly open and we saw someone pop their head into our cell. Usually the guards knew to knock first, so that we could wear our *hijabs*, but this unknown visitor opened the peephole without warning and stared at us with red bloodshot eyes.

"May God punish you," we shouted out in shock and anger.

Some of the women spit in his face. A flurry of yelling filled the room.

"Shut the peephole and get out of here... Who let you in? You sick... disgusting... inconsiderate..."

The man quickly pulled his head back out, shocked at our reaction. A few seconds later, he poked his head back in as if he suddenly remembered that he was the head of the unit and shouted back at us, "Who is the disrespectful one who dared raise her voice?"

Due to his thick accent, made thicker by his drunken state, we didn't recognize the colonel. We got up and pulled the peephole shut in his face.

In the morning, Hajja Madeeha called out to the guard on duty. "Buddy, we have a request for the head of the unit."

"What's the occasion?" asked the guard.

"There was a disgusting officer who opened our peephole in the middle of the night and poked his head in."

"At what hour?"

Hajja Madeeha answered him.

"Let me tell you something for your own good. Don't talk about what happened, because the officer you are talking about is the head of the unit himself."

Hajja Madeeha swung her hand to her chest in shock and said,

"May God punish him."

We found out during "breathing time" from the women in the other cell that after the colonel came to us, he had gone to their cell and tried to talk to Ghazwa. The poor girl just sat there paralyzed with fear, at a loss of how to get rid of him.

## Ebb and Flow

Time passed and it felt as if we were slowly spinning on skewers until December approached. Officers came one morning and read all our names out and told us to get ready. We scurried around with bursts of joy. But the morning arrived and nothing happened. We knocked on the door.

"What happened?" we asked.

"There has been a delay," they said. No explanation.

The next morning, officers came to our cell and called for Um Hassan and her daughters Salwa and Yusra, and little Samia got up with them. They had brought them to our cell the day we arrived, due to overcrowding in their cell. The officers didn't mention release; they simply asked the inmates to follow them. We thought they might be taking them back to the cell they were in before, but later we asked about them and the guards told us they were released. Horrified, we thought that they had received the pardon and release, and we had just missed the train. Hope died again. We plummeted back into a state of pessimism. Azeeza broke down into sobs.

"My heart tells me I will not be released with you," Azeeza whimpered. "You'll see."

Two days later, they called upon Ghazwa, from our neighbouring cell, and released her. We remained in our cell wrestling with the scenarios that flashed through our minds and with our emotions that drifted back and forth, like the ebb and flow of the ocean, until the morning of December the 24th. Officers opened our cell door that morning and told us that the hour of release had truly arrived.

An officer called out all of our names, except for Azeeza's. Her fears proved true. She remained in prison for two more years. The rest of us followed the officers out of the cell towards the reception room where we were supposed to fill out forms. I wondered if they were really going to let us go today. I looked at my cellmates and knew they were wondering the same thing. We barely took a few steps out of the cell, when an officer marched towards us from other end of the hallway.

"There's been another delay," he said. "Take them back to their cell."

At night, the officers returned and took us again to the reception room. We stood in a long line, our hearts full of hope. One of my cellmates leaned over and whispered to the woman in front of her.

"You know, it feels like we're lining up for food rations."

One of the officers overheard her comment.

"Sir," the officer said to Officer Omar, "did you hear what she said?"

"What did she say?"

"Sir, these people don't repent. They're still talking politics."

The officer relayed her comment, in his own words, and Officer Omar walked up to the poor woman and as if suddenly bit by a snake exploded into a storm of curses. Foam formed at the corners of his mouth.

"I swear to God, you people should not be released. You should be buried here until you die," he hollered at her face.

After Officer Omar completed the dictionary of swear words, which he knew by heart, and after we received our confiscated belongings and filled out the forms that needed filling and signed the papers that needed signing, they told us that the matter had been delayed once again until morning due to fog. They took us back to our cell. We huddled behind the door, eyes wide open, tense and alert and unable to

240

relax for a second, let alone fall asleep.

As the night passed, we slipped back into despair. We remembered how they had promised release to the men in Kafar Suseh Prison and how they had transferred them to Tadmur Prison instead. The women and I surrendered half the night to these bitter feelings and the other half of the night to glimmers of hope and sweet thoughts of the possibilities freedom would bring.

As badly as I wanted freedom, I could not imagine what I would do with myself should freedom come. It was as if my mind could no longer comprehend the meaning of freedom and what to do with it. Some of the women talked about how they were going to return to their studies, or their jobs. Others swore they'd never work for the government again and would spend the rest of their lives in the arms of their loved ones.

I couldn't think like my cellmates. I couldn't allow myself those longings. I dared not even imagine such things, although all that stood between me and freedom now was the rising of the dawn.

## Until the Rising of the Dawn

Wednesday, December 25 is a night we will not forget. We will never forget how the men in a neighbouring cell stayed up all night with us, praying, reciting Quran and begging God to let things work out smoothly. We communicated through subtle signs and we felt how they worried about us and feared for us more than they feared for themselves. Despite the clear danger, they continued reciting and praying for us aloud, showering warm light on us in the darkness of the prison. God saved them from the guards that night, and they continued their prayers unhindered until the rising of the dawn.

When dawn approached, we felt exhausted, sleep deprived and starved. But the anticipation for freedom overpowered all other sensations. We knocked on the door over and over again and asked the guards what was going on and when they would finally open this door for good? We asked and asked until one of the guards lost patience.

"Stop knocking! When we want to release you, we will open the damn door and tell you to go."

When they finally did open the door, we were like a towering wave behind a cracking dam. We toppled over each other, racing to get out as if afraid that the door would close on us once again. As we gathered in the hallway, with our eyes locked on the door that led out of the basement to the main hall, they read out our names.

Officers took Hajja Riyad and Hajja Madeeha along with Najwa and Salsabeela to another cell. We didn't know why. They told them that their turn hadn't come yet. The women sank to the ground as if they wanted to die. Hajja Riyad screamed and banged her head against the wall. She thought she'd surely be the first to be released.

The fourteen of us who remained standing in the hall, seven from Aleppo and seven from Hama, followed the guards up to the main hall of the prison. We saw the sun rising through the windows. We walked out of the darkness of the basement and into the light in our torn clothing and with our pale faces, like corpses rising from the grave to walk amongst the living once again. We stood under the warmth of the sun and broke down into heaving sobs. Colonel Kamal Yusuf stared at us strangely.

"What's the matter? Why did you stop walking?" he asked.

"This is the first time in nine years that we see the sunrise," Um Zohair answered. "What do you expect?"

He quickly left and returned with handcuffs and our hearts sank at the sight of them.

"Why the handcuffs?" we asked.

"Those are the rules. You have to be in handcuffs until you pass the suburbs of Damascus."

Our hearts sank after such a high and we started to fear once again that they would only transfer us to another prison. But things began to happen quickly. They read our names again and verified our identities. Then, they handcuffed us and led us onto a bus. Three Mukhabarat officers joined us on the bus, two at the front and one at the back door. The bus began to move.

"Are we really going home?" Majida asked the officer next to her. "Or are we just being transferred?"

"You're being released."

"Tell me, will the men ever be released? And please tell me the truth."

"I don't know. I swear."

Majida continued to prod him until he told her, "Yes, there is hope for the men, but not any time soon. We let you out first so we won't have to worry about you anymore."


## New Year Greetings

The bus moved down the road and we wanted it to fly faster than the clouds and bring us to our homes. But at the same time, our homes and the outside world had become the unknown, and we were scared. We wondered how we'd part from each other and awake tomorrow far from the only faces we've known for nine years, faces that have been with us through the good times and the bad. We wondered where we'd go. We wondered who we'd meet.

I wondered about those who had passed away and those who had been killed. I wondered about my city, Hama, which had been destroyed. I wondered about my neighbourhood that had been flattened. I wondered about the loved ones, now buried under the ground, the loved ones who were the joy of life itself. These questions stormed in my mind until we arrived in Hama.

The bus stopped and the officers removed our handcuffs and told

243

those of us from Hama to get ready to get off. The bus would leave again soon to take the others to Aleppo. We kissed and hugged the ones going to Aleppo and promised to keep in touch and to visit and call regularly.

The bus had stopped in front of the Hama Military Interrogation Unit. An officer from our bus stepped out and walked into the unit to speak to the officers inside, then came back out for us. Three officers from our bus congratulated us on our release.

"Thank God we are done with you and your nagging." They smiled.


## Happy New Year

We watched the bus drive away in the direction of Aleppo. Officers from the Hama Military Interrogation Unit greeted us casually. We heard officers wish each other a happy new year and realized the new year had arrived. We didn't realize that meant we had to wait longer until the head of the unit was done with his new year's greetings. We sat in a cold waiting room, huddled and unable to do anything but stare at each other as we waited and waited for hours and hours.

Finally, an officer came in. He asked each of us to give him the phone number of the family member who would pick her up. Our families had received news of our release a few days before and had gone to Dooma Prison. The warden told them we were transferred to Adra Prison. They had gone to Adra Prison, but found no news of us there and were back to knowing nothing. When they got the call from the Hama Military Interrogation Unit, they weren't sure what to believe.

Soon, the fathers and brothers of my cellmates began to arrive, but nobody came for me. When the officer asked me for a phone number, I didn't know what to say. I couldn't think of any names or numbers of anyone alive.

An officer called Majida's father and told him as he told the rest,

"Come pick up your daughter." Majida's father thought it was a prank and hung up on them. The officer had to go to Majida's father's house and bring him to the unit and all the while Majida's father was still thinking it was all a sick joke. When he saw his daughter with his own eyes, he lost his breath. He held Majida, looked at me and cried.

"And what about you?" he asked. "Who will come for you?"

When the officer returned to ask me again who I wanted to leave with, after many of the women had already left, I told him I'd go with Majida's father. One of the brothers of another cellmate offered to take me home, but I told him I'd like to go with Majida. He later looked through the phone book and found my uncle, from my father's side's, phone number and called him for me. My uncle and his wife were in Homs and the children were alone in the house with their aunt, their mother's sister. She didn't know what to do with the news. She called my uncle, from my mother's side, and told him that I had been released and that he needed to pick me up, but his wife had answered the phone and didn't believe the news.

"Stop lying to us and if you call again I will hang up in your face," my uncle's wife yelled.

My friend's brother then tried calling my uncle's wife himself. "Heba is at her friend Majida's house and you should go pick her up," he told her.

He also got the number of the place where my father's brother was staying in Homs and called him. His wife answered and asked who it was.

"A good doer," he told her.

This scared her and she hung up, but later she decided to call Majida's family just in case. They confirmed the news. She wanted to talk to me before she would really believe it. Majida's mother called me to speak to her on the phone. I found myself unable to carry on a phone conversation, as if I'd forgotten how. As soon as my uncle's wife heard my voice, she sped to Majida's house. She rushed throught the front door and held me and kissed me. I stood frozen, not knowing how to feel, unable to distinguish joy from sorrow. I didn't know what to do next.

The whole neighbourhood seemed to have gathered. Men, women and children welcomed and congratulated us, but a troubled look shadowed their faces as they gawked at Majida and me, all the while thanking God repeatedly for our safe return. My uncle's wife tugged at my hand and led me to the door. Majida's mother followed behind us, teary eyed. She had wanted me to spend the night. I wanted to stay as well, for Majida's mother reminded me of my own mom.

Majida's mother told me how she had seen me in her dream the day before. In her dream, I sent her a post card with a picture of the Aqsa mosque and below it a verse from the holy Quran, "Glorified is He who carried His servant by night from the Inviolable Place of Worship to the Far Distant Mosque." Majida's mother had taken her dream to be a sign of good to come. She had gone to a sheik at the mosque who interpreted her dream and told her that soon we would be released. The next day, we were on our way home.

## Shadows of Tragedy

Toward the end of 1989, at nearly three in the morning, I rode in my uncle's wife's car. I curled up in the back seat, mindful of the chilling cold and the unknown future that lay ahead. As we drove across Hama, I gazed out the window at the unfamiliar scenes we passed. The seven-year-long destruction of the city cast a dark shadow. The empty streets reflected empty hearts. The hum of the windmills' spinning arms had been silenced.

Below the windmills, the Assey River had run dry and the trees and fields around its banks had withered and died. Everything I knew of the city was gone; the unfamiliar scenes seemed lifeless and alien. But one thing remained unchanged. Mukhabarat vehicles still lurked at every street corner, their headlights peeking out of narrow roads, observing, watching, maybe even over the dreams of those sound asleep.

As we drove through the rubble of what remained of Hama, I flashbacked back to New Year's Eve, in 1980, in my apartment in Barmaka, Damascus. Exactly nine years ago, Mukhabarat vehicles screeched onto my street in the middle of the night and the Mukhabarat leader asked for five minutes of my time but took nine years of my life. To this day, I do not understand why.

# Translator's Note

My journey on the translation of this book began in a little bookstore in Toronto. I was looking for books to help improve my Arabic when a completely different type of book caught my attention. I read the title of an Arabic book called, *Just Five Minutes: Nine Years in the Prisons of Syria* and being Syrian, I knew I had to read it. This book would reveal the details of the horrors that took place in Syria twenty years ago, the horrors that most Syrians have learned not to speak of. I spent most of the night and the entire next day reading the book. Usually my reading in Arabic fell into a painfully slow pace and I would abandon books half way through, but this time I couldn't stop reading until I finished the book.

Heba's story shook my soul. I felt an urge to tell her story to the world. I knew translating the book to English would make it accessible to a wider audience. It would also help to build an awareness of the oppression and disregard for human rights in Syria. But I saw more in Heba's story than the pertinent political issues it revolved around. What captured my attention was the story of a young woman who wanted nothing more than to do well in school and please her family until one night she became a hostage in the hands of monsters.

I was thrilled when I found out that Heba shared my desire to make her book available in English and I took on the translation project with enthusiasm. For the next few years, I struggled to find time for my beloved project in the midst of other responsibilities. I am deeply grateful to my family and friends who supported me in so many ways through the completion of this project.

Although Heba and I spoke on the phone regularly during my work on the book, I met her in person only once. During our meeting, I was touched by Heba's gentle nature, her soft and friendly words and the way her eyes lit up when she told me stories about her children. Heba proudly introduced me to her youngest son Warif. "I named him after my brother," she told me. I sensed Heba's need to create ways to remember all that she had lost.

Heba worked as a teacher for some time, but these days she spends most of her time helping her children with their homework and tending to her cherished houseplants and the wide variety of fruit trees in her garden.

Although Heba suffered and lost more than I ever thought one person could bear, she rose up from that darkness and created a new family full of light, love and happiness. The same strength that pulled her through nine years in the prisons of Syria feeds her courage today to love, trust and live again.

The Arabic text of *Just Five Minutes* includes a forward by Zainab Al-Ghazalee, a distinguished Egyptian woman who suffered for her political views for many years in the prisons of the former President Jamal Abd Al-Nasir. Zainab Al-Ghazalee lived a nightmare parallel to Heba Dabbagh's and survived it by grasping tight to her faith and trust in God. In Zainab's forward, she mentions, according to Islamic traditions, that God has forbidden oppression for Himself and has also forbidden it amongst his creation. Zainab writes, "What can be more terrible and more bitter than oppression, especially when the oppressor is a fellow human being?" Zainab's words resonated with me because I wondered about this very question many times as I read the book. I wondered how one human being could treat so brutally another human being, made of the same flesh, blood and emotions.

I find inspiration in the lives of women like Zainab Al-Ghazalee and Heba Dabbagh, who suffered with dignity, strength and courage and who were not afraid to speak out against oppression even as they watched the masses opt for the safety of silence. I am thrilled to do my part in bringing Heba's story to a new audience.

Bayan Khatib

# Glossary of Arabic Terms

Alawi (Alawite)- A religious sect in Syria who makes up a minority of the Syrian population, but holds complete power over the country.

Athan- The call to prayer recited by the muathin.

Baath- A secular Arab nationalist party founded in 1945. The Baath party gained power in Syria in 1963 and still holds a monopoly of political power.

Duha- The time between sunrise and noon when Muslims can pray the voluntary Duha prayer.

Eid Al-Kabeer- Also known as Eid Al-Adha, Eid Al-Kabeer is a four day Muslim celebration at the end of the annual pilgrimage to Mecca.

Fajr- The time of day right before the break of dawn when Muslims pray fajr prayer, the first of the five obligatory daily prayers.

Habeebi- A term of endearment which means my love.

Hajj- The pilgrimage to Mecca and a duty upon every able Muslim to perform at least once in a lifetime.

Hajja- A title of respect used for older ladies.

Hama massacre- The Hama massacre occurred when the Syrian government attacked the city of Hama in 1982, killing thousands of people and destroying the city. The Syrian government makes no official claim about the number of people killed but Amnesty International estimates the death toll to be between 10,000 - 25,000 people.

Hijab- A religious covering for Muslim women for the purpose of modesty.

Islam- A monotheistic religion based upon the Quran. Islam is the second largest religion in the world. Muslims believe that God sent the Quran through the Prophet Muhammad as guidance for humanity. Islam's central premise is faith in only one God and that Muhammad is the final messenger of God. Like Judaism and Christianity, Islam is an Abrahamic religion.

Ikhwan- Also known as the Muslim Brotherhood, the Ikhwan created a resistance movement against the Syrian government and became a banned organization in Syria.

Jihad- The struggle in the way of God.

Jilabiya- A traditional Arab dress.

Ka'bah- The large cube shaped structure in Mecca, Saudi Arabia. It functions as the qibla, the direction Muslims face to pray. During hajj, the annual pilgrimage, Muslims circle the Ka'bah seven times and recite prayers.

Muathin- The person who recites the athan, the call to prayer.

Mukhabarat- Syria's secret service agents. They have many branches all over the country, each of them operating independently. The Mukhabarat branches also operate independent of the Army Interrogation Units.

Mujahid- Someone who struggles in the way of God.

People of the cave- According to the Quran, the people of the cave are

251

a group of people whom God caused to fall asleep in a cave for three hundred and nine years.

Qibla- The direction Muslims face when they pray, which is towards the Ka'bah in Mecca, Saudi Arabia.

Sharia- Islamic law.

Tahajud- Extra prayers performed at night.

Wudu- The ablution or washing of certain body parts. Muslims make wudu to prepare for prayer.

# Map Of Syria

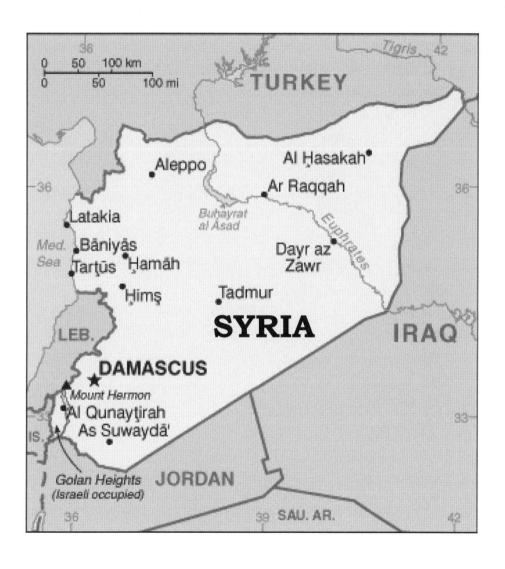